INSIGHT GUIDE

BEIJING

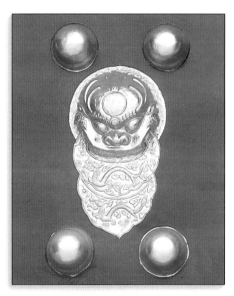

Part of the Langenscheidt Publishing Group

ABOUT THIS BOOK

Editorial

Editor
Tom Le Bas
Editorial Director
Brian Bell

Distribution

UK & Ireland
GeoCenter International Ltd
The Viables Centre , Harrow Way
Basingstoke, Hants RG22 4BJ
Fax: (44) 1256-817988

United States
Langenscheidt Publishers, Inc.
46–35 54th Road, Maspeth, NY 11378
Fax: (718) 784-0640

Canada
Prologue Inc.
1650 Lionel Bertrand Blvd., Boisbriand
Québec, Canada J7H 1N7
Tel: (450) 434-0306. Fax: (450) 434-2627

Worldwide
Apa Publications GmbH & Co.
Verlag KG (Singapore branch)
38 Joo Koon Road, Singapore 628990
Tel: (65) 865-1600. Fax: (65) 861-6438

Printing

Insight Print Services (Pte) Ltd
38 Joo Koon Road, Singapore 628990
Tel: (65) 865-1600. Fax: (65) 861-6438

©2000 Apa Publications GmbH & Co.
Verlag KG (Singapore branch)
All Rights Reserved
First Edition 1990
Fourth Edition 2000

This guidebook combines the interests and enthusiasms of two of the world's best known information providers: Insight Guides, whose titles have set the standard for visual travel guides since 1970, and Discovery Channel, the world's premier source of nonfiction television programming.

The editors of Insight Guides provide both practical advice and general understanding about a destination's history, culture, institutions and people. Discovery Channel and its Web site, www.discovery.com, help millions of viewers explore their world from the comfort of their own home and also encourage them to explore it first hand.

This updated edition of *Insight: Beijing* is carefully structured to convey an understanding of the city and its culture as well as to guide readers through its sights and activities:

◆ The **Features** section, indicated by a yellow bar at the top of each page, covers the history and culture of the country in a series of essays.

◆ The main **Places** section, indicated by a blue bar, is a complete guide to all the sights and areas worth visiting. Places of special interest are coordinated by number with the maps.

◆ The **Travel Tips** listings section, with an orange bar, provides a handy point of reference for information on travel, hotels, shops, restaurants and more. An index to the listings is on the back cover flap.

The contributors

This edition of *Insight: Beijing* was co-ordinated by **Tom Le Bas** at Insight Guides' London office. The book has been completely updated with the invaluable help of a number of China experts.

Bill Smith, a Beijing-based writer and editor, revamped the History and Features sections, including the new People chapter, as well as the chapters on The Great Wall and Chengde. Smith also contributed the features on Pu Yi and Cultural Revolution nostalgia, the material on Mao's Portrait and the opera singer Mei Lanfang, the four picture spreads, as well as fully updating the Travel Tips.

Another Beijing resident, **Hilary Smith** (no relation), updated and reworked the remainder of the Places section, including the new Tianjin chapter. She also wrote the Daily Life

in the Forbidden City text as well as supplying many of the photographs for this new edition.

The current guide builds on the excellent foundations created by the editors and writers of the three previous editions. The project editor for the first edition of the book was **Manfred Morgenstern**, who also wrote many of the original chapters. He fell in love with China during his student years, when he made his first trip that was funded with money earned from holiday jobs. That was in 1977, only a short while after the death of the China's Great Chairman and Helmsman, Mao Zedong. Morgenstern has since made many visits to the city as manager of a travel company, tour guide and travel journalist. As a Sinologist who spoke Chinese, **Helmut Forster-Latsch** spent several years in China working as a translator and consultant to Chinese publishers and editors, and contributed much of the original text. His wife **Marie-Luise Forster-Latsch** contributed to several essays, particularly to the colourful descriptions of Beijing opera. **Marie-Luise Beppler-Lie** wrote the original chapters on Cuisine, Art and Crafts, Museums and Imperial Tombs, while **Elke Wandel** contributed the original chapters on the Imperial Gardens and The Summer Palace. **Klaus Bodenstein** wrote the original Life in the Hutong chapter.

Photographers for the guide include **Manfred Morgenstern, Hilary Smith, Marcus Wilson-Smith, Catherine Karnow, Andrea Pistolesi** and **Bodo Bondzio**.

The text was edited by **Nicholas Inman**, an Insight regular. **Bryony Coleman** proofread the book and **Isobel McLean** indexed it.

Map Legend

▬ ▪ ▪	International Boundary
▬ ▬ ▬	Province Boundary
▬ ▬ ▬	National Park/Reserve
▬ ▬ ▬	Ferry Route
●	Subway
✈ ✈	Airport: International/ Regional
🚌	Bus Station
❓	Tourist Information
✉	Post Office
✝ ✝	Church/Ruins
†	Monastery
☾	Mosque
✡	Synagogue
🏰 🏯	Castle/Ruins
∴	Archaeological Site
∩	Cave
⚊	Statue/Monument
★	Place of Interest

The main places of interest in the Places section are coordinated by number with a full-colour map (e.g. ❶), and a symbol at the top of every right-hand page tells you where to find the map.

CONTENTS

Playing in
the snow by
Houhai Lake

Information panels

Insight on ...

Places

CENTRE OF THE WORLD

Set out according to ancient geomantic principles, modern
Beijing is a dynamic and increasingly sophisticated city

Beijing is, of course, the capital of the People's Republic of China, a 50-year-old political entity with the foundations of one of the world's oldest civilizations. Yet the city was a late starter, of secondary importance to Xi'an and Luoyang, the capitals of the great dynasties for over a millennium. It wasn't until the arrival of the "barbarians" from the north – the Khitan, the Nüzhen, and finally the Mongols – that Beijing came of age.

In the early 20th century, Beijing had missed out on the beginnings of the modern age and the transition from agrarian to industrial society. The heartbeat of that shifting age was already being felt in Shanghai and Guangzhou (Canton), while in Beijing, despite the fall of the emperor, the residue of the court continued to define life.

Beijing entered the modern era on 1 October 1949, when Mao Zedong proclaimed from Tiananmen, the Gate of Heavenly Peace, "China has arisen!" In the 1950s, the area just to the south of the Imperial Palace was demolished to make way for an enlarged Tiananmen Square and some of the ten major construction projects built to celebrate the tenth anniversary of New China. Planners tried to persuade Mao to build a new city to the west, but he insisted on razing the city walls and redeveloping old Beijing.

Ancient and modern

Since the late 1970s, Beijing has progressed on its long march towards a market economy. Although the coastal provinces in the southeast remain ahead in economic daring and prosperity, skyscrapers are beginning to dominate the Beijing skyline. Wide ring roads, which meet in monstrous and tangled intersections, mark new boundary lines between the city's expanding districts.

In the midst of modernisation, however, Beijing's ancient city and its significance give the capital a rock-solid – if not celestial – foundation. Old manuscripts show that the city was divided by a grid in such a way that it reflected the harmony of the universe. Walls were the modules of this cosmic order. The empire had long enjoyed the partly real, partly symbolic safety of the Great Wall just to the north, while the city itself was protected by walls, moats and defensive gates that faced the four points of the compass. The emperor was surrounded by palace walls, and his subjects hid their daily lives behind the walls of courtyard houses in the *hutong*, the narrow alleys of the old city.

Visitors to the Temple of Heaven, standing at the Altar of Heaven, will see a round wall covered with blue-glazed tiles, and beyond it, a second square wall. In Chinese cosmology, Heaven is seen as round

PRECEDING PAGES: Temple of Heaven and visitor; Socialist Realism at the Mao Mausoleum; show of force on the 50th anniversary of the People's Republic in Tiananmen Square, October 1999; same occasion, different choreography.
LEFT: the marble ramp to the Hall of Supreme Harmony in the Imperial Palace.

while Earth is square. Heaven covers the Middle Kingdom and grants its favour to the Sons of Heaven, the Chinese emperors. The "barbarians," generally the Mongolians and other ethnic groups of the steppes north of Beijing, lived in the dark corners of the Earth, where they apparently thrived and belonged, at least until they started descending upon the Middle Kingdom.

The strict orientation of the city's central buildings on a north-south line goes back to the traditional practice of *feng shui*. According to this, *yin* symbolises the north – night, danger, evil, death, coldness and hardness. Therefore, all buildings open towards the south and the sun. There *yang* rules, providing day, life and warmth. This main axis, which slices through today's Qianmen, Tiananmen Square, the Imperial Palace and right up to the Bell and Drum Towers in the north, was once the centre of city life.

Today's Beijing has shifted, however, to a new urban axis: Chang'an Jie, the Street of Eternal Peace. Stretching for 40 km (25 miles) from east to west and dividing the city into northern and southern hemispheres, the boulevard, beautified with trees, grass verges and potted plants, hosted the celebrations of 50 years of communist rule on 1 October 1999. A huge military parade, which featured tanks, missiles and planes, was part of a $10 billion extravaganza. On a more notorious occasion, tanks passed along here on their way to disperse demonstrators in Tiananmen Square in June 1989.

Many old structures that were witness to imperial times – *pailou*, or gate arches, erected in all the major streets – have had to make way for modernisation. Innumerable old temples lie in ruins today, wrecked by Red Guards in the 1970s, or used for irreverent purposes. Whole city districts have been demolished. Pedicabs, taxis and Liberation trucks have replaced the rickshaws and camel caravans that once filled the streets.

The threat to the old city

Deng Xiaoping's bold reforms created rapid economic growth and social change in the 1980s and 1990s, without any concessions to political freedom. Fashionably dressed shoppers stroll along streets once dominated by dark-blue Mao suits. No one knows how much of the old city can be saved. Skyscrapers shoot out of the ground like sun-crazed mushrooms. Yet we should not forget that many people in Beijing prefer high-rise apartments, with kitchens and bathrooms, to their spartan old housing. As is often the case, those who are directly affected view as backward what outsiders perceive as idyllic. And despite the loss of ancient architecture, the most important historic sites, which rival those of any city, have survived: the Temple of Heaven, the Forbidden City, the Summer Palace and the Great Wall.

The United Nations forecasts Beijing's population will grow to 19.4 million by 2015. With a constant stream of enormous construction projects, built by an army of migrant workers, Beijing already feels more like a city of the future than one steeped in the past. Most of its citizens, however, are content to enjoy the present. ❑

RIGHT: cleaning up for the 50th anniversary of the People's Republic.

Decisive Dates

THE EARLY YEARS

circa **3000 BC** Neolithic villages are established in the area around present-day Beijing.

circa **700 BC** Trading between the Chinese, Koreans, Mongols and northern tribes starts to take place around the site of the modern city.

403–221 BC Warring States period. Rise of the city of Ji, the forerunner of Beijing.

221 BC Qin Shi Huangdi unifies China to found the first imperial dynasty, and links existing walls to create the Great Wall. Weights and measures,

currency, and writing are standardised. Beijing (still known as Ji) becomes the administrative centre of Guangyang prefecture.

206 BC Han dynasty founded; capital in Chang'an.

180 BC Eunuchs appear at the imperial court to look after the emperor's wives and concubines.

165 BC Civil service examinations instituted.

AD 105 Traditional date for the invention of paper. Trade between China and Asia/Europe thrives.

2nd century AD The first Buddhist temples are founded in China. Meanwhile, Beijing (Ji) is developing into a strategic garrison town between the warring kingdoms of northern China, and the lands of the Mongol and other nomads.

220 Abdication of the last Han emperor. Wei, Jin, and Northern and Southern dynasties divide China.

581 Following nearly four centuries of division, Sui dynasty reunifies China. New legal code established.

589–610 Repairs of early parts of the Great Wall. Construction of a system of Grand Canals linking northern and southern China.

618 Tang dynasty proclaimed. Government increasingly bureaucratised.

690–705 Empress Wu (627–705) governs China as its first female ruler. Writing of poetry becomes a requisite in civil service examinations.

MONGOL DYNASTIES (916–1368)

907–960 Fall of Tang dynasty. Five Dynasties and Ten Kingdoms partition China. Beijing, now called Yanjing (or Nanjing), becomes the southern capital of the new Khitan (Mongol) empire under the Liao dynasty.

1040 Invention of movable type, but it is not as efficient for printing pages of Chinese characters as wood-block printing. Development of Neo-Confucianism during 11th and 12th centuries.

1125 The Nüzhen, another Mongol tribe, overthrow the Liao dynasty to begin the Jin dynasty.

1153 Beijing, now called Zhongdu, becomes the Nüzhen capital.

1215 Genghis Khan attacks and destroys the city.

1267 Kublai Khan starts construction of Khanbaliq, known in Chinese as Dadu (Great Capital), using Confucian ideals. An imperial palace is built in today's Beihai Park.

1279 Mongols led by Kublai Khan, grandson of Genghis Khan, rout the Song court to establish the Yuan dynasty. Trade along the Silk Road flourishes.

1293 City rebuilding completed. Tonghua Canal links the city with the Grand Canal.

MING DYNASTY (1368–1644)

1368 Founding of the Ming dynasty after Han Chinese overthrow the Mongols. Dadu is renamed Beiping (Northern Peace), but the capital is moved south to Nanjing.

1403 Beiping reinstated as capital of the empire by the emperor Yongle.

1406–20 During Yongle's reign many of the city's famous structures are built. The city is completely rebuilt around the new Imperial Palace and its basic layout, which can still be seen today, is established.

1514 The first Portuguese ships drop anchor off Guangzhou (Canton).

1553 Macau becomes a Portuguese trading port, and the first European settlement in China. Completion of Beijing's city wall.

15th, 16th and 17th centuries Rebuilding of the Great Wall to make the "10,000 Li" Wall.

QING DYNASTY (1644–1912)

1644 A non-Han Chinese people from Manchuria, the Manchu, seize Beijing, to initiate the Qing dynasty.
1661–1722 Reign of Emperor Kangxi.
1736–96 Reign of Emperor Qianlong.
1800 First edict prohibiting the importation and local production of opium.
1838 Lin Zexu, a court official, suspends all trade in opium. The following year, the Qing court terminates all trade between England and China.
1839–42 English forces gather off China's coast. Fighting begins in 1841 in the First Opium War.
1842 Treaty of Nanjing signed. More Chinese ports are forced to open to foreign trade, and Hong Kong island is surrendered to Great Britain "in perpetuity".
1851–64 The Taiping Rebellion.
1858 Conflicts arise between European powers, mainly France and England, and China. Treaty of Tianjin signed, opening more ports to foreigners.
1860 British and French troops burn the Summer Palace in Beijing. Kowloon Peninsula ceded to Britain.
1894–95 Sino-Japanese War, which China loses.
1900 The Boxer Rebellion.
1911 Republican Revolution: Sun Yat-sen is chosen president, but soon steps down.
1912 Abdication of the last emperor, Pu Yi.

POST-IMPERIAL CHINA

1916–28 The president of the republic, Yuan Shikai, considers declaring himself emperor. Several provinces announce their independence. Yuan dies, and China falls apart. Civil war ensues.
1919 On 4 May in Beijing, a large demonstration demands measures to restore China's sovereignty, thus beginning a nationalist movement.
1921 Founding of the Communist Party in Shanghai.
1925 Sun Yat-sen dies.
1934–36 The Long March: Communists forced to abandon their stronghold in southern China. 30,000 of the original 100,000 who began the march arrive at the northern base in Yan'an.
1937 Marco Polo Bridge Incident prompts Communists and Nationalists to unite to fight Japanese.
1945 Japan defeated in World War II; full-scale civil war ensues in China.

PRECEDING PAGES: silk painting depicting the procession of a Ming emperor.
LEFT: watercolour of old China.
RIGHT: President Jiang Zemin addresses the nation.

PEOPLE'S REPUBLIC OF CHINA

1949 Mao Zedong declares People's Republic in Beijing on 1 October; Nationalist army flees to Taiwan.
1950–53 Chinese troops support North Korea.
1957–59 Tiananmen Square and "Ten Great Buildings" constructed in time for tenth anniversary of communist rule.
1958–61 The "Great Leap Forward" causes a mass famine that kills upwards of 30 million Chinese.
1960 Split between China and the Soviet Union.
1966 Beginning of Cultural Revolution.
1969 Fear of Soviet attack grips Beijing; shelters and tunnels are built.
1976 Zhou Enlai and Mao Zedong die, Cultural Rev-

olution ends. Demonstrations in Tiananmen Square.
1978 Deng Xiaoping becomes leader, instituting a policy of economic reform and opening to the West.
1979 The USA formally recognises China. Democracy Wall movement crushed.
1989 Tiananmen Square demonstrations; military crackdown ends with hundreds of deaths.
1992 Deng restarts economic reforms.
1997 Deng Xiaoping dies in February. Hong Kong reverts to Chinese sovereignty on 1 July.
1999 Anti-NATO demonstrations after a bomb hits the Chinese embassy in Belgrade. PRC's 50th anniversary is marked with old-style military parades in front of an invited audience of 100,000. Macau reverts to Chinese sovereignty. ❏

EARLY YEARS TO END OF EMPIRE

Once a frontier town at the edge of fertile lowlands, Beijing served as the capital of imperial dynasties for more than 1,000 years

The geographical position of Beijing has been one of the leading factors in the city's eventful history. Lying at the edge of empire – where the very different cultures of the settled Chinese farmers and the nomads of the northern steppes collided – the city became the prey of each victorious faction in turn, a fact reflected by the many changes to its name throughout the centuries.

The Khitan, who founded the Liao dynasty in northern China, called their capital Nanjing which translates as "Southern Capital". The Nüzhen, who succeeded the Khitan, had a different geographic perception and renamed the city Zhongdu, the "Central Capital". The Mongols, not known for being a modest people, called the residence of their Great Khan, Dadu, or "Great Capital". Later dynasties knew the city as Beijing, "Northern Capital", except for those periods when it was renamed Beiping, "Northern Peace".

Early settlement

However, long before the city had a name or was recorded in history, it already had a far-reaching past. Evidence of human settlement in the area goes back half a million years or so with the discovery of Peking Man (*Sinanthropus pekinensis*). This find, in Zhoukoudian, 50 km (30 miles) southwest of Beijing, revealed that the Peking Man belonged to a people who walked upright and were already using stone tools, and who knew how to light fires. Yet Peking Man marks a point when there is a break in human development, and little is known from then on until about 5,000 years ago.

Around 3000 BC, neolithic villages were established in the area of modern Beijing, inhabited by people familiar with agriculture and the domestication of animals. There is, to this day, dispute as to the existence of the first dynasty recorded in Chinese historical writings, the Xia

dynasty (21st to 16th centuries BC). The dynasty's legendary Yellow Emperor, Huangdi, is thought to have ruled between 2490 and 2413 BC and to have fought battles against the tribal leader Chiyo here, in the "Wilderness of the Prefecture of Zhou". It is presumed that Zhuluo, a town to the west of Beijing, was the earliest urban settlement

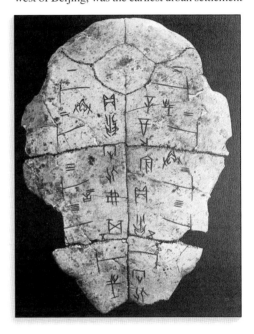

in this area. It was here that Huangdi's successor, Yao, is said to have founded a capital named Youdou, the "City of Calm".

Throughout Beijing's prehistory, the hills to the north, northeast and northwest served as a natural frontier for the people who settled here and who traded with the nomadic tribes living beyond the passes of Gubeikou and Naku. These northern hill tribes also had close ties with the people who occupied the Central Plain, which stretched along the Yellow River to the south and southwest of Beijing. The important role of trading post played by the settlement for the different regions promoted its rise to become the ancient city of Ji. During the period

LEFT: the Emperor Kangxi at his calligraphy.
RIGHT: early Chinese characters on tortoiseshell, Shang dynasty.

of Imperial Conflict (415–221 BC), the count of the state of Yan annexed this area and made Ji his central city. In those times, the city lay to the north of the Guang'anmen Gate near the Baiyuanguan (White Cloud Temple). In the 3rd century BC, the first emperor of the Qin dynasty and of China, Qin Shi Huangdi, made the city an administrative centre of the Guangyang Command, one of 36 prefectures of the unified, centrally-organised feudal empire. Thus, the historically documented city of Ji was established. With the construction of the Great Wall during his reign (221–210 BC), Ji became a strategically important trade and military cen-

an imperial seat when the Khitan conquered northern China and founded the Liao dynasty in AD 936. The Khitan called Ji, their southern capital, Yanjing (it was also known as Nanjing – "southern capital" – not to be confused witj the city of the same name in east-central China, to which the Ming later decamped – *see page 26*). As the southern centre of the nomad empire, this area became a point of support and departure for many expeditions of non-Chinese peoples – Khitan, Nüzhen and Mongols – on their way to the south and the Central Plain.

In relation to today's Beijing, Yanjing lay roughly in the western part of the city. The tem-

tre, a position it retained for about 1,000 years, until the end of the Tang dynasty in the tenth century. During this time, the city was often the subject of war and conflict.

Beijing, the Imperial City

Beijing owed its pre-eminence at the centre of the Chinese empire to repeated invasion by nomadic tribes. At the beginning of the Tang dynasty, Ji was not that different from the other great cities of feudal China. But by the end of the dynasty, the Great Wall had lost much of its protective function, leaving Ji more vulnerable to attack from the north.

The former frontier town began its career as

ple of Fayuansi was in the southeastern corner of the old walls, the Imperial Palace lay to the southwest and the markets were in the northeast corner. Each of the city's four quarters was surrounded by massive walls.

In the early part of the 12th century, the Nüzhen, another nomadic tribe from the northeast, vanquished the reigning Liao dynasty and replaced it with the Jin dynasty. In 1153, they moved their capital from Huiningfu (in the modern province of Liaoning) to Yanjing, and renamed it Zhongdu, "Central Capital". New buildings were constructed, and the Jin moved the centre of their capital – the Imperial Palace – into the area to the south of today's Guang'an

Gate. The ground plan of the city remained square, with three gates on each side. But it only lasted a few decades: in 1215, Mongol cavalry occupied Zhongdu and the city was completely destroyed by fire.

The Great Khan's capital

It was not until 1279 that Kublai Khan made Zhongdu the capital of his Yuan dynasty. He completely rebuilt the city and gave it the Chinese name of Dadu, meaning "Great Capital". In the West, it was mostly known by its Mongol name, Khanbaliq or Khambaluk. In the 14th century, Marco Polo praised this city of

fore they live in the suburbs, and indeed in incredible numbers. There are at least twenty thousand women of pleasure and all of them find custom, for daily, countless traders and strangers come. You may work out the size of the city's population from the number of women who sell themselves... Nowhere in the world are such rare and precious goods traded as in Khanbaliq. I will name some of them for you. The most costly things come from India, jewels, pearls and other precious items... Just imagine, every day more than a thousand wagons arrive, fully laden with silk. In these regions cloth is woven of gold and silk. The city draws

the Great Khan in his journals:

"There are in Khanbaliq unbelievable numbers of people and houses, it is impossible to count them. The houses and villas outside the walls are at least as beautiful as those within, except, of course, for the imperial buildings. And take note of this: if anyone dies in the city, he may not be buried there... And another thing: no wanton women may live in the city, none who take money for their services. There-

FAR LEFT: the imperial bodyguard.
LEFT: print of Qin Shi Huangdi, Qin dynasty.
ABOVE: (from left to right) Kublai Khan and the Ming emperors Hongwu and Wanli.

in wealth from some two hundred towns. From them, people travel to the capital, bringing their wares with them and buying such things as they need themselves."

The Italian explorer was even more enthusiastic about Kublai Khan's grandiose Imperial Palace, the centre of the city, which lay roughly on the site of today's Beihai Park:

"You must know that this is the greatest palace ever built... The hall of the palace is so big that 6,000 people could easily eat therein, and it is truly a wonder how many rooms there are besides. The building is altogether so widespreading, so rich, so beautiful that no man on earth could think of anything to outshine it."

The building of Dadu continued until 1293, while Kublai Khan ruled the empire. The centre of the city at that time was moved to the vicinity of the northeast lakes. In the south, Dadu reached the line of today's Chang'an Boulevard, with the observatory marking the southeast corner. In the north, it reached as far as the present Lama Temple, which was at that time the site of the trade quarters by the Bell and Drum Towers. In 1293, the Tonghua Canal was completed, linking the capital with the Grand Canal and making it possible to bring grain from the south into the city by boat. The circumference of Dadu was

capital back up to Beijing. Thus began the only period in which Beijing was the capital of a Han Chinese empire. At first the city was made smaller. The outer city wall was demolished and rebuilt more towards the south, between today's Deshengmen Gate and Anding Gate. One can still see remains of the demolished northern wall of Dadu outside the Deshengmen gate. Local people call it the Earth Wall, since only a broken row of hillocks remains. From 1406 to 1420, the new Beijing was built, with the Imperial Palace that still exists today as its centre. Yongle conscripted 200,000 labourers to construct the palace, a labyrinth of halls,

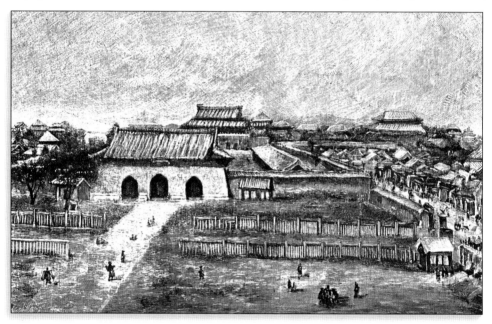

some 20 km (12 miles) and its population about 500,000.

Chinese conquest

Beijing's role as capital city continued during the Ming and Qing dynasties. With the conquest of Mongol Dadu by Ming troops in 1368, Beijing became Chinese once more and was renamed Beiping ("Northern Peace"). Zhu Yuanzhang, founder of the Ming dynasty, at first made the more modern Nanjing, hundreds of miles to the south, his capital and gave Beiping to one of his sons as a fief. When the latter succeeded to the throne in 1403, taking the ruling name of Yongle, he moved the country's

gates, corridors and courtyards now known as the Forbidden City.

Most ancient buildings in today's inner city date back to the Ming dynasty. Like Kublai Khan, the Ming emperors, who ruled over the Middle Kingdom with the Mandate of Heaven, followed the square pattern dictated by the old rules. The main axis ran southwards and the city was completely enclosed by walls with three gates on each side. Civil engineers dug moats and canals, planned Beijing's extensive road network and, in 1553, completed a massive city wall to protect their thriving capital. The ground plan resembled a chessboard, with a network of north–south and east–west streets, at the heart of which nestled the Imperial Palace, surrounded by high red walls. To the south of the palace, starting from today's Qianmen, an Inner City was built.

The decision of the Ming emperor Yongle to retain Beijing as capital may seem surprising, as the city was at the northern edge of the empire and the climatic influence of the steppe was always strongly felt. This position on the borders also brought with it the permanent danger of attack by the Mongols or other nomadic tribes (which did indeed follow in the 16th and 17th centuries). Beijing had become a capital in 1271 under the Mongols, and now, for the first time, it

foundations of which had been laid by the Mongols. This ambition later became the hallmark of the entire Qing dynasty.

The Ming also undertook China's greatest ever public works project: the "10,000 Li" Great Wall. The Ming Great Wall linked or reinforced several older walls, traversing narrow ridges and steep mountains. New, spectacular sections of wall were added, and some strategic passes were guarded by up to 20 parallel walls. But this costly, continuous wall-building ultimately failed to save the Ming empire. In 1644, Li Zicheng led a peasants' revolt, conquered the city of Beijing and top-

was the capital of a dynasty of Chinese origin.

Yongle's decision was, in all probability, an expression of his drive for expansion. Under his rule, the imperial boundaries were pushed as far as the river Amur, and Beijing took on strategic importance for establishing control of eastern Mongolia and the northeastern territories. Moving the capital to the edge of the steppe zone could also be viewed as a sign that the Ming dynasty planned to restore the pre-eminence of the Chinese empire in Asia, the

pled the Ming dynasty. But a mere 43 days later, Manchu troops defeated Li's army and marched into Beijing, making it their capital.

The Manchu rulers

The Manchu did not change the orientation of the city. They declared the northern part of the city, also known as the Tartar City, their domain, in which only Manchu could live, while the Ming Inner City to the south was renamed the Chinese City. The new Qing dynasty left their mark on the architecture of the Imperial Palace, but did not change the basic structure. Outside the city walls, palaces and temples were built – Yuanmingyuan, the

LEFT: an early view of the Imperial Palace.
ABOVE: massive re-building of the Great Wall failed to save the Ming dynasty.

Old Summer Palace, to the northwest; and, at the end of the 19th century, Yiheyuan, the New Summer Palace. A Portuguese priest, Gabriel de Magaillans, described the city in the late 17th century, the early years of Emperor Kangxi's rule:

"The city Pe Kim lies on a plain. It forms a great square, and each side measures twelve Chinese stadia... This city is now inhabited by Tartars and their troops divided under eight banners. Under the previous dynasty the people had increased so much that there was no more space in the city and the nine suburbs outside its gates, and so a new city, also square in form,

"There is a book that can be bought that deals only with the names and the situation of the streets and that the servants of the mandarins use when they accompany their masters on visits or on the way to the tribunal or to deliver gifts. The most beautiful street is called Cham gan kiai (Chang'an Jie), which is 'Street of Eternal Peace'. It runs from east to west, with the wall of the Imperial Palace to the north, and on its southern side there are various state buildings and the houses of great persons. The buildings are all low, in honour of the palace of the emperor. There are some high and splendid buildings of the great lords, but

has been built with each side measuring six Chinese stadia, the northern side adjoining the southern side of the old city. The new city has seven gates with seven suburbs, of which the west-facing ones are the most extensive, as travellers by land arrive on this side.

"Both cities are each divided into five quarters. The main streets run sometimes north to south, sometimes east to west. They are all as long, broad and straight as it is possible to be, having been laid out by design and not by accident, as is the case with European roads. The little streets all run from east to west and divide the space between the main roads into islands of equal size. They all have their names.

these lie within. From the outside, only the great gate and to either side the low houses of servants, workers and traders with their shops can be seen. This has the advantage that right at one's front door one can buy all the necessities of life. The crowds of people on the streets of the new and of the old city are very great, as is only seen in our cities at market times or during processions."

Though the Qing emperors continued the Confucian rites of their predecessors, they also brought their own language and customs. Chinese and Mongolian were both used in official documents. Tibetan Buddhism, which had flourished among the northern tribes since the Mongols promoted it in the 12th and 13th centuries, was the main Manchu religion. The Qing brought the fifth Dalai Lama from Lhasa to Beijing in 1651 to oversee the introduction of Tibetan Buddhism to the capital. The white stupa in Beihai Park commemorates the Dalai Lama's visit, while temples at the Lama Temple, the Summer Palace and Chengde are other legacies of the Qing emperors' religious faith.

During the long rule of this last imperial dynasty, many foreigners settled in Beijing. In 1601, the Italian Jesuit Matteo Ricci arrived, followed in 1622 by Johann Adam Schall von

because of their excellent astronomical and scientific knowledge. In their reports home, the missionaries supplied Europe with much information about China.

Fall from glory

By the beginning of the 19th century, at the time when the Qing empire had reached its greatest power, Beijing had a population of 700,000, including a small foreign community. But signs of decay were beginning to surface – due to corruption within the imperial household, and the gradual wresting of power away from the centre by warlords and princes.

Bell (1592–1666), who in 1650 received permission to build the first Catholic church in Beijing, now known as Nantang, or Southern Cathedral. The dialogue with China begun by the Jesuit missionaries continued throughout the rule of the first two Qing emperors. The missionaries tried to win over the Chinese upper classes and the imperial court by adapting Christian teaching to Confucian philosophy. They quickly won influence at court

LEFT: Matteo Ricci, an Italian Jesuit, was influential in the imperial court.
ABOVE: imperial court ladies-in-waiting.
RIGHT: Johann Adam Schall von Bell

Revolts increased and secret societies sprang up everywhere, rapidly gaining influence. Xenophobia grew with the rise in Han nationalism. The first persecutions of Jesuits and the destruction of churches took place. The emperor Qianlong, still self-confident, supposedly told the ambassador of the British queen that the Middle Kingdom had no need of "barbarian" products, for the Middle Kingdom produced all that it required. And yet, the time of humiliation for Beijing and for all of China was just around the corner, with the advance of foreign colonial powers from the time of the First Opium War (1840–1842) onwards.

At the end of the Second Opium War

(1858–1860), the emperor was forced to flee from the Western armies. Known as the Eight Allied Troops, these forces were led by the British and French but also included German, Italian, American and Japanese soldiers. They completely destroyed part of the city, including Yuanmingyuan, the Old Summer Palace (the ruins can still be seen today), and plundered Beijing's treasuries.

Following defeat in the Opium Wars, the emperor was obliged to grant concessions to the foreign powers. Extra territorial areas were granted and the diplomatic quarter in the southeast part of the imperial city was put at the dis-

posal of the foreigners, which became the Legation Quarter (*see page 117*). Many Chinese, however, were unwilling to accept this humiliation. The hostile attitude towards the foreigners, who were called "the long noses", gradually increased. During the 1880s and 1890s a programme of Chinese "self-reliance", supported by the powerless Emperor Guangxu, was instituted. It centred on the construction of railways, docks and other infrastructural projects that had hitherto been built and controlled by foreigners. The programme met with opposition from the imperial court, and after China's defeat in the Sino-Japanese war of 1894–5 it effectively collapsed. All this added momen-

tum to the demands of extremist groups, and slogans such as "Drive the barbarians from our country!" were to be heard everywhere.

Two years later, in 1900, followers of a secret society named Society for Peace and Justice – known in the West as the Boxers – rebelled. For two months, partly supported by imperial troops, they besieged the foreign embassies. Western countries quickly sent forces to Beijing. The real ruler, the Empress Dowager Cixi, fled to Xi'an and the Boxer Rebellion was crushed. A foreign newspaper based in Beijing reported: "The capital of the emperors was partly destroyed, partly burned down. All that was left was a dead city. The streets were choked with the bodies of Chinese, many charred or eaten by stray dogs."

Once again, the increasingly weak Manchu regime had to pay great sums in reparations, while the foreigners received further privileges. As Beijing continued to decay, the imperial court carried on in the same old way, cut off from reality, bound up as it was in luxury, corruption and intrigue. Neither the Empress Dowager Longyü, nor Prince Chun, regent and father of the child Emperor Pu Yi, were strong enough to resurrect the shaky throne.

End of Empire

In October 1910, an advisory council met for the first time in Beijing. By then the middle-class Xinhai revolution, led by Sun Yat-sen, had become a real threat to the Manchu imperial house. The prince regent recalled the Imperial Marshal, Yuan Shikai, the strong man of Cixi, dismissed earlier in 1909. He was appointed supreme commander and head of the government. However, Yuan Shikai wanted to prepare a change of dynasty in the traditional style. He avoided confrontation with the republican forces in the south, elected himself president of the National Assembly in November 1911, and the next month forced the child Emperor Pu Yi to abdicate, effectively sealing the fate of the Manchu Qing dynasty.

The long rule of the Sons of Heaven was ended. Chinese men could finally cut off their hated pigtails – the external symbol of servitude imposed by the Manchu. However, the city continued to decay and social problems became more acute. ❑

LEFT: Chinese and German troops in battle.

Pu Yi, the Last Emperor

Pu Yi was one of the tragic figures of 20th century China. Born into the imperial family in 1906, he was thrust into the limelight as an infant. When Empress Dowager Cixi died in November 1908, Pu Yi acceded to the throne; he was forced to abdicate just four years later, although he continued living in the imperial palace for another twelve years.

When he was nearly 17, Pu Yi entered a double marriage – to a wife and to a 13-year-old consort. He later took two more consorts. His wife, Wang Jun, grew addicted to opium and died in 1946. Pu Yi remarried in 1962, but remained childless.

Even as an adult, Pu Yi was never in control of his own destiny. Princes, eunuchs and other members of the imperial household ruled him. Warlords manipulated him; the Japanese exploited him; and finally the Communists used him as a model of, and probably an experiment in, reeducation.

A military coup in 1924 forced Pu Yi to leave the Forbidden City. He moved to the port of Tianjin. In his autobiography, *From Emperor to Citizen,* he describes this as a time when he "wavered between different factions and different ideas".

He first thought of emigrating. Then he wanted to persuade warlords to unite in restoring the throne. An attempted Qing restoration in 1917 had already failed, but many warlords and gangland leaders across China proclaimed allegiance to Pu Yi, fearing demise at the hands of either the Nationalists or the Communists.

The growth of anti-Qing sentiments in Tianjin forced Pu Yi to take refuge in the Japanese legation. In 1928, his main warlord ally was murdered, apparently by the Japanese. Yet Pu Yi accepted a deal to become, in 1932, the "chief executive" of the Japanese occupied area of northeast China, which Japan named Manchuria. In 1934, he was made puppet emperor of Manchuria.

After Japan's surrender in World War II, Soviet troops liberated northeast China. Pu Yi was captured at Shenyang airport as he was about to flee to Japan. The Soviets imprisoned him in a hotel at the Siberian spa town of Chita, allowing him to live in relative comfort, surrounded by relatives and former servants. He appeared as a witness at an international war crimes tribunal investigating Japanese atrocities in China. Fearing execution if the Russians returned him to China, he applied to stay in the Soviet Union.

But he was sent back to China in July 1950, and spent ten years in Fushun War Criminals Prison, where for the first time he learnt practical skills like sewing and gardening. He also studied Chinese medicine and communism. After his release, he lived as an ordinary citizen of Beijing until his death in 1967. His life as prodigy, puppet, prisoner and proletarian forms the subject of Bernardo Bertolucci's award-winning epic film *The Last Emperor,* released in 1987.

Pu Yi adopted communism with such zeal that, aged 54, he tried to join a Beijing militia unit. He worked on literature and history for the national committee of the Chinese People's Political Consultative Committee, and later sat on the committee. He even wore the badge of the new "emperor", Chairman Mao.

In 1960, he joined a demonstration in Tiananmen Square, right outside his former palace. He marched in support of "the Japanese people's struggles against the Japan-US Security Treaty". His rebirth was epitomised by his reaction to news of his special pardon in Fushun: "Before I had heard this to the end I burst into tears. My motherland had made me into a man." ❑

RIGHT: Pu Yi as a young child.

POST-IMPERIAL UPHEAVALS

After the warlord years came the brutal Japanese invasion and civil war.

Even the founding of communist China in 1949 didn't end the turmoil

The abdication document of Emperor Pu Yi says: "Yuan Shikai, who some time ago was elected President of the National Assembly in Beijing, now has the opportunity to unite the north and the south. Let him therefore receive all necessary powers to accomplish this and to form a provisional government. Let this be done with the agreement of the representatives of the People's Army, so that peace may be kept and the five races of Chinese, Manchu, Mongols, Muslims and Tibetans may make up one single great state with the name Republic of China."

Pride and poverty

Peace, however, would not come for several decades. First of all, Yuan Shikai failed in his attempt to defeat the Republicans – who had organised themselves as the Guomindang (Kuomintang), the National People's Party, led by Dr Sun Yat-sen. Yuan died in 1916 and the dynasty was overthrown, but the social and political problems remained unsolved. Beijing stagnated in a half-feudal state.

Warlords struggled for control, dashing any hopes of unity and peace. The north and Beijing, which remained the nominal capital of the republic after 1911, were badly affected by these battles. The era of the warlords, which lasted until about 1930, made social and political problems more acute. The misery of the poor was indescribable, further compounded by threats from foreign powers greedy for profit and influence in China.

The foreigners brought new ideas, but they also provoked opposition. In the Treaty of Versailles of 1919, the former German concessions – Kiautschou (modern Qingdao) and the adjacent Jiaozhou Bay – were not returned to China but given to Japan. This deeply wounded national pride. More than 300,000 young Chinese, mostly students and intellectuals, demon-

strated in Beijing on 4 May 1919 to demand national independence and territorial integrity. A manifesto passed at the demonstration ended with the words: "China's territory may be conquered, but it cannot be given to foreign powers. The Chinese people may be slaughtered, but they will not surrender. Our country is in

the process of being destroyed. Brothers, defend yourselves against this!"

As a result of this May Fourth Movement – considered a turning point in modern Chinese history – the Chinese workers' movement grew. Trade unions and the Communist Party came into existence, the latter soon becoming active even in Beijing. At that time, the party's future leader, Mao Zedong, was a librarian at the University of Beijing, or Beida as it is commonly known. In the 1920s, Guomindang and Chinese Communist Party forces still fought side by side against the warlords in the north. But after the right wing of the Guomindang gained the upper hand in 1928, the Communist Party was

LEFT: the Cultural Revolution announces that "the whole country is red".

RIGHT: Sun Yat-sen, the father of the Republic.

banned. Chiang Kai-shek, the Guomindang leader, moved his capital to Nanjing.

Beijing in the 1920s was a vibrant yet poor and chaotic city, with a street life of shops, fortune-tellers, opera troupes, nightclub singers, foreign businessmen and adventurers. Richard Wilhelm, an expert on China, wrote in 1928:

"For centuries nearly everything was permitted in the streets. You could pour out your dirty wash water, throw away scraps, dogs and cats were allowed to die if there was nothing else for them to do – in short, the street generously took in everything and covered anything unpleasant with its dust... Of course there are

demonstrated against the new trams that threatened their livelihood. The modern world was moving into Beijing. The network of streets was extended, water pipes were laid, hospitals were established, and banks opened branches.

The following years, however, were overshadowed by the threat of the Japanese. Already, in 1931, Japan had occupied northeast China, which they named Manchuria. In 1935, huge anti-Japanese demonstrations marched through the streets of Beijing. Following the 1934–36 Long March from the south, the surviving Communist troops regrouped in northern Shaanxi Province, to the southwest of Beijing.

many sick people in Peking, and many die...

"Peking is a city of mysterious freedom... Every person who lives here finds space for whatever work he wants to do. The breeze that blows through Peking is good and free. You can be an eccentric or a sociable person, you can seek to drown your sorrows in the wine of life or you can strive for immortality through ascetic rigour."

Reluctant allies

In 1928, four years after the "Last Emperor" had finally left the Imperial Palace on the orders of the "Christian" warlord, Feng Yuxiang, the rickshaw coolies took to the streets and

The Guomindang, responding to popular pressure, had to make a new alliance with the communists, this time to fight against Japan, the common enemy.

A confrontation choreographed by the Japanese in 1937 on the Marco Polo Bridge, on the western outskirts of Beijing, served the Japanese as a pretext for occupying Beijing and then all of China.

Life became worse for the people of Beijing during World War II, a time when the foreigners remained "neutral" and the Japanese secret police controlled everything. By 1939, Japan had seized all of eastern China and the Guomindang had retreated west to Chongqing in Sichuan Province. The US began supplying the Guomindang troops, hoping that they would oust the Japanese and, later, the Communists – who were then fighting alongside the Guomindang against the common enemy. In 1941 an attack on Communist troops by a rogue Guomindang unit split the alliance, but both sides continued separate action against the Japanese.

Towards the end of World War II, Communist guerrillas were operating in the hills around Beijing. After the Japanese surrender, the Guomindang first took control, supported by the Americans. However, they were eventually

power into part of the Forbidden City, to Zhongnanhai, west of the Imperial Palace.

All government bodies were based in Beijing. Important schools and colleges moved here, and new factories were built. The city, which had just 1.2 million inhabitants in 1949, grew through the incorporation of eight rural districts of Hebei Province in 1958.

Urban re-shaping began in the 1950s. The slum areas were cleared, new buildings erected and the streets widened. Despite pleas by planning experts, Mao insisted on demolishing Beijing's ancient city walls. Grey and dusty Beijing was to become a green city within the decade.

defeated by the People's Liberation Army, due largely to their inability to solve the pressing problems of hunger, inflation, unemployment and the capricious exercise of power.

Communist capital

On 31 January 1949, Beijing was taken without a struggle. On 1 October, Mao Zedong proclaimed the foundation of the People's Republic of China from Tiananmen, the Gate of Heavenly Peace. Just like the emperors before them, the Communists moved their centre of

LEFT: street scene in old Beijing.
ABOVE: the victorious Red Army enters Beijing in 1949.

As the centre of political power, Beijing led several fierce ideological campaigns in the 1950s. During the Korean War from 1950–53, the capital rallied support for its North Korean allies against "US imperialists".

In 1956, Mao issued his infamous edict "Let a hundred flowers bloom, let a hundred schools of thought contend." It sounded too good to be true, but the Hundred Flowers movement soon became a vehicle for flushing out dissenting voices. Many of those who heeded Mao's call were bemused to find themselves purged or arrested. At least 300,000 intellectuals, most of them committed communists, were labelled "rightists" or "capitalist roaders" and sent to remote labour camps for "re-education". Many were from Beijing; some would never return.

Bitter birthday

Khrushchev's 1956 condemnation of Stalin had shocked the Chinese leadership. When the Soviet premier later criticised Mao, shock turned to anger. In July 1960, all remaining Soviet experts left China.

Beijing residents were largely unaffected by the focus of Khrushchev's concern, the Great Leap Forward. Party secrecy also ensured ignorance of the mass famine in the countryside. From 1958 to 1961 some 30 million people

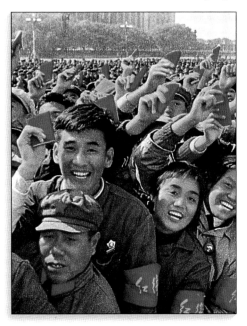

starved to death, mainly due to misguided Great Leap policies. In the middle of this rural catastrophe, in 1959 the capital celebrated the tenth anniversary of communist rule with a huge rally and ten major construction projects, including the Great Hall of the People and the huge museums which flank Tiananmen Square.

Redder than red

As if the traumas of the Hundred Flowers and the Great Leap movements were not enough, in 1965 the first rumblings of the Cultural Revolution began with the launch of a campaign to "Hand over the Khrushchevs sleeping next to Mao". Defence minister Lin Biao orchestrated the rise

of Mao to godlike status. Images of the Great Helmsman decorated Beijing's public buildings and homes, and everyone wore Mao badges. Red Guard groups mushroomed across the capital. Encouraged by Mao, students abandoned their lessons and persecuted their teachers and other authority figures. They took over factories and offices to pursue "class struggle". Some even fought pitched battles with other groups to prove ideological supremacy. The Red Guards also ransacked many of Beijing's ancient cultural sites, and searched homes for "bourgeois" or "feudal" items. Mao's wife, Jiang Qing, and supporters of her Gang of Four used Beihai Park throughout the Cultural Revolution as a private domain.

In 1968, a million Red Guards marched into Tiananmen Square, while Mao waved encouragingly from Tiananmen Gate. Yet even the instigators realized the Red Guard movement was growing dangerously chaotic. As a solution, in 1968, the idea of sending educated urban youngsters to "learn from the peasants" was born. Young Beijingers were sent away with little idea of when they might return, though most came back in the mid-1970s as the fire of the Cultural Revolution was quelled.

At the end of the 1960s a new fear gripped Beijing as soldiers and civilians hurriedly built a vast network of tunnels and air-raid shelters, preparing for possible war with the Soviet Union. The two powers had skirmished along China's northeast border, and Mao was convinced the Soviets planned an invasion.

War was avoided, but the internal struggles continued. In 1971 the heir apparent, Lin Biao, died in a plane crash, allegedly while fleeing China after a failed coup attempt. But Lin's death merely left the way clear for a second faction to manipulate the Mao personality cult. The Gang of Four hijacked Mao's "Criticize Lin Biao and Confucius" campaign, launched in 1973. Zhou Enlai, probably China's most popular premier, became "Confucius" and was removed from office.

US president Richard Nixon made a historic visit to Beijing in 1972, marking the beginning of the end of China's international isolation. But it did not signal the end of the Cultural Revolution, which would last another four years, until the momentous events of 1976. ❑

LEFT: fanatical Red Guards in Tiananmen Square wave Mao's "Little Red Book".

Maomorabilia

Apart from Tiananmen Square, the most likely place you will see the image of the revolutionary leader who rehashed the platitude "A journey of a thousand miles begins with a single step" is hanging from the driving mirror of a Beijing taxi. The role of Chinese St Christopher is just one of many incarnations of an icon that has endured for nearly 40 years. Mao Zedong was already a hero of the Long March and the civil war, and one of the founders of the People's Republic. But the Cultural Revolution (1966–76) elevated him to Messianic status. Pilgrimage sites flourished, especially Mao's hometown of Shaoshan, and the wartime base of Yan'an. Statues of Mao were erected in every city square, while in the countryside some even built small shrines to him. Factories produced some two billion pictures and three billion badges of the Great Helmsman.

In Beijing, Red Guards waved Mao's "Little Red Book" during huge rallies. The book first appeared in 1964. More than 350 million were printed over the next two years, and translations into all major languages followed.

The arms of waving Red Guards became the hands of Cultural Revolution alarm clocks. Rarer models include "scientific socialism" clocks, on which space rockets trace the hour. Double-image Mao medallions, rubber stamps, resin busts, and ceramic ornaments all fuelled the personality cult.

Despite the huge volume produced, some have become valuable collectors' pieces, especially original postage stamps, paintings, papercuts and posters. A few Cultural Revolution paintings have sold for more than $1 million. Many badges were thrown away or used as scrap metal, but Beijing's leading collector has reputedly salvaged more than 100,000.

Shops along Liulichang and the Hongqiao, Panjiayuan and Silk Alley markets sell original Mao badges, as well as modern copies. You may also find ornaments or pictures showing a young soldier wearing a fur-lined hat with earflaps. This is Lei Feng, adopted by Mao as a model of selfless devotion. Lei Feng fixed engines in temperatures of −30°C (−22°F); he worked a 12-hour day but still helped his colleagues; and he gave away much of his meagre pay and rations to those in greater need. Schoolchildren are still taught to follow his example.

RIGHT: Mao collectibles stall at Curio City in Beijing.

Look out, too, for reproduction and original ceramics depicting gun-toting young women dressed in pale blue short suits. *The Red Detachment of Women* was one of seven model stage works allowed by Mao's wife Jiang Qing, a former film actress and self-appointed cultural arbiter.

In the 1980s and 1990s, many artists reworked styles and images from the Cultural Revolution, with varying degrees of irony, including one portrait of *Whitney Houston with the Chairman*. Advertising campaigns and pop music videos also recycle Cultural Revolution pictures and slogans. And Beijing has several restaurants with Cultural Revolution and "Mao hometown" themes.

The cult of Deng Xiaoping has partly continued the Mao trend. Souvenir stalls sell Deng watches, musical lighters, T-shirts, and pendants for car windscreens. But for some people, Deng will always be second best. For them, Mao remains the greatest hero of the 20th century, if not China's entire history. Most people accept the government line that, despite his grave errors, Mao was 70 percent right. Others, however, especially people whose family members died or were imprisoned, find the nostalgia strange, sick even. They hold Mao personally responsible for 30 million deaths from famine after the Great Leap Forward, which began in 1958, and more deaths and persecutions in the Cultural Revolution. ❑

THE MODERN ERA

After the trauma of the Cultural Revolution, Deng Xiaoping's bold reforms created rapid economic growth and social change but little political freedom

In early April 1976, during the week of the Qingming Festival, when the Chinese remember their dead, the silent rage of the people found expression in a massive demonstration. Dissatisfaction had increased because of food rationing and the poor quality of goods available. Support for and trust in the leadership, even in Mao, had evaporated.

The people of Beijing gathered by the thousands for several days in Tiananmen Square, to pay homage to the dead President Zhou Enlai, and to protest against Mao and the radical leaders of the Cultural Revolution. The first demands for modernisation and democracy were heard, signalling the end of the Cultural Revolution. In response to the unrest, a new face was presented to the Chinese people: Hua Guofeng, who was named First Vice-Chairman, second only to Mao.

The Chinese, great believers in omens and portents, have always viewed natural disasters as signs from heaven of great changes to come. In mid-1976, a massive earthquake destroyed the city of Tangshan, to the east of Beijing, and claimed hundreds of thousands of victims. In imperial times this would have been interpreted as a sign that a change of dynasty was imminent.

The Great Helmsman's death

In fact, it was only a few weeks later that another event shook the Chinese people. Their Great Helmsman, Mao Zedong, the man who had led China out of dire poverty and feudal servitude, died on 9 September 1976. Everywhere machines stood still, shops closed and people gathered on the streets. The television showed pictures of mourners weeping. But an acute observer would have concluded that the Chinese were shocked less by the death itself than by the uncertainty of what the future, after Mao Zedong, would bring.

First came the toppling of the Gang of Four, in October 1976. Hua had the four radical

LEFT: the new-look metropolis.
RIGHT: Deng Xiaoping led China into the modern era.

leaders – one of whom was Mao's widow Jiang Qing – arrested during a party meeting. They were convicted of creating and directing the Cultural Revolution. Jiang Qing died in prison.

By spring 1977, the new Chairman Hua's portrait was prominently displayed in the capital. A more than life-sized poster showed him

at the deathbed of the Great Helmsman. Attributed to Mao, the caption read: "You have matters in hand, my heart rests in peace". Hua, however, remained in power only a short time, though he tried to win reflected glory from the Mao cult. A veteran of the revolution was waiting in the wings, one who had twice disappeared into obscurity during the intra-party struggles: former Vice-Premier Deng Xiaoping, who emerged as China's leader in late 1978.

From 1978 to 1980, Beijing was the scene of countless demonstrations by dissatisfied Chinese from all over the country. Most were young students who courageously joined the

"Democracy Wall" movement in spring 1979. On the wall by Xidan market, *dazibao* (big character posters) reappeared. These were familiar from the Cultural Revolution years but were significantly different in their content. Officials were accused of corruption and favouritism, and individuals demanded justice for past wrongs. One concise wall poster merely asked: "Who knows the representative of my district, who is supposed to represent me in the People's Congress?" Space for name, address and telephone number were left blank, a plain pointer to the fact that National People's Congress members in China were chosen

by the higher echelons of the party and in practice no elections took place.

Students at the Xidan wall sold journals that they had produced themselves. It was through these journals that many of the people of Beijing learned for the first time of the mass poverty in the countryside. Delegations of peasants came from the provinces to complain of the disastrous situation. Demonstrators marched in front of the seat of the Central Committee of the Communist Party and on Tiananmen Square. Countless petitions were handed in daily, putting considerable pressure on the party. However, while many of the leaders of these demonstrations were arrested,

some of their ideas became part of official government policy.

The building of Beijing

During the 1970s, Beijing still seemed very much the Forbidden City to the few foreigners staying there. There was practically no tourism until 1977. Visitors were almost all guests of the state or the party. The most modern landmarks were still the "ten great buildings" completed in 1959 to mark the tenth anniversary of communism, including the Great Hall of the People, the museum buildings along Tiananmen, the Minzu Hotel, and the Radio Beijing building.

In stark contrast, tiny brick houses lined many streets, built as refuges after the Tangshan earthquake. There was no hurry to demolish these one-room homes since Beijing still needed the additional living space. For years, almost no new homes were built, although the population had increased explosively. The first skyscrapers, however, started to appear as early as 1977.

Opening the doors

In 1982, a new constitution came into being. An open door policy to foreign countries was one important step in the modernisation programme designed to quadruple China's economic power by the year 2000.

Soon, the first free markets arrived, seen at many major crossroads. In contrast to the state-run shops, these markets were able to offer fresh fruit and vegetables. For years, independent work and private trade had been condemned. Now cooks, cobblers, hairdressers, tailors and carpenters simply started to work for themselves.

Women could have their hair permed in new salons, and street traders offered all sorts of goods in front of the state-run department stores. The city seemed to have awoken from a long sleep, and the pace was hectic. People enjoyed the new beginning. The time of forced participation in political events and campaigns was over and interest in politics faded away. New horizons opened for the young, and never before had they been known to study so eagerly. Careers as scientists, engineers, and technicians, study trips abroad, and freedom and prosperity beckoned.

In the literature of this new decade, young lovers no longer vowed to fight to the death for the revolution and their homeland. Instead, they would study hard and help with the modernisation of their country. The "imperialist archenemies" of previous years became good friends nearly overnight. Television showed pictures from abroad and spread, intentionally or subliminally, the message of the blessings of consumerism. Values previously held firm – a simplistic right-or-wrong view of the world, including indoctrinated slogans – began to topple.

The three "luxury goods" – a bicycle, clock and radio – were no longer enough. Department stores filled up with refrigerators, washing machines, television sets and expensive imported goods. Before long, the first fashion shows and magazines, as well as the success of pop singers and film stars, began to awake the desire of women and men to look attractive and different.

This process of modernisation and reform, however, was not without controversy. After Deng Xiaoping's protégé Hu Yaobang became general secretary of the party and Zhao Ziyang became premier, opposition grew in conservative circles, especially in the army. At the end of 1983, a campaign began against

"spiritual pollution". Many serious criminals were publicly executed as a deterrent, but the fight was mainly against intellectuals and artists, and against fashions like long hair and Western music, which were being imported from Hong Kong.

For some, economic freedom was not enough. At the end of 1986, student protests that began in Hefei reached their peak in Shanghai, where they ended peacefully. This led to conservatives pressurising party secretary Hu Yaobang to retire, as he had sympathised with the students' calls for greater democracy and curbs on corruption. Zhao

Ziyang, who was regarded as a relative liberal, succeeded Hu, and in 1988 Li Peng took over from Zhao as premier.

Tiananmen and after

In April 1989, Tiananmen Square became the focus of the world's media as university students, later joined by workers, aired their grievances against the government at the largest demonstrations since 1949. Most protesters were angered by widespread corruption, and many demanded democratic reform. Hu Yaobang's recent death had ignited rumours and vanquished the hopes of many that political liberalisation was imminent.

LEFT: construction sites are all over the city.
ABOVE: faces of the new China.

The protests gained momentum and spread to other cities until, on 19 May, martial law was imposed on most of Beijing. After several attempts by Deng and other leaders to persuade the protesters to leave, the party lost patience. In the early hours of 4 June, soldiers fired live rounds and used tanks to force the protesters out of Tiananmen Square. At least 300 people are believed to have died, though the government has never given a full account of what happened that night. In the following days, similar protests across the country petered out, mostly peacefully.

Zhao Ziyang, like Hu before him, seemed

Deng's last great act was his "tour of the south" in 1992, when he reaffirmed the party's total commitment to the economic reforms of "socialism with Chinese characteristics". In 1993, Deng officially retired from politics, but remained de facto ruler of China.

After his death in 1997, the torch of economic reform passed to his chosen successor, President Jiang Zemin. The Hong Kong handover and his visit to the United States gave Jiang two opportunities that year to show his new stature to people in China and abroad.

Later in 1997, Jiang consolidated his place as the "core" of the party at the 15th Party

sympathetic to the protesters, and was sacked. Jiang Zemin became party secretary.

Meanwhile, also in May 1989, the leaders of the two socialist superpowers, Deng Xiaoping and Mikhail Gorbachev, who was pushing reforms in the Soviet Union, met in Beijing in an atmosphere of reconciliation after nearly 30 years of division.

To get rich is glorious

Post-Tiananmen, Beijing's growth slowed for a year or two. The massacre had put doubts into investors' minds, but this proved short-lived. By 1992, with Asian economies booming, things were looking up again.

Congress. Qiao Shi, head of the National People's Congress (NPC, China's parliament) and believed to be Jiang's most serious political contender, was pushed out of the all-powerful politburo. Meanwhile, Zhu Rongji strengthened his position as China's chief architect of economic reform.

In March 1999 the NPC enshrined "Deng Xiaoping Thought" in the constitution, giving him a status equal to Mao. The party now publishes several collections of Deng's speeches and reports, and promotes slogans used by Deng, including "To get rich is glorious" and "Some people must get rich first". "Jiang Zemin Thought" is already being developed.

New Asian metropolis

Beijing is well on the way to becoming an international metropolis, though for sheer economic vibrancy it looks increasingly second-best to its great rival Shanghai. The city is changing fast, but essential services do not follow urban renewal in some districts. Many property developers are unscrupulous and corruption is rife. Bicycles are being banished from some roads by the city government and forced off others by traffic conditions. During the middle of the day, the traffic grinds to a standstill on many main roads, adding to the already heavy air pollution.

Some believe the modernisation of the city

ply of retail and office space, the government pushed ahead several showpiece commercial complexes in time for the anniversary.

Today, fashionably dressed people stroll through city streets once dominated by dark-blue Mao suits. Even the most daring styles – tiny miniskirts, fluorescent hair – no longer cause offence or turn heads. Western-style bars and restaurants open almost weekly, especially in the embassy and university districts. Karaoke, which once swept the capital, has lost some of its popularity, but live music is going strong: local bands now have many regular venues, and visiting Western musicians play to full houses. Despite a crack-

has run out of control, and academics and planners have urged the municipal government to protect Beijing's heritage and environment, including its rapidly disappearing old *hutongs*. Some improvements have followed. Canals have been cleaned and pleasure boats are licensed on some. Main roads were given borders of grass and flowers ready for the 50th anniversary of the People's Republic in October 1999. On the other hand, despite an oversup-

down by the government, pirated video and music CDs proliferate on the streets, creating an ongoing international trade issue. Tourists are visiting the city in ever increasing numbers as the bureaucratic frustrations, which once made a visit to China so difficult, become consigned to history.

Private party

Inevitably, the new freedom has limits. "Social disorder" is the biggest fear of the party, which is determined never to allow a repeat of the 1989 demonstrations. The tenth anniversary of the Tiananmen massacre passed without incident. Security in Beijing was extremely tight, especially after the authorities had been sur-

LEFT: the 1989 demonstrations in Tiananmen Square shook China and the world.
ABOVE: glass-fronted skyscrapers increasingly dominate the skyline of the city centre.

prised in April by a protest by 10,000 followers of the quasi-religious Falun Gong movement. Many had travelled from other cities. In the crackdown that followed, thousands of Falun devotees were arrested in Beijing and other cities. Most were released after stern lectures.

Several more unusual bars, clubs and music venues were temporarily closed before the 50th anniversary celebrations. Martial law crept into the capital during September 1999. Most people were instructed to watch the parades from the comfort of their own homes, with an invited audience of just 100,000 actually present.

Everyone saw Jiang Zemin reflect the ideo-

appears poised to play a leading role in world economics and politics in the 21st century. The West's policy of engagement based, cynics claim, mainly on economic interests, led to high-profile state visits to China by US President Bill Clinton and by British Prime Minister Tony Blair in 1998. Jiang paid return visits to both countries in 1999.

Guessing growth

The diplomacy seemed to pay off. In a speech at the end of 1998 to mark the 20th anniversary of economic reform, Jiang promised to uphold the policies introduced by Deng. International

logical contradictions of "socialism with Chinese characteristics" in his behaviour. He put on a business suit to talk to leaders of multinational corporations at the Fortune Global Forum in Shanghai. A few days later Jiang moved to Beijing to play the role of communist patriarch in the 50th anniversary celebrations. On 1 October he donned a grey "Mao" jacket and stood in the back of an old Red Flag limousine to inspect troops and armour lined up along Changan Avenue. The huge military parade, which featured tanks, missiles and planes, was part of a $10 billion extravaganza.

Despite Western concerns over human rights and China's policy towards Taiwan, China

companies continue to beat a path to China's door, drawn by the sometimes premature idea of the world's "largest market". Most leading multinationals have bases in Beijing, Shanghai, and Hong Kong.

Yet the growth of China's gross domestic product slowed from regular double digits in the early 1990s to seven percent in 1998. The financial crisis that started in Southeast Asia and quickly swept through Hong Kong, Korea and Japan in the second half of 1997 also hit Beijing. China's markets plunged, but its ability to maintain the value of its currency and relative economic stability led many other governments to see China, not Japan, as

Asia's economic stabiliser in the 21st century.

Yet the widening gap between rich and poor is clearly visible. On the street, men in faded old clothes pedalling heavily laden tricycles are passed by German-made saloon cars driven by businessmen in expensive suits. And the ranks of unemployed are growing – especially among low-skilled workers over 40 years of age.

The March 1999 National People's Congress session further enhanced the role of the private sector, and confirmed that priority will be given to the development of central and western provinces under the Tenth Five Year Plan (2001–2005). But major questions remain over

again turbulent, partly due to ongoing issues over trade, human rights and Taiwan, and partly due to two particular events in 1999. First came allegations that China had stolen US nuclear weapons technology, which China denies. Then, in April, US planes on a NATO mission in Serbia bombed the Chinese embassy in Belgrade. Though the US insists this was an accident, and President Bill Clinton offered a personal apology, many Chinese remain angry. Demonstrators attacked embassies of several Nato countries in the week following the bombing. Reaction to the bombing was orchestrated by the party, which benefited from the wave of

the slow reform of state enterprises, how to deal with the resultant unemployment, and how to boost consumer spending. Through economic policies and media campaigns, the government still tries to persuade people to spend – sometimes deeming it a "patriotic duty" – especially in key sectors such as housing.

Shadow boxing

At the close of the 20th century, relations between China and the United States were

patriotism. On a more positive note, China seems likely to negotiate entry into the World Trade Organisation.

In September 1999, a major earthquake in Taiwan temporarily halted the growth of cross-straits hostility, prompted, according to the mainland, by Taiwanese President Li Denghui's attempts to move Taiwan towards formal independence. In his 50th anniversary speech in Beijing, Jiang reiterated China's determination to push forward "peaceful reunification" with Taiwan. The Chinese government still reserves the right to use force to take back the island, though it has promised not to use nuclear weapons against its "renegade province". ❏

LEFT: JJs disco packs in the crowds.
ABOVE: a show of military force during the 50th Anniversary celebrations of the PRC.

PEOPLE

Beijingers, with their distinctive burr, love to talk. And the economic and social changes of recent years have certainly given them plenty to talk about...

Defining the typical Beijinger gets harder by the day. In the early years of communist China, enforced uniformity made such description a relatively simple task. Everyone worked for the state. Men and women wore identical "Mao" suits and lived in spartan, state-supplied apartments. They rode bicycles, attended compulsory meetings organised by the Party, and had little time or money for leisure.

Phenomenal economic growth has brought unprecedented social liberation to China's cities, and families enjoy larger apartments, with facilities and consumer goods undreamed of before 1978. As government control has focussed on the political sphere and relaxed in other areas, a new generation has grown up less constrained by the straitjacket of communism.

Lifestyles, too, have diversified. Some work all day, others play all night. Like most capital cities, Beijing attracts leading entrepreneurs, actors, singers, models, bureaucrats, politicians, generals, scientists, and sports stars. Members of this elite step briefly into public view as they emerge from the dark glass of their cars to spend the monthly wage of an average factory worker on a single meal at one of Beijing's many expensive restaurants.

Public space

Shopping vies with watching television and eating out for the title of number one leisure pursuit. During the 1980s and early 1990s, people rushed to open small businesses like shops, market stalls, restaurants, hairdressers' salons, and garages. Large shopping centres and chain stores have since displaced some of their smaller competitors. Wangfujing, which underwent major redevelopment in 1998 and 1999, is again the capital's premier promenading street.

Lack of public and private space means many activities still take place on Beijing's busy streets and hutongs. Walk around a major inter-

PRECEDING PAGES: rush hour; relaxing in the park.
LEFT: an elderly Beijing gent.
RIGHT: Beijingers dote on their children.

section and you will see families flying kites over the road, boys kicking a football around on the grass verges, and elderly people chatting on bridges. On summer evenings, along the pavements and under the bridges sit barbers, bicycle repairers, fruit and vegetable vendors, neighbourhood committee wardens, and fortune-

tellers. *Qi gong* practitioners and *Yang Ge* dancers (*see pages 54–55*) use whatever space remains. And there, keeping order among the motley procession of pedestrians, cyclists, drivers and passengers, are the ever-watchful eyes of authority; the police, flag-waving traffic wardens, and bicycle and car park attendants.

Made in China

Individuality has flourished in tandem with the economy, as fashion and pop culture have taken Beijing by storm. Many of the Western-style fashions once reserved for export now fill clothes shops and markets. Although foreign brand designer clothes remain popular with more affluent consumers, exclusive "Made in China" labels are gaining recognition. Bold, modern designs incorporate traditional Chinese motifs, often using imperial style fabrics.

Earrings and dyed hair are de rigueur for hip young men, while platform soles and hotpants are the norm for their girlfriends.

The Communist Party is definitely not trendy, and members under the age of 30 suffer "young fogey" taunts from their peers. For chic, affluent youngsters, the Party has made way for the party.

Countless karaoke venues and small discos form the backbone of Beijing's nightlife. Older

and wealthier people head for huge cabaret and restaurant complexes. Frequent reports of a "Beijing Spring" are at best exaggerated, but many new cultural forms and styles have taken root, including Western theatre, jazz, punk rock, performance art, and tattoo parlours. The first Chinese novel to portray openly lesbian relationships was published in 1999.

Mobile phones, pagers, home computers, sound systems, VCD players and 36-inch TVs keep the culture vultures in touch with the latest trends, and with each other.

English, compulsory in schools, also helps the spread of Western culture. Many middle-class parents pay for extra private lessons for their children. "Crazy English," in which students are told to shout out the words, has caught on after promotion at evangelist-style rallies, and traditional rote-learning methods are gradually being cast aside.

Born free

After three decades of rapid population growth encouraged by Mao, the one-child policy was initiated in 1979. Couples having more than one child were penalised with fines and other disincentives. In rural areas, some overzealous officials used forcible sterilisation and abortion. Abandonment and female infanticide became common, as did spoilt male offspring, so-called "little emperors" (*see box below*).

Implementation was weaker in Beijing and other large cities. Parents still theoretically require permission to conceive, but those outside the state sector can avoid the bureaucracy, while many state employers seem to have abdicated their responsibility. Chemist's shops, private hospitals, and a few semi-independent counselling centres offer more choice for contraception.

The future of the one-child policy remains uncertain. In the 1980s, the party promised that by 2000 the policy would be over. Yet in 1999, state media warned that tougher enforcement might follow in the early 21st century.

Lavish weddings are another reflection of greater affluence. Many Beijingers marry in Western dresses and suits, sometimes arriving in limousines. More money, of course, does not guarantee greater happiness. Beijing's divorce rate reached over 25 percent in 1998, nearly twice the national average and higher than that of many developed countries.

NOT-SO-LITTLE EMPERORS

Since the one-child policy was introduced in 1979, a single child often has a monopoly over two parents and four doting grandparents. Boys, seen as inheritors of the family line, are spoilt more. Memories of famine, and the desire to get the most out of one offspring, mean many parents believe bigger is better. Obesity has become common among urban children puffed up by Western fast food and countless brands of snacks and sweets.

In return for all the attention, the Little Emperors face increasing pressure to succeed in their exams. Yet sympathy is in short supply: "Many of them are selfish, lazy, arrogant and uncaring," wrote *China Daily*.

Second and third marriages are common. Couples marry later and have children later. Some decide not to have children at all. Younger people who can afford their own apartment often live together before marriage.

These trends appear to be tolerated by the authorities. The state-run China Central Television has reported uncritically the increases in the number of couples living together, in single parent families, and even in homosexual relationships.

New sexual freedoms

More liberal attitudes to sex have had one negative side-effect: they have brought a huge rise in prostitution. Prostitutes seldom solicit on the street. Instead, they work in massage parlours, hairdressers' salons, bars and clubs. Often they present themselves in nightclubs as *san pei* – "three accompaniments" women. Officials who licence the activity claim san pei means providing customers with companions for eating, drinking and dancing. But the privacy of windowless karaoke rooms hides much more.

Rates of HIV infection and AIDS remain low by world standards, though some fear the relative ignorance of young Chinese people about sex, long a taboo subject, could prove dangerous when combined with rapid social change. The first condom machine in a Chinese college was installed at Beijing's Qinghua University in 1999, heralding official recognition of the need for safe sex among students.

Much of Beijing's "disorder" – from unplanned births to crime and pollution is blamed on migrants. Using family connections, savings, or sheer persistence, an estimated 2–3 million migrants have managed to find a niche in the capital.

Most are men who clean toilets, transport waste on heavy tricycle carts, unblock drains and canals, or construct roads, housing and shopping centres. Some sell fruit and vegetables, often sleeping under their makeshift stalls in summer. Many women find live-in jobs as waitresses or servants. Tibetan merchants,

> **AUSPICIOUS DATES**
>
> Despite the liberalisation of recent years, some marital superstitions endure. On 9 September 1999 (9/9/99) hundreds of Beijing couples married, many at 9:09am.

standing out from the crowd in their sheepskin robes, sell gazelle horns and yak skulls.

Apart from the occasional, incongruous sight of these nomads strolling through central Beijing, Hui Muslims are the capital's most visible minority. Beijing has several mosques and Islamic cultural centres, as well as Muslim districts like Niu Jie (Ox Street).

Hui women wear headscarves, and men usually wear white skullcaps similar to those worn in Muslim countries. The men often grow

beards, but otherwise resemble China's Han majority. The capital's other main Muslim group, Uighurs from Xinjiang in the far west of China, look more Turkish than Chinese.

Beijing's Yuan and Qing dynasty rulers were Mongolian and Manchu, respectively, from ethnic groups which form two of China's 56 official minorities. Some minority families have lived here for centuries, but, despite the addition of 100,000 foreigners, the city is not yet multicultural.

For the visitor, however, restaurants run by Dai, Uighur, Hui, Korean, Mongolian and Tibetan people offer a glimpse of what lies on the rim of China's great rice bowl. ❏

LEFT: a "little emperor" at a fashion show.
RIGHT: a Fourth of July celebration is held every year in the United States Embassy.

BEIJING'S MORNING EXERCISES

From 5am, early morning exercisers begin to fill parks, pavements, alleys, grass verges and any space large enough to swing a leg or bat a shuttlecock. It's a fascinating spectacle

Walk along any Beijing street early one morning, and you will see old men shuffle out of their homes to escape the chaos in their tiny apartments. In their hands are bird cages, which they swing back and forth as they make their way to the nearest park, where they join people of all ages enjoying a myriad of activities.

Stroll through one of the larger parks, such as Longtan, Tiantan or Ditan, and watch the fascinating mixture of martial arts, breathing exercises, Beijing opera, calligraphy, ballroom dancing, *Yang Ge* dancing, badminton, jogging, hanging from trees, shouting exercises, meditation, kite-flying and, the newest addition, walking the dog. *Taijiquan* shadow boxers draw the eye with slow, flowing movements as they practice "monkey's retreat" or "send the tiger over the mountain."

As the exercisers disperse, elderly people spread out chessboards, mah-jong tiles, dominoes or playing cards. Spectators roll jangling steel balls around their hands, a practice said to prevent rheumatism. By now, the streets are crowded with commuters on buses, taxis and bicycles.

▷ **FOLK FANS**
Yang Ge dancing, originating from folk dances, is one of the most popular forms of exercise for middle-aged and elderly women.

▷ **SLOW MOVERS**
Qigong practitioners use slow, precise breathing exercises that focus their strength. *Qi* means vital energy or life-force, which adherents believe can be positively channelled.

△ **CALLIGRAPHY**
Writing large characters on paving slabs helps exercise both mind and body. The characters are usually painted with plain water, so the fine brushwork quickly disappears.

△ **HAVING A BALL**
Ballroom dancing is popular with older people, who see it mainly as a form of exercise, and with younger people who take the art form seriously.

▷ **FULLY EQUIPPED**
Many retired or unemployed people vacate crowded homes to spend whole days in a park, joining activities with their friends, and taking books, food, drink, birds, and radios.

SPRING FESTIVAL YANG GE DANCING

Yang Ge literally means "dancing during the planting season." This is why it plays an important role in Spring Festival temple fairs at Chinese new year, when dancers wear traditional style robes and heavy make-up. Most dancers are women, with a few male characters. Some troupes include more men in large bands of drummers or stilt-walkers. A prancing fool and a wealthy woman riding a hobby-horse are among the most common characters. Drums, gongs and the *sona*, an ancient wind instrument that sounds like bagpipes, accompany the dancers.

Yang Ge originated in the farming villages of northern China. The stories are based on traditional legends and classical literature. Different areas have different styles, with the northeast the best known. In rural areas, larger Yang Ge groups include stilt walkers and acrobats. Children balanced on long poles appear to float in the air above the processions.

For daily practice in Beijing, dancers rarely wear costumes but they do use fans, the standard Yang Ge prop. Shops and restaurants sometimes hire groups in full costume, to add colour to special promotions.

◁ **FIGHTING FIT**
Sword drills are one of the key elements of *wushu*, the general name for martial arts. Standard movements build concentration and improve suppleness.

△ **MEDITATION**
In order to clear the mind, some people stand for tens of minutes, even hours, apparently staring at a tree. Others balance on bricks to maintain a precise position.

LIFE IN THE HUTONG

The heart of Beijing lies behind its modern steel and glass facade, in the tranquil hutong, narrow alleys that have been the hub of the city's street life for 700 years

In a region protected by the Great Wall, Beijing was hidden behind its own city walls until 1949. And within those walls, its citizens lived within yet more, built around their own homes. For hundreds of years, Beijingers built single-storey homes with tiled roofs, facing into a central courtyard and protected by high back walls. Wealthy merchants and mandarins enjoyed entire courtyards, or *siheyuan*, while ordinary families usually occupied a single room – or a lean-to against an outside wall.

Today, soaring walls of mirrored glass flank the main ring roads, taking over the function of the city wall, itself a victim of town planning. Yet in the city centre, faceless buildings of the 1950s protect the inner core, a labyrinth of crumbling old grey alleyways between the courtyards, some dating back several centuries. These are the *hutong*.

Once the hub of Beijing life, hutong are now threatened with eradication and replacement by modern high-rise housing estates. But many remain and, for now, offer a fascinating glimpse into the past.

Hutong history

Beijing is a Mongol city. The conquerors who first made the city their capital brought with them their customs, way of life and language. Genghis Khan had wanted to turn the plains around Beijing into pasture, an extension of the vast Mongolian grasslands. But the Mongols did not complete their conquest of China until the reign of Genghis' grandson, Kublai Khan, who had other ideas. In the new capital of the Yuan dynasty, deep wells were dug and horse-troughs, *hut* or *hot* in Mongolian, were set up.

Mongols or no Mongols, Beijingers could hardly leave their houses and homes lying unprotected amid the wells and horse-troughs. So, they would close up the small spaces between the houses with a wall and privacy was

restored. It was even simpler to build on to the wall of their neighbours, although no one was allowed to block another householder's route to water. In this way, the tangle of hutong grew, just wide enough to let a rider through.

The houses and courtyards, hidden away and boxed in, are themselves closed off with

wooden gates, on which one can often see carved characters intended to bring good fortune to the occupants. If you try to take a look at such a house – the gates are almost always invitingly open – you will find your view blocked by yet another wall: the ghost wall. Apparently, a Chinese ghost can only move straight ahead, and once it has crossed the wooden threshold between the carved stone gateposts, the wall bars any further progress.

Inscribed tablets are set into some ghost walls. These carry messages ranging from the philosophical "Hail jewel in the lotus" to more recent proclamations of patriotism – "Long live Chairman Mao".

LEFT: view over hutong rooftops in western Beijing.
RIGHT: hutong resident and pipe.

Courtyard culture

Hutong form the heart of traditional Beijing. They are the domain of old men who fill the parks every evening with their bird cages, wrapping themselves in thick blue clothes to protect against the weather, with grey beards and laughter lines framing their last remaining teeth. The women wear black hats like those in the Beijing opera, and can produce a three-minute tirade of curses with ease before they even think of drawing a breath, then fling a convincing "It's all true!" as their opponent withdraws into a courtyard. These are the secret lords of the city, who at five in the morning,

before going to work, prefer *taijiquan*, a form of shadow boxing, to jogging.

You really shouldn't miss visiting one or two of these unique courtyards as the introverted architecture reveals more about the Chinese family and the psyche of the people of Beijing than any books or lectures. In an ideal situation, you will pass the ghost wall and see a courtyard full of flowers and cacti and a few trees – usually apricot, walnut or pomegranate. And of course, the family bicycles. Three or four single-storey buildings surround the courtyard, the lower halves of their windows covered with paper to obstruct the view of nosy

WHAT'S IN A NAME?

The name of each of Beijing's hutong has its own story to tell, by describing the life it contains. Some names indicate professions or crafts: Bowstring Makers' Lane, Cloth Lane, Hat Lane. Other lanes, if mostly populated by a single family, are named after that family: the lane of the Liu family, the front and rear lanes of the Gao family, and even the village of the Zhuang family.

Many hutong are given names according to their shape. The Buffalo Horn Curve is, of course, curved, as is the Dog Tail Lane, of which there are at least eight in Beijing. Horse Tail, Goat Tail and Pig Tail Lanes all have similar shapes. Trousers Lane has a "belly" section and two branching

"legs", as does East Trousers Lane. Sesame Lane (not Sesame Street!) is simply a very small lane.

Sometimes the names still carry echoes of the military organisation of the Qing dynasty Manchu state. Nearly all the names ending in "camp", such as Mongol Camp, Muslim Camp, or Camp by the Incense Burner, go back to former troop positions. In lanes carrying the most esoteric monikers, it's up to the visitor to find out the origin of the name – if such a thing is possible. How did Chicken Claw Lane, Western Crutch Lane, Heart's Point Lane, Sausage Lane, Coffin Lane, Mother Sow Lane, Donkey's Hoof Lane and Big Ears Lane get their names?

passers-by, the upper half glazed. Inside the rooms you can still find ornately carved wood panels and furniture, and ancient calligraphy.

In the siheyuan of families higher in the social order, a second and third courtyard may adjoin the first. There may be two small "ear courtyards" to the sides, which contain the kitchens or serve as storage spaces. These more finely-constructed homes have curved roof tiles, wooden pillars on stone pedestals, and often carved details on the external brickwork. But such housing has become a rarity, as space is needed for the ever-growing population.

At the main gate, the carved stone *mendun'r* ("door pairs") also reflect the status of the occupants. Many designs feature lions, which were originally reserved for homes connected with the imperial household. Drum-shaped stones marked the homes of military officers, while square stones indicated a civil servant. Bats symbolise good luck, pears longevity, and fish

SELFISH MOTIVES

Siheyuan preservation was set back by the failure of the 1990s Ju'er reconstruction project, which saw poor residents moving out and sneakily renting their rebuilt homes to the wealthy.

prosperity. Three goats stand for peace, and a lotus flower ensures a happy marriage.

You can sense the spirit of the Great Helmsman, as Mao was known, in the lanes of Beijing. In 1950, the city had 1.7 million inhabitants, and the population was growing only slowly. The population movements of the 1950s saw the population grow, while the early years of the Cultural Revolution (1966–76) brought a huge influx. Still more people arrived during the economic boom of the

1980s and 1990s. Large single-family dwellings were adapted to house four or five families. Smaller rooms were added to the outside of some courtyards, narrowing the hutong further. Most courtyards became hopelessly overcrowded. Trees and flowers were replaced by huts and cooking fires, bicycles and prams. But even in such courtyards, there is always space to spread out a chessboard.

Preservation versus progress

The worst slums were demolished to make way for apartment blocks, but large areas of courtyard housing remained until the late 1980s. As in the West, housing policies have

LEFT: relaxing over a game of *xianqi* (Chinese chess).
ABOVE: remnants of the Cultural Revolution are tucked away in the city's alleyways.

fluctuated between wholesale redevelopment and sensitive renovation. Now siheyuan and hutong are bearing the brunt of the drive to create a concrete metropolis of mirrored-glass skyscrapers and ivy-covered flyovers. Many hutong families occupy just one or two small rooms – most are combined kitchens, living rooms, bedrooms and washrooms. The families use a public toilet in the alley, even when the temperature drops to –10°C (14°F). A 15th-floor apartment with all mod cons naturally holds great appeal.

Yet some families prefer to stay put, fearing exile from the city centre to distant suburbs

with poor infrastructure. Others believe hutong should be preserved for their historical value.

In a country where, because of the political climate, public debate normally tackles only the most trivial issues, the fate of Beijing's hutong caused a stir in the late 1990s. Academics wrote articles stressing the importance of the hutong to Beijing's cultural heritage. Residents wrote to officials and attempted court action. Some even staged small protests. And local media reported both sides of the story. Though the demolition continues, the ongoing debate seems likely to save some hutong.

The best way to approach the hutong these days is through an organised tour. Starting from

the north end of Beihai Park, these tours will expose travellers to the history and culture that lies behind these ancient and curious structures. They take you to the hutong around Qianhai and Houhai lakes, one of Beijing's most picturesque areas. They give you a chance to see past the hutong walls and enter the siheyuan, perhaps even to have a chat, if lucky, with a local inhabitant.

Unguided tour

If you want to take a walk through the hutong on your own, it's no problem. Many typical lanes are in the south of the city, where the Chinese were permitted to live (the north was reserved for the Mongol and later for the Manchu conquerors and their allied peoples), such as around the bird market near Longtan Park. Like many visitors, you'll probably end up in Liulichang, a gentrified lane of shops with art and antiques for sale; head off south or southeastwards from here into any lane and just walk around. No one gets lost doing this. Another possible starting point is the acrobatics theatre in Dazhalan Street. However, allow at least half a day for such an excursion.

On a typical summer's evening, young and old sit under the lantern in front of the house entrance, their sleeves rolled up, fanning themselves and chasing the flies off the chessboard. The husks of melon seeds are piled up where they've been spat. The housework is done and the children have been sent to bed. The chamber pots have been taken, together with a fly-swatter, to the public toilet (its presence can be sensed from afar). Now is the time for old tales to be told, deep in the tangle of grey alleyways.

If you can speak Chinese, or can find a friend to interpret, go and join the old Beijingers. Guests are always welcome. The curious inquiry of "What country do you come from then?" is your ticket of entry to a long conversation. Everyone in the hutong has a story to tell; no one will admit to being the one who doesn't know how this particular hutong got its name. You will certainly not leave without hearing a charming or exciting story, and given local hospitality, you'll probably be sitting there long into the night. ❑

LEFT: clearing away the snow.
RIGHT: life in a hutong near Qianmen.

RELIGION

Daoism, Buddhism and Confucianism are slowly regaining popularity, after the
Cultural Revolution abruptly halted one the world's richest spiritual traditions

China is the cradle of some of the most profound and enduring religious beliefs and practices. By the time Buddhism and Islam flourished along the ancient trade routes that became known as the Silk Road, an indigenous religion was already well established.

The earliest forms of Daoism grew out of cultural practices associated with shamanism and ancestor worship. Chinese astrology, astronomy and medicine all have their roots in this early Daoism, influenced by ideas that reached China from Babylon and other ancient civilizations of the Middle East. On Daoist holy mountains, the path was not simply a route from one place to another; it also symbolised the journey from the physical to the spiritual realm, an important stage in a lifelong moral quest.

Sacrificial altars, reserved for emperors and priests, topped the most sacred Daoist mountains. Originally both humans and animals were sacrificed, as in many ancient religions, and later just animals. In China, the most important sacrifices were to ancestors, both real and legendary, rather than deities.

Ancestor worship

The ancestor worship of the Chinese is based on the belief that a person has two souls. One of them is created at the time of conception, and when you die, this soul stays in the grave with the corpse and lives on the sacrificial offerings. As the corpse decomposes, the strength of the soul dwindles, until it eventually leads a shadow existence by the Yellow Springs in the underworld. However, if no more sacrifices are offered, it will return to earth as an ill-willed spirit and cause damage.

The second soul only emerges at birth. During its heavenly voyage, it is threatened by evil forces, and is dependent upon the sacrifices and prayers of living descendants. If the sacrifices cease, then this soul, too, turns into an evil spirit. But if the descendants continue to make sacrificial offerings and maintain the grave, the soul of the deceased ancestor may offer them help and protection.

Originally, formal ceremonies of ancestor worship were exclusive to the king. Later inscriptions on oracle bones from the Shang

dynasty (1600–1100 BC), and on bronze dating from the Zhou period (1100–476 BC), reveal an ancestor worship of high nobility, a cult of a high god called Di, and an animistic belief in numerous gods of nature.

By around 500 BC peasants began to honour their ancestors. At first, people believed the soul of the ancestor would search for a human substitute, and created an abode for the soul during the sacrificial ritual. It was usually the grandson of the honoured ancestor who took on the role of substitute. About 2,000 years ago, genealogical tables were introduced as homes for the soul during sacrificial acts. Until then, the king and noblemen had used human sacrifices for

LEFT: the Jade Emperor.
RIGHT: ancestor worship.

ancestral worship. Today they offer their ancestors sacrifices of food, for example, during the Qingming Festival.

Popular beliefs

The original popular Chinese religion focused on the worship of natural forces. Later on, people began to worship the Jade Emperor, a figure from Daoism; from the 14th century onwards the Jade Emperor became the most important god in popular religion. Guanyin, the goddess of mercy, originated in Mahayana (Great Wheel) Buddhism. There were also earth deities, and every town, large or small, wor-

Daoism

Two of the central concepts of Daoism are *dao* and *wuwei*. *Dao* means the way or path, but also means method or principle. *Wuwei* is sometimes simply defined as passivity, or "swimming with the stream". The concept of *de* (virtue) is closely linked to this, not in the sense of moral honesty, but as a virtue that manifests itself in daily life when *dao* is put into practice. The forces of *yin* and *yang* determine the course of events in the world. The masculine, brightness, activity and heaven are considered *yang* forces; the feminine, weak, dark and passive elements of life are *yin*.

shipped its own town god. Demons of illness, spirits of the house, and even the god of latrines had to be remembered. The deities of streams and rivers were considered particularly dangerous and unpredictable.

Until the founding of the Qin Empire in 221 BC, China had been divided into a considerable number of small states, with a variety of contending schools of philosophical thought. From these myriad doctrines, only Confucianism and Daoism had gained wide acceptance. Buddhism, China's other major religion, arrived from India in the 1st century AD, though it remained small-scale for several more centuries.

In popular religion, Laozi is seen as the founder of Daoism. He lived at a time of crises and upheavals. Some early Daoists were opposed to feudal society, yet they did not fight actively for a new social structure, preferring instead to live in a pre-feudal tribal society.

Experts today still argue about Laozi's historical existence. He was born, it is said, in a village in Henan province in 604 BC into a distinguished family. For a time, he held the office of archivist in the then capital, Luoyang. But he later retreated into solitude and died in his village in 517 BC. According to a famous legend, he wanted to leave China on a black ox when he foresaw the decline of the empire.

The classic work of Daoism is the *Daodejing*. It now seems certain that more than one author wrote this work. The earliest, and most significant, followers of Laozi were Liezi and Zhuangzi. Liezi (5th century BC) was concerned with the relativity of experiences, and he strived to comprehend the *dao* with the help of meditation. Zhuangzi (4th century BC) is especially famous for his poetic allegories. But the abstract concepts of Daoism did not attract ordinary people. Even in the Han period (206

believed to be governed by the Queen Mother of the West (Xiwangmu) and her husband, the Royal Count of the East (Dongwanggong). Without making any changes to it, the Daoists also took over the idea of hell from Buddhism.

Religious Daoism developed in various directions and schools. The ascetics retreated to the mountains and devoted all their time to meditation, or else they lived in monasteries. Daoist priests had important functions as medicine men and interpreters of oracles. They car-

BC–AD 220), there were signs of a popular and religious Daoism. As Buddhism also became more popular it borrowed ideas from Daoism, and vice versa, to the point where one might speak of a fusion between the two.

Paradise found

The Daoists and Buddhists both believed that the great paradise was in the far west of China, hence the name, Western Paradise. It was

ried out exorcism and funeral rites, and read mass for the dead or for sacrificial offerings. Many of these practices drew on ancient shamanism and Daoist magic.

Confucian influence

For Confucius, too, *dao* and *de* are central concepts. For more than 2,000 years, the ideas of Confucius (551–479 BC) have influenced Chinese culture, which in turn sculpted the worldview of neighboring lands such as Korea, Japan and Southeast Asia. It is debatable whether Confucianism is a religion in the strictest sense. But Confucius was worshipped as a deity, although he was only officially made equal to the heav-

LEFT: the forest ghosts and spirits altar at the Daoist Dongyue Temple.
ABOVE: statue of Laozi.
RIGHT: a Daoist monk.

enly god by an imperial edict in 1906. (Up until 1927, many Chinese offered him sacrifices.)

Mencius, the most famous Confucian scholar, describes the poverty at the time Confucius was born as follows: "There are no wise rulers, the lords of the states are driven by their desires. In their farms are fat animals, in their royal stables fat horses, but the people look hungry and on their fields there are people who are dying of starvation."

Confucius himself came from an impoverished family of the nobility who lived in the state of Lu (near Qufu in western Shandong province). For years, Confucius – or Kong Fuzi

(Master Kong) – tried to gain office with one of the feudal lords, but he was dismissed again and again. So he travelled around with his disciples and instructed them in his ideas. He is said to have taught 3,000 disciples. A number of them, including Mencius, were highly-gifted and are still worshipped today. Some legends say that Confucius and Laozi once met, though most scholars discount this possibility.

Wisdom and gentility

Confucius significantly re-interpreted the idea of the *junzi*, a nobleman, to that of a noble man, whose life is morally sound and who is, therefore, legitimately entitled to reign. He believed that he would create an ideal social order if he reinstated the culture and rites of the early Zhou period (1100–700 BC). Humanity (*ren*) was a central concept at the time, based on fraternity and love of children. A ruler would only be successful if he could govern according to these principles.

Confucius defined the social positions and hierarchies very precisely. Only if and when every member of society takes full responsibility for his or her position will society as a whole function smoothly. Family and social ties – and hierarchy – were considered fundamental: between father and son (filial piety); man and woman (female subservience); older brother and younger brother; friend and friend; and ruler and subordinate.

Confucianism has had many incarnations. After the Han dynasty emperors adopted it, Confucianism became a religion of law and order. This ensured its popularity with subsequent dynasties. Just as the universe is dictated by the world order, and the sun, moon and stars move according to the laws of nature, so a person, too, should live within the framework of world order. This idea, in turn, is based upon the assumption that man can be educated. Ethical principles were turned into central issues.

In the 12th century, Zhu Xi (1130–1200 BC) succeeded in combining the metaphysical tendencies of Buddhism and Daoism with the pragmatism of Confucianism. His systematic work includes teachings about the creation of the microcosm and macrocosm, as well as the metaphysical basis of Chinese ethics.

This system, known as Neo-Confucianism, reached canonical status in China; it was the basis of all state examinations, a determining factor for Chinese officialdom until the 20th century. Mao tried to annihilate Confucianism – and all religion – in the Cultural Revolution. But non-religious Confucianism is slowly finding favour with a new breed of pragmatic communists who value the ancient religion's emphasis on order and social hierarchy.

Buddhism

The Chinese initially encountered Buddhism at the beginning of the first century AD, when merchants and monks came

ROOT OF LEARNING

Confucius is regarded as the founder of scholarly life in China. The Chinese word *ru* – as a rule translated as Confucian – means "someone of a gentle nature", a trait attributed to a cultured person.

able opposition to Buddhism, which contrasted sharply with Confucian ethics and ancestor worship. At the time of the Three Kingdoms (AD 220–280), the religion spread in each of the three states. The trading towns along the Silk Road as far east as Luoyang became centres of the new religion. After tribes of foreign origin had founded states in the north, and the gentry from the north had sought refuge in the eastern Jin dynasty (317–420), Buddhism developed along very different lines

to China over the Silk Road. The type of Buddhism that is prevalent in China today is the Mahayana (Great Wheel) school, which – as opposed to Hinayana (Small Wheel) – promises all creatures redemption through the Bodhisattva (redemption deities).

Two aspects were particularly attractive to the Chinese: the teachings of karma provided a better explanation for individual misfortune, and there was a hopeful promise for existence after death. Nevertheless, there was considerable

LEFT: portrait of Confucius.
ABOVE: worshipper lighting incense at a Buddhist temple in Beijing.

in the north and south for about two centuries. During the rule of Emperor Wudi (502–549), rejection and hostility towards Buddhism spread among Confucians. And during the relatively short-lived northern Zhou dynasty (557–581), Buddhism was officially banned (from 574 to 577).

Imperial approval

Buddhism was most influential during the Tang dynasty (618–907). Several emperors officially supported the religion; the Tang Empress Wu Zetian, in particular, surrounded herself with Buddhist advisors. During the years 842 to 845, however, Chinese Buddhists also experienced the most severe persecutions in their entire history: a total of 40,000 temples and monasteries were destroyed, and Buddhism was blamed for the economic decline and moral decay of the dynasty.

Despite this setback, ten Chinese schools of Buddhism emerged, eight of which were essentially philosophical in nature and did not influence popular religion. Only two schools have remained influential: Chan (School of Meditation or Zen Buddhism) and Pure Land (Amitabha-Buddhism). The masters of Chan considered meditation to be the only path to knowledge.

redeemer of the world). In Chinese monasteries, Sakyamuni greets the faithful as a laughing Buddha in the entrance hall. Since the 14th century, the Amitabha School had dominated the life and culture of the Chinese people.

Chan (Zen) Buddhism began at the Shaolin temple in Henan province, now more famous for its martial arts. It preached redemption through buddhahood, which anyone is able to reach. It despised knowledge gained from books or dogmas, as well as rites. Liberating shocks or guided meditation are used to lead disciples towards the experience of enlightenment. Other techniques used to achieve final

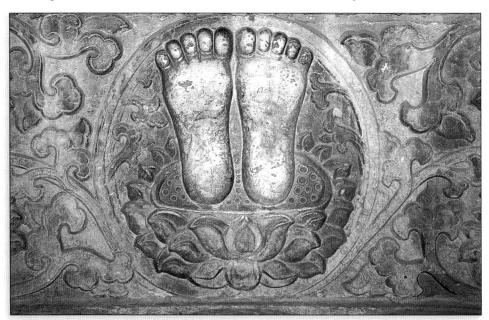

In Mahayana Buddhism, worship focused on the Bodhisattva Avalokiteshvara. Since the 7th century AD, the ascetic Bodhisattva has been a popular female figure in China. She is called Guanyin, a motherly goddess of mercy who represents a central deity for the ordinary people. Guanyin means "the one who listens to complaints."

Heart of the faith

In Chinese Buddhism, the centre of religious attention is the Sakyamuni Buddha, the founder of Buddhism who was forced into the background in the 6th century by the Maitreya Buddha (who was called Milefo in China, or

insights were long hikes and physical work.

The most important method was a dialogue with the master, who asked subtle and paradoxical questions, to which he expected equally paradoxical answers. In 1949, the year the People's Republic of China was founded, there were approximately 500,000 Buddhist monks and nuns, and 50,000 temples and monasteries. A number of well-known Buddhist temples were classified as historical monuments.

In the 7th century AD, Buddhism was introduced into Tibet from India. With the influence of the monk Padmasambhava, Tibetan Buddhism incorporated shamanist beliefs and rituals from the indigenous Bön religion. Apart from the Buddhist and Bön deities, Tibetan Buddhism includes Brahman and Hindu gods. Magic, repetitive prayers, movements, symbols and sacrificial rituals are all means to achieve redemption.

The monasteries in Tibet developed into centres of intellectual and worldly power, Yet arguments – theosophical and political – were common and only the reformer Tsongkhapa (1357–1419) succeeded in rectifying the chaos. He founded the Gelugpa (Virtuous) order, which re-introduced strict rules, including

LOST HERITAGE

The Cultural Revolution hit Buddhism hard, especially in Tibet. Only a few important monasteries and cultural objects could be protected or partly preserved.

hisattva of Mercy (Avalokiteshvara), is also worshipped as the patron god of Tibet. The Panchen Lama is higher in the hierarchy of the gods and the embodiment of Buddha Amitabha. The 14th Dalai Lama – enthroned in 1940 – fled to India after an uprising in 1959. He still lives in exile.

The tenth Panchen Lama died in Beijing in January 1989, at the age of 50. He remains a controversial, ambiguous figure. Some Tibetans still see him as a traitor, while others believe his collabora-

absolute celibacy. The Chinese often call Gelugpa the Yellow Hat order.

According to legend, Tsongkhapa predicted that two of his disciples would be reborn as heads of the church. He had anticipated the continuous transfer of powerful positions within the church – for instance, the position of the Dalai Lama and the Panchen Lama. The Dalai Lama (Ocean of Wisdom), a title first conferred by the Tibetans' Mongol overlords in 1578, represents the incarnation of the Bod-

tion with Beijing was in the best interests of the Tibetan people. To add the controversy, he now has two rival reincarnations, both discovered as six-year-olds in 1995. Many Tibetan monks refuse to recognise the state-sponsored 11th Panchen Lama. His unofficial rival, the candidate approved by the Dalai Lama, is believed to be held in Beijing – perhaps the world's youngest political prisoner.

The arrival of Islam

Islam probably reached China in the 7th century, via two different routes: one was the famous Silk Road, the other by sea to the southeast coast. During the Yuan dynasty

LEFT: Buddha's footprints are honoured in the Temple of Five Pagodas (Wutasi).
ABOVE: the Lama Temple.

(1271–1368), Islam finally became permanently established in China. Expansion of the empire into central Asia brought more Muslims into China.

Muslims have perhaps suffered more persecution then other religious groups in China, partly because their faith is still considered "foreign," unlike Daoism and Buddhism. The policies of the Qing dynasty were – though it may be oversimplified to say so – hostile to Muslims. In the 18th century, slaughtering animals according to Islamic rites was forbidden, and the building of new mosques and pilgrimages to Mecca were not allowed. Some Muslim sects were banned. Marriages between Chinese and Muslims were illegal, and relations between the two groups were made difficult. Several Muslim rebellions took place, especially in the southwest.

After another round of persecution during the Cultural Revolution, Chinese Islam has been allowed to revive its influence. Today, ten of the 56 recognised nationalities in China profess themselves to Islam – a total of 14 million people – and there are around 21,000 mosques in China. Muslims again celebrate their traditional festivals, and Chinese-Muslim societies organise pilgrimages to Mecca. But relations

FALUN GONG VERSUS THE STATE

Since the Cultural Revolution, when religion was banned and most sacred sites desecrated, the Chinese government has attempted to harmonise socialism and religion. It guarantees freedom of worship, but exercises control through state-sponsored "patriotic" religious associations.

The Party fears the revival of mass popular religion, a fear heightened by the huge growth of the quasi-religious Falun Gong movement. Devotees claim Falun Gong, a blend of traditional *qi gong* (breathing exercises) and mystical beliefs drawn from Taoism and Buddhism, has 100 million practitioners in China. All large cities, including Beijing, had organised Falun groups but these were banned in 1999. As a result, Falun Gong practitioners have staged frequent small protests in Beijing and other cities.

In the West, opinion is divided as to whether Falun Gong is a destabilising influence or merely a harmless cult. However, the Chinese authorities have taken a hard line. Most of those identified as leaders have been arrested, and the government has mounted a huge media campaign against Falun Gong. People in the movement claim some members have been beaten to death in police custody. The Chinese government claims 1,400 people have died as a result of Falun Gong, mainly from refusing medical treatment but also from suicide and self-mutilation.

between Muslims and Han Chinese soldiers and settlers remain tense in Xinjiang, the autonomous region in the far west of China.

Christianity

Christianity was first brought to China by the Nestorians in 635 AD. The Nestorians disseminated their teachings with the help of a Persian called Alopen, who was their first missionary. The symbol of Nestorianism was a cross with two spheres at the end of all four beams.

For a period, in spite of religious persecu-

EARLY CHURCH

The first Catholic church in China is believed to have been built when John of Montecorvino, a Franciscan monk from Italy, arrived in Beijing in 1295.

The Jesuits used their excellent knowledge of Western sciences to forge links with Chinese scholars. Other Catholic orders were more dogmatic and caused tensions. The Chinese emperors, fed up with the squabbling, persecuted them all.

At the onset of the 19th century, the Protestants began their missionary activities, and despite some fairly unscrupulous practices, the number of people converted remained negligible. In 1948, the year before the founding of communist China, there were 3

tions, pockets of Nestorian Christianity had spread to all regions of the empire. In some parts of the country it was practised until the end of the Yuan dynasty. At the same time, initial contacts were made between China and the Roman Catholic Church.

During the Ming period, Catholic missionaries began to be very active in China. The Italian Matteo Ricci was one of the leading Jesuit missionaries to China. When he died, there were about 2,000 to 3,000 Christians here.

LEFT: Beijing has a sizeable Muslim population.
ABOVE: the Virgin Mary shrine.
RIGHT: inside the South Cathedral (Nantang).

million Catholics and 1 million Protestants.

The Vatican adopted an extremely anti-communist stance after World War II, and as a result, the Chinese government ordered that the Catholic church in China should no longer consider itself accountable to the Vatican. To this day, the Vatican recognises only the Taiwan government.

However, relations are slowly improving. According to government figures, China now has 10 million Protestants and 4 million Catholics worshipping in state-sanctioned churches. This does not include an unknown number of Christians who attend independent – and therefore illegal – house churches. ❏

CUISINE

Eating is one of the main pleasures in a city that not only offers its own specialities but also acts as a melting pot for cuisine from all over China

Beijing cuisine has traditionally existed in two, largely separate, forms; the imperial food of the royal court and the less refined dishes enjoyed by the ordinary citizen.

Over the centuries, the imperial capital attracted people and food from across the empire. The emperor called the finest cooks to his court, and the best among them could count on being given the rank of minister. In the palace kitchens, cooks created dishes that belong at the pinnacle of world cuisine, dishes made from rare ingredients and prepared with great culinary artistry – both of which only the emperor could afford. They were altered and adapted in kitchens all over the country, but the basic recipes remained true to their original forms. This is where dishes that belong to every sophisticated Chinese kitchen originated: Peking Duck, Phoenix In The Nest, Mandarin Fish, Lotus Prawns, rice soup, Mu Shu Pork, Thousand Layer Cake. Even today, the ordinary citizen can get to know imperial dishes only in special restaurants.

Standard fare

The traditional cuisine of the capital's workers, peasants and soldiers was simple, with plenty of onions and garlic, but not the great variety of vegetables used in the rest of China. In winter, it was common to see nothing but cabbages filling the markets. Improved transportation means that today's residents can get pretty much anything they need, albeit at a slightly higher price.

Beijing's modern cuisine is a mixture of the refined imperial cuisine, the everyday food of northern China, and culinary skills from across the country. The main meal of a family of four usually consists of rice, noodles or steamed bread, soup, and three or four freshly-prepared hot dishes. Most families will eat three cooked meals a day, which makes for a lot of domestic

work, which is why many working people – especially those on lower incomes – eat in workplace canteens.

"Food first, then morals," wrote the dramatist Bertolt Brecht, a maxim particularly appropriate to China. During its long history, it has suffered repeated famines. Even today, the

problem of an adequate food supply is by no means solved, despite the generous supply of goods in Beijing's stores and free markets.

The great importance of eating in China is expressed in everyday speech. A common greeting is *"Chiguolema?"* or *"Chifanlema?"* (Have you eaten?). The government constantly reminds its critics that China feeds 22 percent of the world's population on just 7 percent of its arable land. Only about 10 percent of China is suitable for agriculture, which explains why in fertile areas every square metre is used for growing something edible, even in spaces barely large enough for a single head of cabbage. Pasture or fallow land is rarely seen.

LEFT: Imperial-style cuisine is served at many of Beijing's restaurants.
RIGHT: fried grasshoppers are not to everyone's taste.

Western palates generally have little difficulty adjusting to and thoroughly enjoying Chinese cooking. However, with the influx of so many foreigners in recent years, it was inevitable that Western-style restaurants and bars would follow. Today, you cannot walk a block in either the Sanlitun or Jianguomenwai embassy districts without passing at least one Western-style bar or restaurant. Many locals, especially the young, enjoy the novelty of Western food and leading fast-food multinationals such as McDonald's, Pizza Hut and

Kentucky Fried Chicken are here in force, each with numerous branches in Beijing.

The perfect guest

The people of Beijing are noted for their hospitality, but how do you behave when invited to a private party or an official function? First of all, it is usual to bring a gift for the hosts. This could be in the form of alcohol or cigarettes, but small presents typical of your home country are always well-received. Flowers are popular among the younger generation. Shake hands when greeting people, a custom adopted from the West. It is no longer usual for the sexes to be separated; in rural areas, however,

the women of the house might eat only after the men and the guests have finished.

There will be bowls and chopsticks on the table, sometimes with smaller plates for sauces or leftover food. Cold hors d'oeuvres, like pickled vegetables, meat and small delicacies, are neatly arranged on serving dishes. These snacks provide the accompaniment to the alcoholic drinks, which on special occasions – and on not so special occasions – are imbibed freely, according to the capacity of each guest.

After the appetisers, several hot dishes are served, with at least one per person. As soon as the host has noticed which foods appeal most, he or she will keep on placing more of them on to the guest's plate. You can expect such a large quantity of food to be served that you will be unable to eat even one-third. But don't worry; if the guests at a banquet should succeed in clearing every dish, the host would lose face.

When the menu is put together, great care is taken to provide contrasting flavours and colours by serving a selection of meat dishes with vegetables, one dish of vegetables only, and usually a fish dish as well. In this way, a hot dish can be followed by a less spicy one, and a sour one by a sweet one.

Hot dishes are served freshly prepared, one after the other — which means that if you are a guest at a private house, whoever is cooking will spend most of the time in the kitchen. Eat slowly and steadily, tasting a bit of everything. "*Man man chi*" (eat slowly) is the local equivalent of bon appetit.

At the same time, people drink, chat and smoke between courses. It is mostly men who smoke since, except in the northeast and among younger women, it is still considered improper for a woman to smoke. Foreign women, however, are generally excused as "honorary men".

Mifan, or rice, is one of the last dishes to be served, but not until all glasses of alcohol have been drained. This can sometimes be difficult, as during the meal, you will probably find your glass is never allowed to be less than three-quarters full. If you simply can't manage any more, don't be embarrassed to ask the person next to you to help finish your drink.

Light soup ends the meal. There is no dessert in the Western sense, since sweet dishes are

DOUBLE SERVINGS

Fish dishes are favourites at banquets; the word for fish, *yu*, sounds the same as the auspicious word for abundance.

served as part of the main meal, though some restaurants serve slices of fresh fruit at the end of your meal.

A liking for liquor

Alcohol is often an integral part of the meal. A warning to take care is not unwarranted here, as Chinese men often drink very strong grain liquor. The expensive *Maotai*, named after its place of origin, is famous, as is *Wuliangye* from Sichuan. *Erguotou*, the most popular Beijing brand, gives you 56 percent alcohol by volume for just a few *kuai*. Spirits are usually found in every restaurant and home, and are in special abundance at any type of official gathering. Many wealthy Beijing business people now prefer *Remy Martin XO* or similar luxury brandies. In property, construction and many other industries, bottles of brandy are used as small gifts to oil networks of *guanxi* (connections), especially among officials.

Sweet liqueurs, more popular in the south, are also drunk, as is beer, which is a standard mealtime drink. Chinese beer is generally good, while several Sino-French joint ventures produce passable, inexpensive wines. Dragon Seal and Dynasty are among the better brands.

At the meal, the host will encourage guests to help themselves to food and will drink toasts to them. *"Ganbei!"* (empty cup) means you should empty your glass in one shot, and turning your glass upside down shows that you have followed this instruction. But don't be too quick to do this; watch what your host does first. From time to time, eat a few of the snacks, but if you don't want to seem greedy, put your chopsticks down now and again. Refusing to drink can be tricky. One way is to turn your glass upside down or hold your hand over it. If your host insists on pouring more, citing health reasons should get you off the hook.

Mealtime customs

Westerners may, at first, be a little put off by the fact that everyone eats with fairly audible enjoyment, but in time most people get used to it. You may even come to appreciate the lack of restraint and practise the same yourself. However, remember that eating is a communal act here. Demonstrate proper social etiquette while eating by taking care of your neighbours at the table, and serving them some of the food, especially from dishes that they cannot reach easily. Remember also not to pick out the best pieces on each dish, but to take food from the side of the dish closest to you.

Apart from such customs, almost everything that furthers your enjoyment is allowed, and if at a loss as to where to discard the bones, simply place them on the table beside your bowl. Many a Chinese table looks like a battlefield after a meal. In fact, the success of three-day wedding celebrations has often been measured

COOKING BY DESIGN

Scarcities of land and fuel and itinerant lifestyles have dictated the way the Chinese handle food and prepare meals. Usually the ingredients are cut small, so that they do not take too long to cook. Few utensils are used in cooking, and often the stoves are small, portable affairs, fuelled by bricks of compressed coal dust. This means that they can be set up anywhere outside the house, especially if there is no kitchen. Most Beijing apartments, however, have mains gas cookers. Ovens, which need a lot of fuel, hardly exist in private households. This explains why, until recently, China produced almost no Western style bread.

LEFT: noodles are one of Beijing's staple foods.
RIGHT: even the most simple meal is a social occasion.

by the height of the piles of discards – sweet wrappers, fruit peel, cigarette butts, water melon and sunflower seed husks – left on the floor. Nowadays, though, you should take care not to throw away any litter or to spit in the street and other public places.

Tea may be served both during and after the meal, mostly green tea scented with fragrant jasmine blossom. Boiling water is poured onto the leaves, which are not strained. With green tea, water can be poured on several times, and it is said that the second brew is better than the first. However, if water has been poured more than three times onto the same tea leaves, you may take this as a delicate hint that the meal is over and it is time to leave.

Beijing specialities

The most famous Beijing dish is unquestionably Peking Duck, but many other culinary styles and specialities have found fame here. Indeed, many dishes use older recipes from different parts of China. Traditional Beijing haute cuisine is said to reflect two styles of cooking: imperial, which is based on Qing dynasty palace dishes; and Tan, a synthesis of salty northern cuisine with sweeter southern cuisine, named after the Tan family.

CHANGING CHOPSTICKS

Chopsticks, or *kuaizi*, date back thousands of years. Although bone, ivory, gold, jade and steel have all been used, most chopsticks are now made of wood, and thrown away after each meal. The main production area, the northeast, produces around 75 billion pairs a year from 68 million cubic meters of birch wood – enough to build a chopstick Great Wall every five years.

Once a luxury, disposable chopsticks are now standard, and are found in all but the most expensive restaurants. This is primarily for reasons of hygiene; greasy chopsticks have in the past helped spread epidemics of hepatitis and other diseases.

For northern China's *laobaixing* (ordinary people; literally, 100 old surnames), the most common specialities are *jiaozi* (meat and vegetable filled pasta parcels), *baozi* (steamed buns stuffed with mincemeat and vegetables), noodles, cornbread and pancakes – rice is not grown in the harsh climate of the north. Stir-fried and boiled dishes often feature cabbage and potatoes.

Hotpot, sometimes called Mongolian hotpot – although Mongolians claim it originated in Korea – is another speciality. This combines fondue-style cooking – usually in a communal hotpot – with unlimited meat and vegetables. A newer challenger has also caught on: Sichuan "yin-yang" hotpot, divided into two compartments. Beware the fiery *yang* half.

"Thousand year-old" eggs remain one of Beijing's most popular appetisers. These are duck eggs that have been packed raw into a mass of mud, chalk and ammonia and left for two weeks or so – not a thousand years. When fully preserved, the egg white turns a transparent, dark greenish black and the yolk turns milky yellow-green. The eggs are then cut into wedges, sprinkled with soy sauce and sesame oil, and

MODERN TASTES

Westernisation has made its mark on Beijing in many ways. Despite the Chinese intolerance to dairy products, many shops now stock milk, cheese, and yogurt.

slaughter, plucking and cleaning, air is carefully blown through a hole in the neck, so that the skin is loosened from the flesh. This process helps to make the skin as crisp as possible after roasting. The duck is then painted with a mixture of honey, water and vinegar and hung up in an airy place for three days to dry. Afterwards, still hanging, it is slowly grilled in a special oven.

Equally important to the Peking Duck experience are the dishes served alongside: very thin pancakes, little sesame seed rolls, spring onions

served with pickled ginger. To many Westerners the taste is an acquired one, but nonetheless worth trying at least once.

The city's signature dish

A prerequisite for true Peking Duck is a special kind of duck bred in and around Beijing, which is force-fed for about six months before it is slaughtered. Preparing the duck so that it has the perfect, world-renowned melt-in-the-mouth crispness requires great skill. After

LEFT: noodles come in various different sizes.
ABOVE: multi-course banquet at a Peking Duck restaurant.

and *haixian* (or *hoisin*) sauce, a sweetish bean sauce flavoured with garlic and spices.

An authentic meal of Peking Duck begins with a selection of appetisers, most of which derive from various parts of the duck: fried liver, deep-fried heart with coriander, intestines, boiled tongues, and the webbed skin of the feet cut very finely – in Chinese cooking, little is wasted. Next, the cook brings the roast duck to the table and cuts it into bite-sized pieces of skin and meat. Take one of the pancakes, use the chopped spring onion to spread *haixian* sauce on it and put a piece of duck over the spring onion. Then roll the whole thing up, and eat it using your fingers.

It is this combination that provides the

highest gastronomic pleasure and makes the often rather fatty meat digestible. For the final course, you will be served a soup made of the remains of the duck – mostly bones.

Full duck banquets don't come cheap; in fact, they are too expensive for most Chinese families, and reserved for special occasions. There are a number of cheaper duck restaurants in Beijing, but sadly many have become pure mass production centres.

Gastronomic melting pot

Just as new forms of Italian, Indian and Chinese food have become standard in Western

countries, Beijing has assimilated food from many Chinese regions into its *jia chang cai* (home-style dishes). These are the standard dishes you will find in restaurants and homes. Sichuan, Guangdong (Canton), Dongbei (the Northeast), Shanghai, Shandong and Hunan are some of the regions that continue to influence typical Beijing menus. Milder Sichuan dishes, such as *Mala Doufu* (spicy tofu) and Gongbao Chicken (with chilli and peanuts), can be found in most large restaurants. Sizzling rice-crust, called *guoba*, also originated in Sichuan.

Apart from the dishes that have already joined the ranks of the city's *jia chang cai*, Bei-

jing has many restaurants specialising in cuisine from different regions of China, especially Sichuan, Hunan and Guangdong. You can eat lean, grilled mutton and beef at restaurants run by China's Korean and Uighur minorities. The Uighurs, from Xinjiang in China's far northwest, make flatbreads and kebabs similar to those found in the Middle East. Hand-cut, stir-fried pasta pieces served in spicy tomato sauce, called *chaopian'r*, are another Xinjiang speciality. Restaurants run by Dai (from Yunnan), Mongolian and Tibetan people offer further tastes of China's remote frontiers.

Indian, Middle Eastern, Italian, French, Mexican, African, German and many other foreign restaurants have joined the melange, though many lack the quality of food found in their equivalents in the West. Some Chinese restaurants even serve their own versions of fruit salad, chips and curry.

Fast food

Against this culinary invasion, "Old Beijing" fast food and the lively dining style common before 1949 have made a comeback. Traditionally-dressed waiters shout across the restaurant, announcing those coming and going. Diners order a range of dishes, which are whisked through the restaurant and clattered down. Noodles, usually eaten with a thick sesame and soy based sauce, are standard fare.

Countless snack restaurants, some open 24 hours, offer a relaxed atmosphere in which you can try much more than noodles. You will also find an endless choice of snacks like red bean porridge, sesame cakes, jiaozi, baozi, *hundun* (wonton, like jiaozi soup), and *guotie* (fried jiaozi "pot stickers"). Many department stores and shopping malls, such as Parkson and Sun Dongan Plaza, feature Hong Kong style food courts serving snacks from around China.

For a quick breakfast try *jian bing* (egg pancakes), sold at roadside stalls. Or sample *youtiao*, deep-fried bread sticks (like doughnuts) usually eaten with hot *dou jiang* (soy milk). They are a delicious traditional start to the day and the ideal fuel for a hard morning exploring all that the city has to offer. ❑

LEFT: McDonalds are rapidly expanding their presence in China.
RIGHT: *jiaozi* dumplings are a local favourite.

BEIJING OPERA

The unique tradition of Beijing opera faces an uncertain future, threatened with the more immediate appeal of popular Chinese and Western culture

Beijing opera, or *Jingju*, has only existed in its current form for about 200 years, although the origins of theatre in China go back much further. Descriptions of dances dating from the Tang dynasty (618–907) show striking similarities to present-day Beijing opera, while many elements of the song, dance and music of Beijing opera can be traced back to *Kunju*, a form of musical drama developed during the Ming dynasty (1368–1644).

In the old days, permanent theatres were a rarity, even in Beijing and the major ports. As a result, Beijing opera was performed on the streets and in the market places – a sign of its popularity with ordinary people. Opera was a useful way for them to learn about life outside the narrow circle of their own day-to-day existence, and was probably an important source of Chinese history. Hardly a single temple festival lacked a theatrical performance, although the operas generally had no direct connection with any religious occasion.

The art of opera

The four main elements of Beijing opera are song, dialogue, mime and acrobatics – disciplines normally separated in European theatre. According to the particular form of Beijing opera, music and song might be predominant, or sometimes mime. Other pieces might feature acrobatic fight scenes, while in some the spoken word gets centre stage.

The main division is between *wenxi* (civilian plays), and *wuxi* (military dramas), but there are also comedies and skits. *Wenxi* pieces are more like Western drama, and describe daily life. The *wuxi*, on the other hand, consist mainly of fights, and tell of historical wars and battles, making great use of acrobatics.

Many Beijing operas draw upon popular legends, folk or fairy tales, or classical literature;

LEFT: a common character in Beijing opera is Sun Wu-kong, the King of the Apes.
RIGHT: mask colours provide information about the character.

tales such as *The Three Kingdoms*, *The Dream of the Red Chamber*, or *Journey to the West* are much better known in China than their equivalent literary classics in the West.

Beijing opera orchestras also have a distinctive style, using a scale composed of five notes rather than the Western eight-note scale. The most common instruments are the *erhu*, a two-stringed instrument played with a bow; the *zheng*, a zither; the *dizi*, a bamboo flute; and the *pipa*, a four-stringed instrument similar to a lute. Gongs and cymbals provide percussion, especially during fight scenes.

The players

There are four different types of role in Beijing opera: *sheng*, male lead roles; *dan*, female roles; *jing*, painted-face roles; and finally *chou*, male or female clowns. Each major group is divided into sub-groups and there are a host of additional characters such as soldiers, guards and ladies-in-waiting.

Foreigners often have difficulty understanding the individual roles. For instance, the *xiao sheng*, or young male lead role of the Beijing opera *The White Snake*, had to be turned into a *lao sheng* (old man) role for tours abroad, due to inappropriate laughter during some performances. The xiao sheng role calls for rouged cheeks, soft movement, a very high speaking voice and falsetto singing and the overall effect came across as comically effeminate to many non-Chinese audiences.

CAST OF CHARACTERS

Make-up artists of the Beijing opera are remarkable not only for their artistry but also for their repertoire; more than 300 different characters.

Jing, or painted-face roles, portray warriors, heroes, statesmen, adventurers and supernatural beings. Their stage make-up is skilfully-applied to resemble a mask.

Finally, the *chou* (clowns) are easily recognised by their white make-up around their eyes and noses. The eyes are also sometimes enclosed in a black square frame.

Only comedies have *chou* in leading roles; in other pieces they take secondary parts. They often appear as peasants, servants or other menials, and their coarse, col-

Of all the roles in the Beijing opera, the *dan* or female role is the most important, for two reasons. Firstly, in most of the dramas, stories and novels that form the basis of the operas, a woman is the focus of interest. Secondly, the central figure in Chinese dramas has been a woman ever since the Yuan dynasty (1271–1368).

In general, the *dan* – who were traditionally played by men – have their faces made up with a white base and various shades of carmine, and a little pale pink around the eyes. They move gracefully with soft, flowing steps. Another characteristic is their half-sung, half-spoken dialogue, which sometimes sounds a little like mewing.

loquial speech makes the audience laugh. What the other roles achieve through expressive, elevated speech, the *chou* gains by making use of everyday slang. The jokes of the *chou* are easy even for a Beijing opera novice to understand, as they are similar to comic characters in theatres worldwide.

Masks and costumes

The costumes of Beijing opera are based on the court attire of the Han, Tang, Song, and especially the Ming (1368–1644) and Qing (1644–1911) dynasties. However, despite their roots in history, the costumes are not intended to be realistic; their symbolic characteristics are particularly obvious in the beggar costumes made of silk with colourful patches.

While the colours and patterns of their stage make-up might be used purely for aesthetic reasons, more often they represent details of character. Red is the colour of loyalty and bravery; black represents a good, strong nature – albeit with a touch of the rough diamond; blue symbolises courage, but with a slight recklessness and arrogance, while yellow indicates a diminished version of the same failings; green is the sign of an unstable character, orange and grey the signs of age, and a golden mask is worn by gods and goddesses.

lines painted over his face. This shows not only his great age but also his disgraceful character, as white symbolises treachery, poor self-discipline, cunning and guile.

The art of seeing

In China, you never say you're going to see a Beijing opera, rather, that you are going to listen to one. A famous performer wrote in his memoirs: "If, in earlier years, anyone had ever said he was going to see a Beijing opera, he would have simply sounded ridiculous, for connoisseurs went to listen to an opera. During a lengthy sung portion, they would not watch the

Patterns of behaviour

Good characters are made up with relatively simple colours, but enemy generals and hostile characters use complicated patterns in their masks. Mysterious characters in the *jing* roles are denoted by all kinds of colour and pattern combinations. Cao Cao, one of the main figures from the time of *The Three Kingdoms* and who often appears on the Chinese stage, is made up in white, with thin eyebrows and sometimes with zigzagging

stage, but sit with their eyes closed and listening, clapping to the rhythm and thinking about every word in the song."

Beijing opera is a complete work of art, rather than a realistic drama. In recent years the use of scenery, lighting effects, and more props has led to some changes, but the form and performances remain essentially the same.

The emphasis is on the essential, with the unnecessary left out. Props are used sparingly. An oar in the hand of a boatman is enough to make it clear that the scene takes place in a boat. A chair can be just a chair, but it can also be high ground in a landscape. An unlit candle can be the sign that evening is coming on.

LEFT: a female general.
ABOVE: the fascination lies in the brilliant masks and magnificent costumes.

Every soldier carrying a banner represents a whole regiment, while riders will often also portray the horse through mime and gesture, rearing, trotting and galloping like a centaur.

There is an art to understanding and enjoying this unique type of theatre, and if you want to get the most from your experience of Beijing opera, it is important to understand some of the conventions.

The style of acting is typical of the "non-reality" of Beijing opera. The aim of the actor is

---

FRIGHT MASK

The tradition of mask-like make-up stems from legendary 3rd-century hero, Zhuge Liang. He had fine, feminine features, so he painted his face to terrify his enemies.

---

alone. The smallest movement of the eyes, the mouth, a single finger, is full of significance. Every gesture has been carefully and painstakingly rehearsed, every movement of hand, foot and body precisely laid down. And they vary from role to role. When a *sheng* walks, he lifts his feet up and places them slightly to one side. A *dan*, on the other hand, walks in a slow glide, with little steps, one foot hardly separated from the other. The painted faces take big steps and adopt an upright, proud posture.

not, as in Western drama, to become the character portrayed. The actor distances him or herself from the role and tries to quote it, to portray events that are connected to the role. The closest parallels in the West to the ritual style of operatic performance with its fixed gestures are to be found in classic mime, in ballet and among circus clowns.

Intricate acting

Beijing opera is most enjoyable when the technique of the performers is perfect and when you can follow the stylised methods of expression. Not that this is always easy; there are more than twenty different ways of laughing and smiling

In contrast to the other three roles, which demand an upright position, the *chou* uses his whole body in an expressive, lively fashion. Given the symbolic nature of Beijing opera, this theatrical skill demands excellent coordination from the actors. Just as in a good piece of calligraphy, movement must be both stylish and correct, so every symbol must have its exact counterpoint in real life. The actor has to follow the rules and conventions. How far he or she is able to deviate from them – with delicacy and certainty, without in any way breaking them – is a measure of talent.

Using the medium of Beijing opera, actors can swim on the stage, or a battle can be portrayed taking place in water or in darkness. Embroideries can be created or tea prepared using the art of mime. Everyday things can be translated into the language of the stage. Enacting them, the performer of the Beijing opera shows three things: how the portrayal follows the rules, what the character feels about it, and finally, his or her own interpretation of the action.

With its arcane structures and unique form, Beijing opera is relatively inaccessible, even to foreigners who speak Chinese. However,

ANCIENT AND MODERN

To learn more about the opera, visit the Mei Lanfang Memorial (*see page 186*), which celebrates the work of China's best-known modern performer of *dan* roles.

house, performed in Western Europe and Japan.

In the meantime, Western dramatists have also found an audience in China. Successful performances include Brecht's *Galileo Galilei* and *The Caucasian Chalk Circle*, Arthur Miller's *All My Sons*, as well as various Shakespearean plays.

Young dramatists and directors have been trying to break with old conventions. London University's production of Su Liqun's *Zhuang Zi Tests his Wife* was the first play to be staged in English by local actors in over eighty years,

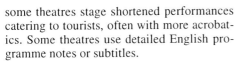

some theatres stage shortened performances catering to tourists, often with more acrobatics. Some theatres use detailed English programme notes or subtitles.

Modern competition

Under the influence of foreign culture, modern forms of theatre have only begun to develop in China over the last few decades. Among the influential dramatists are Cao Yu, Tianhan, Guo Moruo and Lao She. The latter wrote *The Tea-*

LEFT: a traitor is accused.
ABOVE: elegance and grace on roller skates.
RIGHT: novel use of chairs, Beijing Acrobatic Theatre.

while the truly innovative Experimental Theatre of Modern Drama's *Lay Down Your Whip, Woyzeck* combined Chinese street theatre with a German anti-fairy tale to deal with issues such as violence against women.

Today, Beijing opera aficionados are pondering the future. How can they allow innovation to move the art form forward without destroying the unique tradition? Can such an art form, which relies on convention and stereotype, really adapt itself to deal with modern issues? It will take time, but perhaps modern Chinese ballets like *Red Detachment of Women,* and Western operas like *Nixon in China* can point the way. ❑

ART AND CRAFTS

Silk, jade, porcelain and cloisonné epitomise China's rich artistic heritage,

yet the Chinese consider painting and calligraphy their highest art forms

Painting, like so many other cultural pursuits in China, has an ancient and fascinating history. Murals in tombs, temples and palaces, as well as scroll paintings, are known to have been created from the 3rd to 1st centuries BC onwards. But perhaps more worthy of note is the country's long enchantment with watercolour and calligraphy, and the extraordinary value the Chinese have always placed on the art of brush painting.

Brush painting

Writing and painting have always enjoyed an intimate association due to the original pictographic nature of the Chinese script. China has countless local dialects but, as Chinese writing is not phonetic, anybody who is literate in whatever region will be able to understand a written text. This nationwide, unifying and historically continuous script was therefore always more important than the spoken language; the art of rhetoric – as practised, for instance, in ancient Greece – never developed in China.

The close connection between writing and Chinese painting is evident from the customary incorporation of written words into most Chinese pictures, such as a poem, the name of the painting, the painter's name and date of completion, as well as the painter's and collector's name stamp. There are also examples of calligraphy where the ideograms stray so far from the characters as to virtually become paintings themselves.

In China, painting comprises various different disciplines: calligraphy; monochromatic and coloured work in ink on fabric or paper; mural reproductions such as wood-block prints and other related techniques, such as embroideries, woven pictures, and purely decorative paintings.

Writing and painting materials are referred

to in China as the Four Treasures of the Study, consisting of the brush, ink stick, rubbing stone and paper. Such tools have long been held in high esteem by Chinese poets, scholars and painters; there are reliable records which show that brush and ink were being used as early as the 1st century BC, during the Han period. Chi-

nese ink was only taken up in Europe as a distinct kind of paint in the 17th century.

The art of ink

Solid ink gained early cult significance because it was esteemed as the most important calligraphic material. It is made from the soot of coniferous resin with the addition of glue, and, in ink of good quality, perfume; traditionally musk was added, but these days it is likely to be cloves. The mixture is pressed into the shape of slabs, bars or prisms in wooden moulds.

Ink in solid form is used both for writing and painting, although it is now also available in liquid form. However, it is commonly felt that this deprives the painting process and calligraphy of some of their contemplative attraction. The rubbing of ink – dripping water onto a stone pestle, rubbing solid ink on it and, if necessary, diluting the solution with water – is not just a practical procedure, but also attunes one to the artistic activity and aids concentration.

Today, a paintbrush consists of a bundle of rabbit fur set in a slim bamboo tube; finer brushes are made of pine marten fur. These brushes differ from the European watercolour brushes by their softness and,

above all, in the way they taper to a very fine point at the end, which allows a brushstroke to be broadened gradually by a movement of the wrist – from a hairline to the full breadth of the brush.

Paper is the usual medium on which to paint. In former days, silk and fine linen were often used; they have become less common as they do not allow as much technical refinement as paper. Paper – itself another ancient Chinese invention, developed by Cai Lun and used from AD 106 onwards – is now produced in different qualities, each offering alternative possibilities depending on absorption and texture.

In China, painting skills are learned in much

ARTISTS' SUPPLIES

Liulichang is one of the best places to buy traditional brushes, paper, ink sticks, rubbing stones and other artists' materials.

the same way as writing: through copying old masters or textbooks, of which *Flowers from a Mustard Seed Garden* is one of the most famous. A painter is considered a master of his art only when the necessary brushstrokes for a bird, a chrysanthemum or a waterfall can flow effortlessly from his hand. The strong emphasis placed on perfection quickly leads to specialisation by painters on specific subjects. In this way, for instance, Xu Beihong (1895–1953) became known as the painter of horses, just as Qi Bai-Shi (1862–1957) was famous for his shrimps. Many of Xu's best works are displayed at the Xu Beihong Museum in Beijing.

One of the most favoured painting forms in China was landscape painting. Notable characteristics of this form are perspectives that draw the viewer into the picture, plain surfaces (unpainted empty spaces) that add a feeling of depth, and the harmonious relationship between man and nature, with man depicted as a small, almost vanishing, figure in nature.

Part-time paintings

A peculiar feature is the presentation of the picture as a hanging scroll. It is first painted on silk or on extremely thin paper, backed with stronger paper and mounted in a complicated way on a long roll of silk or brocade. Then a wooden stick is attached at the lower end, or left end if the scroll is to be displayed horizontally. Typically, the picture was stored away rolled up and brought out only on special occasions to be slowly unfurled, revealing only parts of a scene, subtly drawing the observer into the picture. After it had been displayed, the scroll was carefully put away again.

Thus, the picture was handled while being scrutinised. With horizontal scrolls, always unrolled little by little, the hands were in constant movement. The same applies to the two other formats for classical painting – the fan that needed unfolding and the album leaf that needed pages turned. The underlying idea was to create a bond between picture and observer, whereas Western painting on panel or canvas imposes a rational distance. In keeping with this, a landscape painting often has a path or bridge in the foreground to draw the viewer in.

Silk and the less-noble arts

Calligraphy, painting, poetry and music are regarded in China as the noble arts. Applied arts are considered merely an honourable craft. All the same, in the West, these skilled crafts have always held a special fascination. When thinking of China, one thinks of silk, jade and porcelain.

The cultivation of the silkworm is said to go back to the 3rd century BC. Legend has it that the wife of the mythical Yellow Emperor Huangdi began the tradition of planting mulberry trees and keeping silkworms. For centuries, silk held the place of currency: civil servants and officers as well as foreign envoys were frequently paid or presented with bales of silk. The precious material was transported to the Middle East and the Roman empire via the famous Silk Road.

The Chinese maintained a monopoly on silk until about 200 BC, when the secret of its manufacture became known in Korea and Japan. In the West – in this case the Byzantine empire – such knowledge was acquired only in the 6th century AD. The Chinese had prohibited the export of silkworm eggs and the dissemination of knowledge of their cultivation, but a monk is said to have succeeded in smuggling some silkworm eggs to the West.

Today's centres of silk production are areas in the east of China around Hangzhou, Suzhou and Wuxi. Hangzhou has the largest silk industry, while Suzhou has the finest embroidery.

The story of porcelain

The Chinese invented porcelain sometime in the 7th century AD – a thousand years before Europeans began producing it. The history of Chinese ceramic artefacts, however, goes back to neolithic times. Along the Huanghe (Yellow River) and the Yangzi (Changjiang), 7,000- to 8,000-year-old ceramic vessels, red and even black clayware with comb and rope patterns have been found. The Yangshao and Longshan cultures of the 5th to 2nd millennia BC developed new types of vessels and a diversity of patterns in red, black or brown. Quasi-human masks, stylised fish, and hard, thin-walled stoneware, were created with kaolin and lime

LEFT: modern brushes.
RIGHT: a classic Chinese painting on display at the Summer Palace.

feldspar glazes. Later, light-grey stoneware with green glazes, known as *yue* ware – named after the kilns of the town of Yuezhou – was typical of the Han period. Even during the Tang dynasty (618–907), China was known in Europe and the Middle East as the home of porcelain.

A world of colour

The most widespread form of ancient Chinese porcelain was celadon – a product of a blending of iron oxide with the glaze that resulted, during firing, in the characteristic green tone of the porcelain. *Sancai* ceramics – ceramics with three-colour glazes from the Tang dynasty –

became world-famous. The colours were mostly strong greens, yellows and browns. *Sancai* ceramics were also found among the tomb figurines of the Tang period in the shape of horses, camels, guardians in animal or human form, ladies of the court, and officials. The Song period celadons – ranging in colour from pale or moss green, pale blue or pale grey to brown tones – were also technically excellent.

As early as the Yuan period, a technique from Persia was used for underglaze painting in cobalt blue to distinctive effect. These days, wares decorated in such a way are generically known as Ming porcelain. Common themes seen throughout the subsequent Ming period were figures, landscapes and theatrical scenes. At the beginning of the Qing dynasty, blue-and-white porcelain attained its highest level of quality.

From the 14th century, Jingdezhen in Jiangxi province has been the centre of porcelain manufacture, although today, relatively inexpensive porcelain can be bought throughout China. However, antique pieces are still hard to come by because, in order to protect the country's valuable heritage, the Chinese government prohibits the sale of articles predating the First Opium War of the 19th century.

translucence and hardness, as well as its rarity. Nephrite is similar, but not as hard and is more common. During the 18th century, nephrite was quarried in enormous quantities in the Kunlun mountains of Xinjiang province. It comes in various shades of green (not the luminous green of jadeite), white, yellow and black.

Mystical significance

The oldest jades so far discovered come from the neolithic Hemadu culture (about 5000 BC). The finds were presumably ritual objects. Circular disks called *bi*, given to the dead to take with them, were frequently found. Centuries

China's cherished stone

With its soft sheen and rich nuances of colour, the Chinese have valued jade since antiquity; but it became widely popular only in the 18th century. Colours vary from white to green – in China, a clear emerald-green stone is valued most highly – but there are also red, yellow and lavender jades. According to legend, *Yu*, as the jewel is known, came from the holy mountains and was thought to be crystallised moonlight. In fact, jade came from Khotan, along the southern Silk Road.

Jade is not a precise mineralogical entity but comprises two minerals: jadeite and nephrite. The former is more valuable because of its

later, the corpses of high-ranking officials were clothed in suits made of more than 2,000 thin slivers of jade sewn together with gold wire. Since the 11th century, the Jade Emperor has been revered as the superior godhead in Daoist popular religion. Today, the ring disk – a symbol of heaven – is still worn as a talisman; more prosaically, jade bracelets are believed to protect against rheumatism.

In the jade carving workshops in present-day China, there are thought to be as many as thirty kinds of jade in use. Famous among these workshops are those in Qingtian (Zhejiang province), Shoushan (Fujian province), and Luoyang (Hunan province). Masters of jade work include Zhou Shouhai, from the jade carving establishment in Shanghai, and Wang Shusen in Beijing, the latter specialising in Buddhist figurines. In government shops, jade can be trusted to be genuine. On the open market and in private shops, however, caution is advised. Genuine jade always feels cool and cannot be scratched with a knife. Quality depends on the feel of the stone, its colour, transparency, pattern and other factors. If in doubt, consult a reputable expert.

CASKET CASE

Emperor Qianlong (1734–1795) had a special liking for carved lacquerware, he was even buried in a coffin magnificently carved using this technique.

back to the 5th millennium BC. Bowls, tins, boxes, vases, and furniture made of various materials (wood, bamboo, wicker, leather, metal, clay, textiles, paper) are coated with a skin of lacquer. A base coat is applied to the core material, followed by extremely thin layers of the finest lacquer that, after drying in dust-free moist air, are smoothed and polished. In the dry lacquer method, the lacquer itself dictates the form: fabric or paper is saturated with lacquer and pressed into a wooden or clay mould. After dry-

Protective beauty

The glossy sheen of lacquerware is not only attractive to the eye but is also appealing to the touch. The bark of the lacquer tree (*rhus verniciflua*), which grows in central and southern China, exudes a milky sap when cut, which solidifies in moist air, dries and turns brown. This dry layer of lacquer is impervious to moisture, acid, and scratches, and so is ideal protection for materials such as wood or bamboo.

The oldest finds of lacquered objects date

LEFT: souvenirs on Liulichang.
ABOVE: an intricate and extremely expensive ivory carving.

ing, the mould is removed and the piece is coated with further layers of lacquer. Vessels, boxes and plates were already being made in this way during the Han period.

If soot or vinegar-soaked iron filings are added to the lacquer, it will dry into a black colour; cinnabar turns it red. The colour combination of red and black, first thought to have been applied in the 2nd century BC, is still considered a classic. In the Song and Yuan periods, monochromatic lacquerware in simple shapes was most highly valued.

During the Ming period, the manufacture of lacquered objects was further refined. The cities of Beijing, Fuzhou, Guangzhou, Chengdu, Suzhou and Yangzhou were renowned for their lacquerware, which was enriched and decorated with fine carving, fillings, gold paint and inlay.

The carved lacquer technique, which began in the Tang dynasty, when large lacquerware Buddhist sculptures were produced, reached its highest peak during the Ming and Qing periods. The core, often of wood or tin, is coated with mostly red layers of lacquer. When the outermost coat has dried, decorative carving is applied, with the knife penetrating generally to the lowest layer so that the design stands out from the background in relief. Today, lacquerware is mainly produced in Beijing, Fuzhou

and Yangzhou; best-known is the Beijing work, which goes back to the imperial courts of the Ming and Qing dynasties.

Lost and found

The cloisonné technique – used to create metal objects with enamel decor – reached China from Persia in the 8th century AD, was lost and then rediscovered in the 13th century. In cloisonné, metal rods are soldered to the body of the metal object. These form the outlines of the ornamentation, while the spaces between the rods are filled with enamel paste and fired in the kiln, usually four or five times. Finally, metal surfaces not already covered with enamel

are gilded. During the Yuan dynasty, Yunnan was the centre of cloisonné production. However, the golden age of this technique was the Ming period, when the techniques of melting enamel onto porcelain was developed.

Art and endangerment

As a craft material, ivory is as old as jade, and early pieces can be traced to as far back as 5000 BC. During the Bronze Age, wild elephants were not a rarity in northern China – some of them were tamed during the Shang dynasty. The old artist carvers regarded elephant tusks as a most desirable material from which to make jewellery, implements and containers. The once-large herds of elephants in the south of China thus shrank to a small remnant, and eventually ivory had to be imported. Ming dynasty carvings exemplified the excellent craft skills and superior taste; then during Qing times, ivory carving was even further refined. Today's centres for ivory carving are the cities of Beijing, Guangzhou and Shanghai. All the ivory is imported from Thailand and various African countries.

If you buy ivory in China, bear in mind that its import is prohibited in many countries.

Craft of the people

Papercutting is one of China's most important folk arts. In rural areas poor peasants, who often could not afford any other form of decoration, would make their own papercuts. In the cave houses of Shanxi province, to the west of Beijing on the Loess Plateau, papercuts were traditionally pasted onto the windows – which were also made of paper. The technique for making the intricate designs involves folding, cutting and pressing. Some designs require hundreds of tiny cuts. The thin paper is usually plain red but sometimes ink or watercolour is added. Chinese New Year papercuts remain the most common designs.

Other popular subjects include "double happiness" symbols (normally for newlyweds), door guardians, animals from the Chinese zodiac, cats and peonies. Yet, despite its ancient origins, it is an artform that has certainly moved with the times. In some shops you may find modern papercuts showing PLA soldiers, ships, tanks, oil refineries, or even Chairman Mao. ❏

LEFT: making a cloisonné pot at an "Industrial Art" factory in the northern suburbs.
RIGHT: carving in nephrite.

THE ANCIENT TRADITION OF CHINESE MEDICINE

Based on Daoist philosophy and the know-how that comes from 5,000 years of experience, traditional holistic medicine continues to play a central role in Chinese healthcare

The theoretical foundations of China's healing arts, like those of the martial arts, are rooted in the cosmic concepts of *yin* and *yang*, the five elements (earth, water, metal, wood and fire) and *qi*, or vital energy. Using herbs, acupuncture and other methods, the doctor maintains the patient's health by establishing the optimum internal balance of vital energies and restoring harmony among the body's vital organs. The main form of examination is an extended feel of the patient's pulse.

Traditional Chinese medicine, which dates back 5,000 years, approaches disease and therapy in a fundamentally different way to modern Western medicine. The Chinese regard medicine as an integral part of a comprehensive system of health and longevity called *yangsheng*, "to nurture life." This holistic system includes proper diet, regular exercise, deep breathing, and regulated sex, as well as medicinal therapies and treatments.

Modern medical care in China uses both traditional and Western treatments. Designed to produce weak effects that stimulate the body's natural defences, Chinese medicines are used to treat minor ailments, while Western medicines are used for more serious or acute illnesses.

▷ ESSENTIAL BALANCE
The concept of balance is considered key to understanding diagnostic techniques and preparing blends chosen from some 6,000 ingredients.

▽ MOXIBUSTION
The powerful effect of moxibustion stimulates *qi*, or vital energy. Small pieces of dried herb are ignited to heat focal points, sometimes with the addition of suction cups.

▽ PRESSURE POINTS
The ancient Chinese text *Huangdi Neijing* describes the 356 sensitive points used in acupuncture, in addition to the 12 major conduits of the human body.

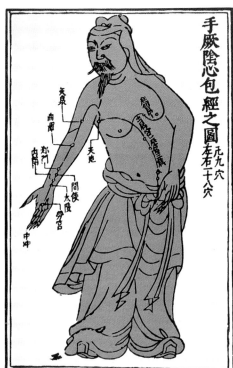

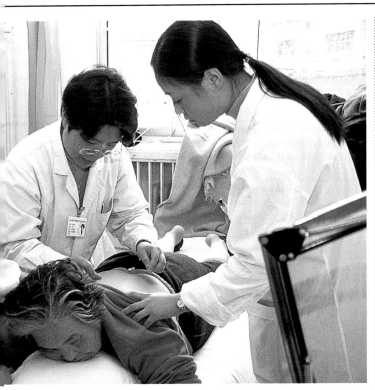

APHRODISIACS TAME THE TIGER

The use of animal parts in traditional medicine has a long history in Asia. Many nomads on the northern steppes still use wolf parts as the mainstay of their pharmacopoeia. Yet killing for medical use is a major reason why three of the world's five remaining tiger subspecies have been driven to the verge of extinction. In China, tiger eyeballs are used to treat epilepsy, the tail for skin complaints, and whiskers for toothache. But the bones are the most valuable part. They are used to treat rheumatism and are added to many standard concoctions. Increasing medicinal use of tiger parts has left as few as 30 South China tigers in the wild, a population already too low for long-term sustainability. The global tiger population may be as low as 5,000.

The craving for male potency also fuels demand for tiger parts. Various animal penises, rhinoceros horn, and deer antlers are other common ingredients for potent brews. The sale of tiger parts is now officially banned in China, but you can still find them at illicit market stalls and even in medicine shops.

△ **ACUPUNCTURE**
The flow of positive energy is essential for maintaining good health. Acupuncture helps stimulate this flow, and can relieve pain and cure allergies.

△ **SNAKE TONIC**
Various ingredients, often including snake and ginseng, are marinated in grain liquor to produce different kinds of *yaojiu*, or medicinal wine.

△ **THE PHARMACY**
Herbal prescriptions come in a variety of forms, including powders, infusions, ointments, tablets and wines, and usually contain at least six ingredients.

▷ **KITCHEN CUPBOARD**
Like medicinal herbs, foods are categorised according to their effects. Many medical herbs are also used in Chinese cuisine.

PLACES

A detailed guide to the city and its surroundings, with the main sights cross-referenced by number to the maps

In traditional Chinese thought, the world was not imagined as the flat, circular disk of the Ptolemaic system familiar in the West, but as a square. A city, too – and especially a capital city – was supposed to be square, a reflection of the cosmic order; in no other city in China was this basic idea realised as completely as in Beijing.

However the city did not develop its typical form, which still survives today, until the Ming dynasty. The Emperor Yongle is considered its actual planner and architect. In 1403, he moved the seat of government to the city of Beiping (Northern Peace), renaming it Beijing (Northern Capital), which became known as Peking in the West. Yongle's layout for the city followed the principles of geomancy, the traditional doctrine of winds and water that strives to attain a harmonious relationship between human life and nature.

Screened from the north by a semicircle of hills, Beijing lies on a plain which opens out to the south. In an analogy to this position, all important buildings in the city are built to face south, thus protecting them from the harmful *yin* influences of the north – be they the vicious Siberian winter winds or enemies from the steppes. Coal Hill (Jingshan), behind the Imperial Palace, is today a favourite viewpoint over the city, but it was proabably created out of geomantic considerations as a barrier against such harmful northern influences. It was in the south that the generosity and warmth of the *yang* sphere was thought to reside. It was not by chance that Qianmen Gate, the outer or southern entrance to the city, was built to be the largest and most beautiful gateway, and was held to be the most sacred.

East and west

A line from north to south divides the city into eastern and western halves, with a series of buildings and city features laid out as mirror images to their equivalents on the opposite side of the city. For instance, the Altar of the Sun (Ritan), in the east, has its equivalent in the west, the Altar of the Moon (Yuetan). Planned in an equally complementary way were Xidan and Dongdan, the eastern and western business quarters, which today still serve as shopping streets.

Some notable buildings of old and new Beijing are on the north-south axis of this symmetry. If you were to walk along this axis from the north you would begin at the Bell and Drum Towers (which acted as two huge clocks) and shortly come to Coal Hill. From the south you would pass through the Qianmen Gate to enter Tiananmen Square. Within the square two modern monuments, the Mao Mausoleum and the Monument to the Heroes of the People also fall on the axis. These

PRECEDING PAGES: a restored section of the Great Wall; winter scene at Houhai; lofty woodwork in Tiantan, the Temple of Heaven.
LEFT: the Imperial Palace bathed in golden light.

northern and southern approaches converge at the Imperial Palace, which the meridien line bisects, passing through the Hall of Supreme Harmony and, within it, the Dragon Throne – facing south, of course. From here, the emperor ritually mediated between Heaven and Earth.

The throne of the emperor was considered the centre of the physical world. The Earth was imagined as a gigantic chessboard. Each of its square elements was given a clearly defined place in the hierarchy of existence, depending on how far they were removed from the centre.

Crowded around the Imperial City was a sea of mainly single-storey houses: the Inner City. Its roofs, curved like the crests of waves, were not allowed to rise above the height of the Imperial Palace. Here were to be found the elegant private residences of princes and wealthy and influential officials. Only a few of the monumental gateways through the mighty defensive walls that once surrounded it have survived – notably the Qianmen and, in the north, the Deshengmen.

Adjoining the Inner City to the south was the Outer City. In Qing times, these two residential areas were known as the Tartar City and the Chinese City respectively. In the Outer or Chinese City, the doors of the houses were lower and the *hutong* (alleys) narrower. The rice bowls of the people living here were less well filled; hot water was drunk instead of tea; and people wore straw sandals on their feet instead of boots.

However, bored officials and wealthy merchants liked to flee their respectable surroundings and come here where tea and opera houses, baths and brothels, restaurants and bazaars – all competed for the favours of tipsy literati, mahjong-playing monks, lusting mandarins and the occasional prince in disguise. This southern area is still one of the liveliest parts of Beijing. Further south is the Muslim area, centred around Niu Jie. To the east of the Inner City a commercial area developed, and this is still to be seen in the modern shopping centres and malls of Wangfujing and Sanlitun. In the northwest lies the scientific and intellectual quarter with the city's most famous universities – Beijing and Qinghua.

Preserving religious buildings

Although transformed, Beijing retains some of the spirit of Ming and Qing times. Here and there you will find Buddhist, Daoist, and Tibetan shrines, plus a few mosques and churches. Many small temples, mostly dedicated to local gods, were destroyed after 1949, or turned into factories, barracks or schools. But there has been a shift towards preserving and restoring old religious buildings and opening them to the public.

Many interesting places are within reach of Beijing on a day or two's excursion. The so-called Summer Palaces, old and new, are now practically within Beijing's suburbs. Not much further away is the attractive Fragrant Hills Park, which can be combined with a trip to see the home of the ancient hominid Peking Man. The monumental tombs of the Ming emperors can be visited on a day trip while those of the Qing emperors require an overnight stay away.

The world-famous Great Wall can be seen in a variety of places, the closest being an easy return trip on the new expressway. Other places to visit include the Imperial Resort at Chengde, where the emperor and his court spent the summer, and the old treaty port of Tianjin, where foreign merchants built houses in the 19th century. ❏

RIGHT: stone tablet on the Marco Polo Bridge.

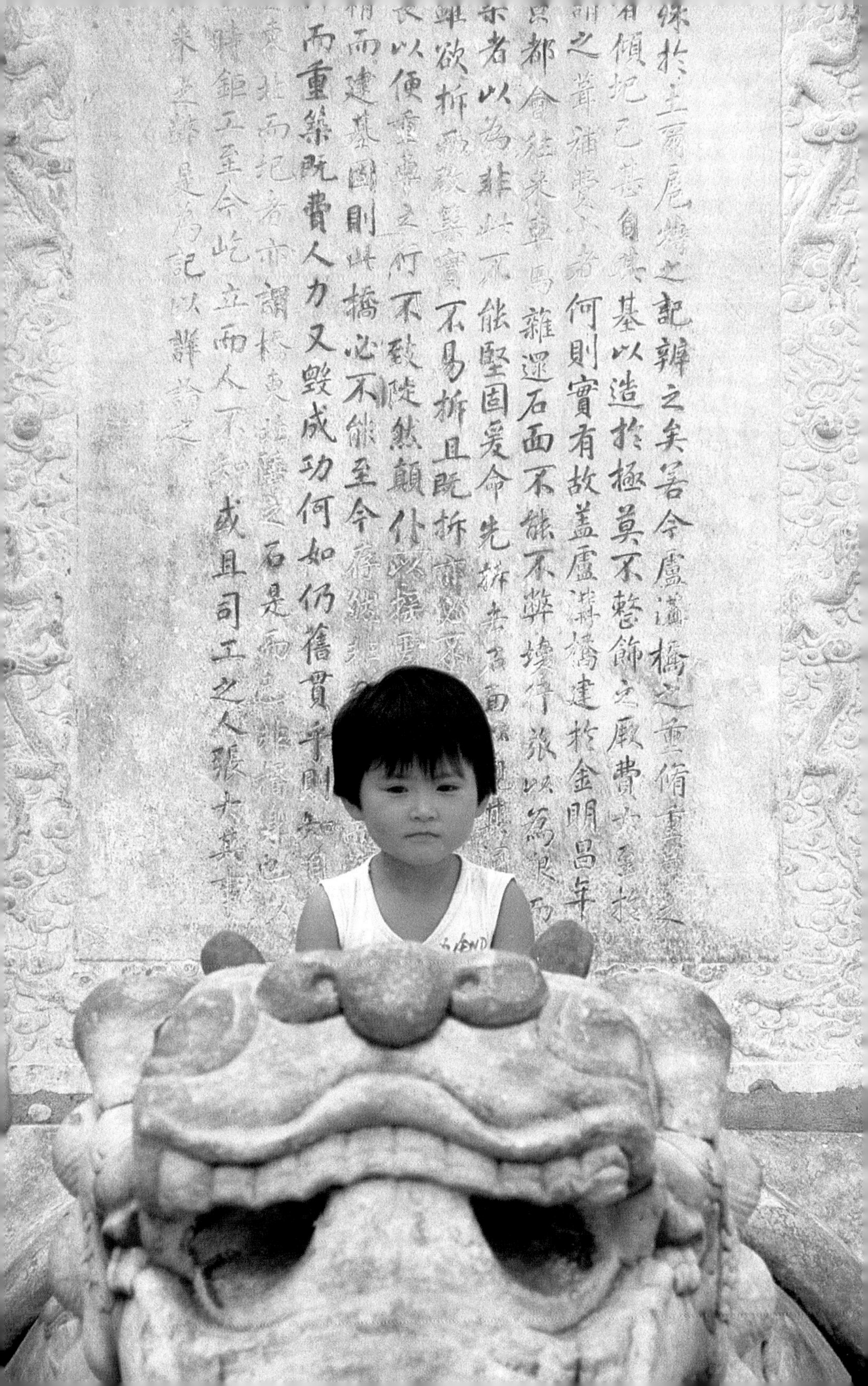

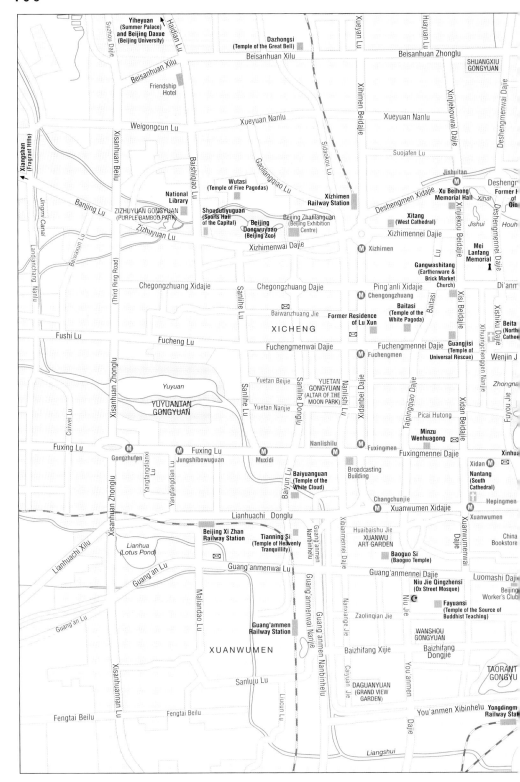

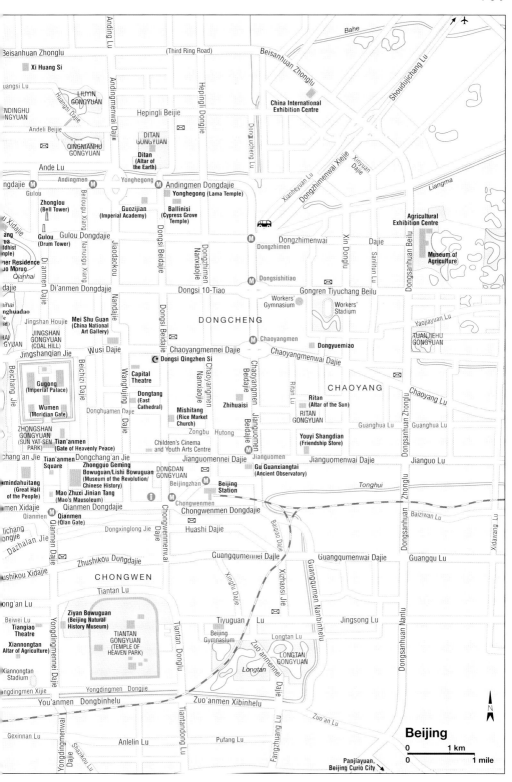

Beisanhuan Zhonglu
(Third Ring Road)
Beisanhuan Zhonglu
Bahe
Shoudujichang Lu

Xi Huang Si

uangsi Lu
LIUYIN
GONGYUAN
Huangsi Dajie
Andingmenwai Dajie
Hepingli Dongjie
Hepingli Beijie
China International
Exhibition Centre

NDINGHU
NGYUAN
Andeli Beijie

QINGNIANHU
GONGYUAN
Hepingli Beijie
DITAN
GONGYUAN

Ande Lu
Andingmen
Ditan
(Altar of
the Earth)
Xiatiheyuan Lu
Dongzhimenwai Xiejie
Xinyuan
Dajie
Liangma

ngdajie
Gulou
Yonghegong
Andingmen Dongdajie
Yonghegong (Lama Temple)
Dongchengcheng Lu

Zhonglou
(Bell Tower)
Guozijian
(Imperial Academy)
Ballinisi
(Cypress Grove
Temple)
Agricultural
Exhibition Centre

u Xidajie
ang
ua
ddhist
nple)
ner Residence
o Moruo
Gulou
(Drum Tower)
Gulou Dongdajie
Belouogu Xiang
Nanuogu Xiang
Jiaodaokou
Dongsi Beidajie
Dongzhimen
Nanxiaojie
Dongzhimenwai
Dajie
Xin Donglu
Sanlitun Lu
Dongsanhuan Beilu
Museum of
Agriculture

Qianhai
Di'anmen Dongdajie
Nandalie
Dongsi 10-Tiao
Dongsishitiao
Gongren Tiyuchang Beilu

eihai
nghuadao
e
id)
Jingshan Houjie
DONGCHENG
Workers'
Gymnasium
Workers'
Stadium
Yaojiayuan Lu

HAI
GYUAN
JINGSHAN
GONGYUAN
(COAL HILL)
Mei Shu Guan
(China National
Art Gallery)
Dongsi Beidajie
Chaoyangmen
Dongyuemiao
TUANJIEHU
GONGYUAN

Jingshanqian Jie
Wusi Dajie
Chaoyangmennei Dajie
Chaoyangmenwai Dajie

Beichang Jie
Beichizi Dajie
Wangfujing
Dongsi Qingzhen Si
Capital
Theatre
Chaoyangmen
Nanxiaojie
Chaoyangmen
Beidajie
Ritan Lu
CHAOYANG
Chaoyang Lu

Gugong
(Imperial Palace)
Dongtang
(East
Cathedral)
Zhihuaisi
Ritan
(Altar of the Sun)
Dongsanhuan Zhonglu

Wumen
(Meridian Gate)
Donghuamen Dajie
Mishitang
(Rice Market
Church)
Jianguomen
Beidajie
RITAN
GONGYUAN
Guanghua Lu
Guanghua Lu

ZHONGSHAN
GONGYUAN
(SUN YAT-SEN
PARK)
Tian'anmen
(Gate of Heavenly Peace)
Zongbu Hutong
Children's Cinema
and Youth Arts Centre
Youyi Shangdian
(Friendship Store)

chang an Jie
Tian'anmen
Square
Dongchang'an Jie
Jianguomennei Dajie
Jianguomen
Jianguomenwai Dajie
Jianguo Lu

mindahuitang
(Great Hall
of the People)
Zhongguo Geming
Bowuguan/Lishi Bowuguan
(Museum of the Revolution/
Chinese History)
DONGDAN
GONGYUAN
Gu Guanxiangtai
(Ancient Observatory)
Tonghui

men Xidajie
Qianmen
Mao Zhuxi Jinian Tang
(Mao's Mausoleum)
Beijingzhan
Beijing
Station
Dongsanhuan Nanlu
Baiziwan Lu

Qianmen
(Qian Gate)
Qianmen Dongdajie
Chongwenmen
Chongwenmen Dongdajie

lichang
ongjie
Qianmen Dajie
Dongxinglong Jie
Chongwenmenwai Dajie
Huashi Dajie
Baijiao Dajie

Dazhalan Jie
Zhushikou Dungdajie
Guangqumennei Dajie
Xingfu Dajie
Xizhaosi Jie
Guangqumenwai Dajie
Guangqumen Nanbinhelu
Guangqu Lu

ushikou Xidajie
CHONGWEN
Tiantan Lu

ong'an Lu
Yongdingmennei Dajie
Ziyan Bowuguan
(Beijing Natural
History Museum)
Tiantan Dongllu
Tiyuguan
Lu
Jingsong Lu

Beiwei Lu
Tiangiao
Theatre
TIANTAN
GONGYUAN
(TEMPLE OF
HEAVEN PARK)
Beijing
Gymnasium
Longtan Lu
LONGTAN
GONGYUAN

Xiannongtan
Altar of Agriculture)
Zuo'anmennei Dajie
Longtan

Xiannongtan
Stadium
Yongdingmen Dongjie

ngdingmen Xijie
You'anmen Dongbinhelu
Zuo'anmen Xibinhelu
Zuo'an Lu

Gexinnan Lu
Shazikou Lu
Anlelin Lu
Tiantandong Lu
Pufang Lu
Fangzhuang Lu

Beijing

0   1 km

0   1 mile

N

Panjiayuan,
Beijing Curio City

TIANANMEN SQUARE AND SURROUNDINGS

Map on page 110

This giant open space at the centre of the city reflects China's tumultuous history. To the southeast, the former Legation Quarter is a reminder of the city's brief colonial period

Most visitors to Beijing make their way first to **Tiananmen Square ❶**, the vast plaza at the heart of the city where old and new China meet. It is in this square – bounded by the Great Hall of the People to the west, the Museum of Chinese History to the east, the Imperial Palace to the north and the "ordinary" city to the south of Qianmen Gate – that classical heritage and revolutionary symbolism meet head on. Imperial gateways, representing the feudal centuries of the Middle Kingdom, now face the monuments and museums erected by the Communist regime.

The square took on an increased significance in 1949, when Mao Zedong proclaimed the People's Republic from the balcony of the Tiananmen Gate. Many other public events have taken place since the square was quadrupled in size in 1959 to 50 hectares (120 acres), creating room for over a million people to assemble. As well as the mass parades organised by the government and the immense gatherings of the Cultural Revolution, the square has also witnessed the demonstrations of April 1976, and the infamous democracy rallies of the summer of 1989. On 1 October 1999 it served as a stage for the government's 50th anniversary commemorative parade. Upwards of 500,000 people marched along Chang'an Jie in front of the Tiananmen Gate, watched by Jiang Zemin and other leaders. This day capped monumental spending efforts to spruce up the square, which had been closed to the public from October 1998 to June 1999 in order to replace old cement blocks with new pink granite slabs intended to withstand the weight of parading tanks. The stone-paved slabs in the square are numbered in series, so that soldiers taking part in parades can quickly find their places.

LEFT: keeping watch at Tiananmen Gate. **BELOW:** queues outside the Mao Mausoleum.

The monument and the mausoleum

In the middle of Tiananmen Square is the **Monument to the People's Heroes ❷**, an obelisk dedicated in 1958 to the remembrance of soldiers who fell in the Revolution. It stands on a double pedestal and at a height of 37 metres (123 ft) is 4 metres (14 ft) taller than the Tiananmen Gate. The lower part of the base is ornamented with bas-reliefs portraying the stages of Chinese revolutionary history, from the first Opium War (1839–42) to the founding of the People's Republic.

To the south of the memorial, in front of the Qianmen Gate, is the **Mao Mausoleum ❸** (open Tue, Thur and Sat, 8.30–11.30am, and Mon, Wed and Fri, 2–4pm). After the death of Mao Zedong in 1976, political circumstances dictated the building of an

*Kite flying has long
been a popular
pastime at
Tiananmen Square.*

everlasting memorial to the leader of the Revolution, founder of the state and party Chairman. In contrast, President Zhou Enlai, who died in the same year, had his ashes scattered to the winds. Mao's body was embalmed – by Vietnamese experts, it is said – and placed on display here. The mausoleum was built in only nine months in 1978 and also contains rooms commemorating other state and party leaders. It was renovated in 1999 for the the 50th anniversary. Nowadays, some Chinese regard the monument as an unfortunate remnant of the personality cult of Mao.

There are massive group sculptures by the front and rear entrances to the mausoleum, depicting the people's common struggle for socialism – typical examples of the style of Socialist Realism. The small open space to the south of the mausoleum was a busy market area known as Chessboards Street under the Ming dynasty. Only the ground floor of the two-storey building is open to the public. Visitors have to queue in lines of four in front of the building, and no bags, cameras or other objects may be taken inside. In the entrance hall is a

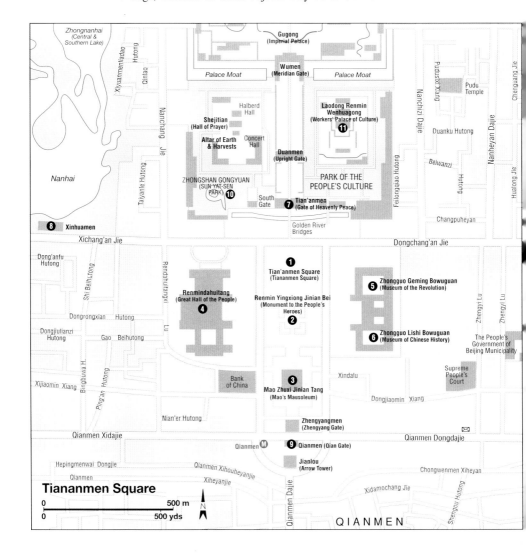

Tiananmen Square

marble statue of Mao. The wall behind it is covered with a 24-metre (79-ft) long tapestry depicting the rivers and mountains of China.

The body of Mao lies in state in a crystal coffin in the Central Hall of Rest. He is dressed in the typical blue suit and covered with the flag of the Communist Party. In the southern hall beyond, calligraphy by Mao himself can be seen, bearing the title "Reply to Comrade Guo Moruo". The mausoleum was visited by countless Chinese in the months after it was opened, with people queuing patiently across Tiananmen Square. These days it is rather less frequented, although it can still be busy. While the mausoleum was being renovated in 1999, rumours circulated that Mao's body is to be removed from here and returned to his birthplace in Hunan province in southern China.

Two museums

Tiananmen Square is flanked by massive, Soviet-style edifices dating from the days of close relations between the two countries in the 1950s. The **Great Hall of the People** ❹ (Renmindahuitang; open daily, 8.30am–2pm), on the west side of the square, is the largest of these behemoths. The National People's Assembly, the Chinese parliament, meets in the 50,000-square-metre (19,300-sq-ft) building. Various official departments are also housed here. In addition, the Hall is used to receive political delegations from abroad.

Behind the Great Hall to the west is the future site of the National Theatre. People are being relocated, and homes demolished, to make way for French architect Paul Andreu's chosen design – a colossal complex of theatres shaped like a pearl which is due to open in 2003.

On the eastern edge of Tiananmen Square, opposite the Great Hall of the People, are two museums housed in the twin wings of a four-storey building erected in 1959. Two pillars on either side of the entrance are shaped like torches, symbolising the words of Mao Zedong: "A spark can start a fire in the steppe".

BELOW: The Great Hall of the People (Renmindahuitang).

From the entrance hall, walk north into the Museum of the Chinese Revolution or south into the main hall of the Museum of Chinese History. The central hall is dedicated to the memory of Marx, Engels, Lenin and Stalin – busts of all them are on show.

The **Museum of the Chinese Revolution** ❺ (Zhongguo Geming Bowuguan; open Tues–Sun, 8.30am–5pm; entrance fee) provides information about the history of the Communist Party in China, the revolutionary civil wars, and the campaign of resistance against the Japanese. During the time of the Cultural Revolution, the displays had to be constantly readjusted to fit in with whatever was the current campaign (rather like the Ministry of Truth in George Orwell's *1984*), but today the aim is to provide an objective record.

The **Museum of Chinese History** ❻ (Zhongguo Lishi Bowuguan; open Tues–Sun, 8.30am–3.30pm; entrance fee) was opened in 1926. After 1949, the objects on display were increased to more than 30,000. A few came from state sources such as the Department of the Administration of the Cultural Objects of Northern China, but more than 16,900

Map on page 110

BELOW: Mao Zedong's portrait, symbol of the People's Republic.

pieces came from private collections in China and elsewhere in the world. Among them is a valuable blue-glazed lamp from the Southern Dynasties period (420–589 AD), Tang figures and an embroidered silk portrait of the Celestial Kings. Ancient bronzes, jade pieces and bones, and ceramics from the Tang and Song dynasties are also on show. The museum also features Chinese discoveries such as printing, gunpowder, the compass and paper manufacture. Temporary exhibitions have included those on Peking Man, Lantian Man from Shaanxi, and Yuanmou Man, whose remains were found in Yunnan Province.

Imperial gateways

The **Tiananmen Gate** (The Gate of Heavenly Peace) ❼ itself was reserved for the emperor to pass through. Today, traffic roars past it along the 38-metre (125-ft) wide Chang'an Jie. The first gate here, the Guomen (Gate of the Empire), was built out of wood in 1417. When this was damaged by fire in 1465 it was rebuilt in stone. In 1651, the gate was rebuilt again after destruction by Manchu troops and renamed Tiananmen. The side gates were demolished in 1912 to open up the square. This was the meeting place of the divided city, where the levels of the traditional pyramid of authority – the city to the south of Qianmen, the Imperial City, and the Imperial Palace (or Purple City, the actual Forbidden City) – touched.

When the emperors left the Forbidden City to celebrate the New Year rites at the Temple of Heaven, they made their first offerings at the Tiananmen Gate. On important occasions, imperial decrees were lowered from the gate in a gilded box. The civil servants, kneeling, were to receive them, copy them, and then distribute them all over the country. Thus it was in a decidedly imperial manner that

MAO'S PORTRAIT

As Mao's body lies in its mausoleum, his seemingly ageless likeness looks down from the Tiananmen Gate. The gigantic portrait of the leader measures 6 metres by 4.5 metres (20 ft by 15 ft) and weighs nearly 1.5 tons. It is cleaned every year before Labour Day (1 May) and replaced before National Day (1 October), when Mao is joined by the founder of the Republic, Sun Yat-sen. The portrait first appeared at the founding of the New China in 1949 and was originally hung only for these two occasions, but it became a permanent fixture during the Cultural Revolution – though a black-and-white picture briefly replaced it after Mao's death in 1976.

Ge Xiaoguang, the latest of four artists who have maintained the image, has painted 19 giant portraits of the Great Helmsman altogether. Each one takes about two weeks. The paintings are reinforced with plastic and fibreglass and have to be lifted into place by crane. Used portraits are apparently kept in case of demonstrations like those in 1989, when paint bombs added a touch of Jackson Pollock to Ge's work. Ge, incidentally, became a minor celebrity after he appeared on TV in 1994. As an employee of Beijing Art Company, he receives no extra payment for his special assignment.

Mao Zedong proclaimed the People's Republic of China from this spot on 1 October 1949, and in the same way received the adulation of millions of Red Guards during the Cultural Revolution. Following in Mao's footsteps, President Jiang Zemin attempted to recapture that symbolism, by ushering in the 50th year of the People's Republic of China from the gate on 1 October 1999.

The gate has become the symbol of Beijing, and, indeed, for the whole of the People's Republic. It is the only public building still to display the portrait of Mao, the founder of the state, on the outside. To the left of this portrait is a sign in Chinese characters: "Long live the People's Republic of China". The sign on the right says, "Long live the great unity of all the peoples of the world".

Five marble bridges lead to the five passages through the gate. The central one follows the imperial route and was reserved for the emperor. Subjects are said to have put up petitions to the emperor, along with suggestions for improvements, on the marble pillars.

Follow Chang'an Ji west for a few hundred metres. On the right-hand side, framed by red walls, is **Xinhuamen ❽,** the gate leading into Zhongnanhai, the seat of the Communist Party of China and a modern day Forbidden City. It was here that Mao Zedong used to reside as the Great Leader; today this area is still the inner sanctum of the party leaders (*see page 157*).

At the southern end of Tiananmen Square, the **Qianmen Gate ❾** was once the outer, southern entrance into the old Inner (Chinese) City from the Outer (Tartar) City and dates from 1421 during the reign of Yongle. The gate is in fact comprised of two separate structures; the stone Arrow Tower (Jianlou), which burnt down in 1900 and was reconstructed in 1903; and the main gate, the wooden Gate Facing the Sun (Zhengyangmen), just to the north, to which the

Map
on page
110

BELOW: Tiananmen Gate, lit up at the 50th anniversary celebrations of October 1999.

city wall itself was connected. Just looking at the breadth of this gate gives you an idea of how thick the former wall was. The area to the immediate south of Qianmen is one of the liveliest in the city (*see page 135*).

Sun Yat-sen Park

To the west of the promenade leading from Tiananmen Gate to the Meridian Gate, and separated from the Imperial Palace by a wall and a moat, **Sun Yat-sen Park** ❿ (Zhongshan Gongyuan; open daily, 6.30am–8pm; entrance fee) is a fine example of the fusion of imperial architecture and garden design.

Sun Yat-sen was one of the great figures of the 1911 revolution, which brought about the fall of the Manchu dynasty and the end of imperial China. After the successful revolt, he became the country's provisional first president (until stepping aside for Yuan Shikai in 1912) and chairman of the Guomindang, the National People's Party, at its base in Guangdong in China's deep south.

Sun Yat-sen's widow, Song Qingling, came from one of the wealthiest and most powerful families in the country. She remained in the People's Republic of China, where her name is still greatly respected today. Sun himself is still known with great respect by all Chinese on both sides of the Straits of Taiwan as the "Father of the Country".

Sun Yat-sen Park received its name in 1928. Originally – more than 1,000 years ago – this was the site of the Temple of the Wealth of the Land. None of that building remains, and only the ancient cypresses are reminders of that time.

From the main entrance to the park in the south, the path first goes through a white **marble arch**. In 1900, the German ambassador Baron von Ketteler was shot dead on Hatamen Street (modern day Chongwenmen), on his way to the

BELOW: family gathering in Tiananmen Square.

Chinese Foreign Ministry by one of the rebellious Boxers. In reparation, the imperial family were required to build a triumphal arch on the spot, with the inscription: "In memory of the virtuous von Ketteler". However, after 1919, Germany no longer existed as an imperialist power, and the arch was moved to its present position and inscribed: "Justice will prevail". In 1953, it was reinscribed again. The present calligraphy is the work of the famous poet Guo Moruo, and reads: "Defend peace".

Further north, in the centre of the park, is a great square area, where in 1421 the Ming Emperor Yongle had the **Altar of Earth and Harvests** built. It stood directly opposite the Temple of the Imperial Ancestors (*see page 116*). The altar's shape is a reminder of the old Chinese concept of the earth as square. Twice a year, in the grey light of dawn, the Ming and Qing emperors brought their offerings here in the hope of obtaining divine support for a good harvest. During the sacrifice, the altar was covered with five different types of coloured earth, and these colours can still be seen today, repeated in the tiles that cover the low surrounding walls. The symbolism of the five colours is not clear. It may be that they stand for the five points of the compass (north, south, east, west and centre), or the five elements of metal, wood, water, fire and earth, which, according to traditional Chinese thought, form the basis of all beings. To the north of the altar is the **Shejitian** (Hall of Prayer), built of wood, a typical example of Beijing's classical architecture.

A palace for culture

To the east of Sun Yat-sen Park, on the other side of the promenade connecting the Tiananmen and Meridian gates, is the **Workers' Palace of Culture**

Map on page 110

BELOW: the marble arch at the entrance to Sun Yat-sen Park.

(Laodong Renmin Wenhuagong)  – the grounds of which are used for temporary exhibitions and cultural events. In the centre of the complex is a venerable temple dating from the 15th and 16th centuries – the **Temple of the Imperial Ancestors** (Taimiao). Five times a year, the wooden ancestor tablets, upon which the names of the dead forefathers of the imperial family were recorded, were taken from the central hall in which they were kept to the southern hall, where the emperor paid his respects to his forefathers. The rear (northern) hall was reserved for the ancestor tablets of those "posthumously" declared to be "imperial ancestors". In other words, they were members of families who were not the ruling dynasty at the time when they were alive.

The veneration of ancestors is one of the oldest practices in the Chinese spiritual tradition. Central to it is a belief in the mutual interdependence of the physical and spiritual worlds. The transcendental well-being of those in the spirit kingdom depends upon the offerings and the veneration of their descendants. Equally, however, they can influence the fates of their children and their children's children. The living therefore try to gain the loyalty of their ancestors by being as generous as possible with their offerings, and dutiful in the observance of rituals.

This ancestor worship is part of the daily life of every Chinese household. The imperial ancestors received extraordinary honours and respect, of course, as they were believed to be responsible for the well-being of the whole country. The Taimiao was thus one of the country's most important ritual sites.

After 1949, the temple complex was restored and equipped for its new life as a workers' college and pleasure garden. Now, the "sacred halls" are used for leisure activities and further education courses.

BELOW: children's playground at the Workers' Palace of Culture.

The Foreign Legation Quarter

In contrast to Shanghai and neighbouring Tianjin (*see page 259*), European traders never established much of a presence in Beijing. Yet after the Second Opium War, the British and the French, followed by various others, were grudgingly permitted to establish a concession in the heart of the city. At first they made use of existing palace buildings, and the quarter where they lived was integrated into the rest of the city. But during the 1900 Boxer Rebellion, which culminated in a 55-day siege on the quarter, almost the entire area was destroyed. In the subsequent rebuilding, high walls were added for protection, and colonial-style edifices replaced the older Chinese buildings. Eventually evicted from the premises by the victorious Communist government in 1950, the foreigners left behind these anomalies of colonial style architecture, which to most Chinese are unwanted reminders of an embarrassing period in their country's recent history.

Buildings that were not deemed useful by the communists were allowed to decay, or were razed to the ground to be replaced by utilitarian modern structures. Other buildings, however, were put to use by the government and are still well maintained, but they are off limits to the public and hidden behind high walls and guarded gates. Yet the area is well worth strolling through in order to get a glimpse of a bygone colonial age. The villas and mansions remain ensconced in quiet, tree-lined streets, a world away from the crowded, jostling arteries of downtown Beijing.

To the north and south the Legation Quarter borders Dongchang'an Jie and Qianmen Dongdajie / Chongwenmen Xidajie (formerly Legation Street); to the east it runs as far as Dongdan Park and Chongwenmennei Dajie.

Maps on pages 110 & 117

Mobile phones are everywhere in Beijing, another indication of the city's rapid modernisation.

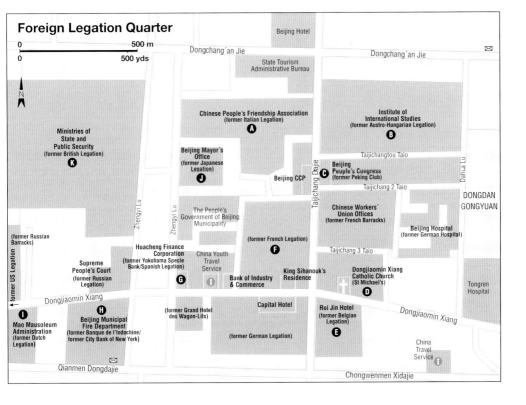

Map on page 117

A stroll around the quarter

Towards the northern end of Taijichang Dajie (formerly Rue Marco Polo) the grand red brick towers of the former **Italian Legation** Ⓐ are now the head-quarters of the Chinese People's Friendship Association. The building was also used to accommodate "foreign friends" who supported the Chinese Revolution. Two well-known residents in the past have been the American writer Anna Louise Strong, and the New Zealander Rewi Alley. Down the hutong to the east is the grey and white, Greek-temple facade entrance to the **Austro-Hungarian Legation** Ⓑ, now housing the Institute of International Studies. Back on Taijichang is the grey-blue walled **Peking Club** Ⓒ. Built in 1902, complete with tennis courts and a swimming pool, this is the exclusive haunt of high-ranking Chinese Communist Party officials.

Further south, on Dongjiaomin Xiang, is **St Michael's Catholic Church** Ⓓ, built by the French Vincentian fathers in 1902. It was nearly destroyed during the Cultural Revolution but renovated in 1989 by the Chinese Patriotic Catholic Church and renamed the Dongjiaomin Xiang Catholic Church.

The rear entrance to the expansive grounds of the former **Belgian Legation** Ⓔ is across the street. The buildings, originally modelled after a villa belong-ing to King Leopold II (1835–1909) now function as a state guest house. Nearby is the old **French Legation** Ⓕ, the Beijing residence of Cambodia's King Sihanouk, distinguished by an imposing grey gate with red doors and two large stone lions standing guard.

Further down the street is the large red and white brick building of the **Yoko-hama Specie Bank** Ⓖ, where Cixi supposedly took out a loan. It is now the Huacheng Finance Corporation. Looking south is the site of the **Grand Hotel des Wagon-Lits** which was razed to make way for a new Chinese hotel that bears no resemblance to the original. The Wagon-Lits was *the* fashionable place to stay in Beijing, and was close to the old railway station outside the wall. The station still stands, just southeast of Tiananmen Square, but is now used as a shopping mall.

On Qianmen Dongdajie are the buildings of the **Banque de l'Indochine** and the **City Bank of New York** Ⓗ, both now used by the Beijing Municipal Fire Department. Further west, barely noticeable, is a bricked up gate. This is all that is left of the **Dutch Legation** Ⓘ; the offices behind the gate now house the Mao Mausoleum Administration. Across the street is the site of the **Russian Barracks**, where many old buildings still remain. Further along on the left is the former **US Legation**.

Back on Zhengyi Lu is the **Japanese Legation** Ⓙ, fronted by an impressive red towered gate. It was here that the Chinese were forced to accept the infamous "Twenty-One Demands" on 7 May 1915, whereby the Japanese obtained special rights over Manchuria. It is now the offices of the Beijing Municipal People's Government. Opposite is the old **British Legation** Ⓚ. Previously a prince's palace, this building was the city's largest foreign legation. Many sought refuge here during the siege of 1900. It is now occupied by the Ministries of State and Public Security. ❏

BELOW:
the former City Bank of New York.
RIGHT:
looking south across Tiananmen Square from Tiananmen Gate.

THE IMPERIAL PALACE

The great palace complex at the heart of Beijing, also known as the Forbidden City, was more than the abode of the emperor. It was the fulcrum of the ordered cosmos that was imperial China

Map on page 126

When the capital of the Ming Empire was moved to Beijing in 1421, the emperors of the Middle Kingdom took up residence in the **Imperial Palace** (Gugong). This "city within a city" goes under a variety of names. Officially it is now the Palace Museum. Hitherto it was called the Forbidden City – hinting at a world removed from everyday life and the common people. It was also described as the Purple City, after the constellation of purplish stars around the pole star, implying that the rulers' residence was not only at the centre of the Chinese world but also the hub of the entire universe.

Sacred geometry

The Imperial Palace was not meant to be a home for a mortal king but for the Son of Heaven, the divinely-appointed intermediary between heaven (*yang*) and earth (*yin*), who was responsible for peace, prosperity and the orderly life of the world. According to legend, the Ming emperor Yongle, who began the building of the palace in 1409, received the plans from the hands of a Daoist priest who had descended from heaven especially for that purpose. The complex is sometimes jokingly referred to as the "place with 9,999 and a half rooms", as only heaven has 10,000. (In fact there are only 8,706 rooms and halls.)

The architecture of the palace raised the court above all earthly things. Huge red walls enclosed the inner sanctum, an area forbidden to ordinary mortals. No building in the city was permitted to be taller than the walls of the palace nor to outshine them in splendour. The exact, grid-like, geometric pattern of the palace complex reflects the strongly hierarchical structure of imperial Chinese society, with its fixed and ordered harmony as an expression of cosmic order. The buildings were aligned on north-south lines, the most important of them orientated to face south, towards the sun. Many of them have names based on Confucian philosophy – endless combinations of "harmony", "peace" and "quiet" – which were considered to have fortunate connotations.

History of the palace

The Mongols (Yuan dynasty, 1279–1368) built their palace to the west of today's Imperial Palace, before moving the capital to Nanjing in central China. In 1403, the third Ming emperor, Yongle, decided to move the capital back to Beijing. He ordered a new palace to be built and the basic structure has remained to the present day. Between 1406 and 1420 some 200,000 people were occupied in building the palace. The stones had to be brought on wagons from quarries in the countryside around Beijing. In winter, they were drawn on ropes over the icy ground. The buildings of

PRECEDING PAGES: view across the Imperial Palace from Coal Hill. **LEFT:** the Golden Water River. **BELOW:** lions guard the palace gates.

There are several sundials in the Imperial Palace, symbols of heaven and the yang *element.*

BELOW: huge urns were filled with water to safeguard against fire.
RIGHT:
a quiet pavilion.

the palace were mostly wooden and were constantly being altered; the wood came from the provinces of Yunnan and Sichuan in the southwest of China. Their main enemy was fire, and often entire great halls burned down. For this reason, there were a number of large water containers in the palace, many made of gilded copper. Most of the present buildings date from the 18th century. Even as late as 1987, one of the smaller buildings in the palace fell victim to fire.

Until the overthrow of the last emperor, the general public had no access to the Imperial Palace. Although the older parts were made into a museum as early as 1914, the last emperor and his court lived in the rear parts of the palace until 1924. The first tourists were admitted in the 1920s, but after 1937 there was not much left to look at, as items were removed to Nanjing and Shanghai for safekeeping from the advancing Japanese. From there, palace treasures were in turn "removed for safekeeping" to Taiwan, during Chiang Kai-shek's retreat in 1949.

Following the founding of the People's Republic, extensive restoration work was undertaken. Zhou Enlai is credited with protecting the renovated palace from zealous Red Guards during the Cultural Revolution. Today, this complex of imperial buildings is officially designated a "palace museum", and is protected by law.

The Imperial Palace covers an area of 720,000 square metres (861,000 square yards), running a distance of 961 metres (3,150 ft) from north to south and 753 metres (2,470 ft) from east to west. It is surrounded by a broad moat (drained and repaired for the 50th anniversary of the People's Republic), and is protected by a rectangular wall 10 metres (35 ft) high, with mighty watchtowers standing at the four corners. The palace is divided into two main areas – the southern (front) section or Outer Courtyard, comprising three large halls, in

which the Ming and Qing emperors held state ceremonies, and the residential northern (rear) section or Inner Courtyard, consisting of three large palaces and a few smaller palaces and a few smaller ones, and the Imperial Gardens.

Map on page 126

THE OUTER COURTYARD

To the north of the Tiananmen Gate (*see page 112*) is the **Meridian Gate ❶** (Wumen; open daily 8.30am–5pm; ticket window closes at 3.30pm in winter and 4.30pm in summer; entrance fee), the entrance to the Imperial Palace. At 38 metres (125 ft) it is the tallest gate of the palace. Because of the five pavilions on its U-shaped base, this gate was also known as the Gate of the Five Phoenixes. As everywhere in the palace, the number five is of great symbolic importance as it represents the five Confucian cardinal virtues. The emperor could only represent the *dao* of heaven, the order that pervades the world, and bring harmony on earth if he walked the path of these virtues. From a throne in the middle pavilion, the emperor reviewed military parades, announced new calendars and ordered rebellious officials to be punished. The only people apart from the emperor allowed to use this gate were the empress on her wedding day, and scholars who had passed the palace examinations. Nowadays, however, streams of foreign and Chinese visitors pass between the huge gates with their large lion-head door knockers.

Inside the Meridian Gate, five marble bridges representing the five Confucian virtues (humanity, justice, refinement, education and trust) cross the **Golden Water River** (Jinshahe) **❷**. This waterway dissects the first courtyard you enter and then runs along the palace's west wall . Across this first courtyard to the north is the **Gate of Supreme Harmony** (Taihemen) **❸**, which was rebuilt in

For an additional fee you can be guided around the palace by a cassette tape audio tour. This was once narrated by Peter Ustinov; currently the voice is that of Roger Moore. The tapes are available for rental in the first bookstore as you enter the main square.

BELOW: the Court of the Imperial Palace.

Imperial Palace

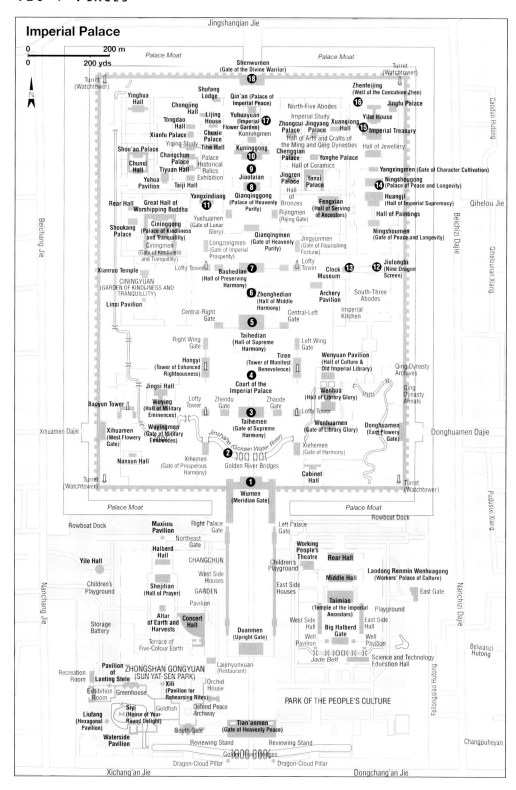

1890. Inside it there is a large map of the palace. Beyond this gate is the largest courtyard in the complex, the **Court of the Imperial Palace** ❹, where the imperial shops selling silk and porcelain were situated.

There are three large audience and throne halls at the end of this courtyard: the Hall of Supreme Harmony, the Hall of Middle Harmony, and the Hall of Preserving Harmony. They stand on a marble platform more than 8 metres (26 ft) high, which is divided into three levels. The balustrades on each level are decorated with dragon heads that spout water when it rains.

Halls in harmony

The **Hall of Supreme Harmony** (Taihedian) ❺ is the largest of the three halls and in the time of the Ming and Qing dynasties, its 35 metres (115 ft) made it the tallest building in Beijing. Within the hall stood the **Dragon Throne**, from where the emperor ruled. Only he could enter the hall by walking up the ramp adorned with dragon motifs. On the platform in front of the hall are two symbols – a grain measure on the left and a sundial to the right – representing imperial justice and agriculture. Also present are bronze figures of cranes and tortoises – symbols of good luck and longevity.

On state occasions, such as a coronation, the first day of the New Year, or the empress' birthday, a formal court ceremony was conducted in the hall. Outside the hall, officials and the more important dignitaries lined up according to their rank, waiting to be summoned before the emperor. Incense and bells strengthened the impression of the other-worldly nature of the emperor.

The roof of the hall is supported by 72 pillars, with the inner six adorned by dragons. The hierarchy of Chinese feudal society was even reflected in roofs, which were designed to indicate the social position of the householder. The roofs of the Imperial Palace symbolized the highest degree of power through their colour, construction and material. Their breathtaking beauty makes it worth taking the time to see them again and again from different perspectives. The U-shaped corbels typical of Chinese wooden buildings – all built without the use of nails – were reserved for great palaces and temples.

The Hall of Supreme Harmony has the most imposing roof in the palace, with a horizontal ridge, four rooftrees and double eaves. The varnished ornaments are also a sign of the building's status. Its dragons, for instance, at a weight of 4.5 tons and a height of 3 metres (11 ft), are the largest in the palace. These dragons are supposed to attract clouds and water and so protect the building from fire. Altogether, there are the figures of 10 animals on the roof, and one immortal, to serve as protection against evil spirits.

In the smallest of the three halls, the **Hall of Middle Harmony** ❻ (Zhonghedian, behind the Hall of Supreme Harmony), the emperor prepared for ceremonies before entering the main hall. Visitors can see an imperial palanquin here. The last of the three great halls, the **Hall of Preserving Harmony** (Baohedian) ❼, was used in lavish New Year's banquets, as well as for examinations.

Once beyond the Hall of Preserving Harmony, stairs

Map on page 126

The bronze tortoise in front of the Hall of Supreme Harmony symbolises longevity, and thus the permanence of the ruling dynasty.

BELOW: a guard in Qing dynasty attire during a costume drama performance.

The Golden Prison

I t may not be obvious from a visit to the Imperial Palace that although the emperor and his court moved daily around buildings of stunning beauty, contemplated extraordinary collections of art and played in gardens beyond compare, their privileged life of luxury came at a price.

Reginald Johnston, tutor to Pu Yi, wrote: "If ever there was a palace that deserved the name of a prison, it is that palace in the Forbidden City of Peking, in which emperor Shunzhi pined for freedom, and in which the last, but one, of his successors, the emperor Guangxu, ended his dismal days nearly twelve years ago."

From the first, a Chinese emperor was a slave to a system built around the cult of his divine personality. His life, and the lives of his empress and concubines, were effectively not their own. From the moment they rose to the moment they went to sleep – and even while they slept – they were kept under

scrutiny by attendant eunuchs, so that they never experienced any real privacy.

The emperor could not leave the confines of the palace grounds without official escort and usually not unless it was to attend an official function or to travel to another palace. Empresses and concubines led even more sheltered lives because their sex made it impossible for them to be seen by any other males outside the immediate family circle.

Days in the palace were governed by routine. Rising early, sometimes at three or four in the morning to ready themselves for official audiences, they would be bathed by eunuchs and maidservants who carried water from the Golden Stream. When necessary, a chamber pot was brought, placed in the corner of the room, and emptied immediately.

The young sons of the emperor, and perhaps a privileged cousin or two, spent their days in lessons with the most learned of Confucian scholars, learning Chinese language, calligraphy, and the Confucian classics, the philosophy on which the civil service was based and which governed official life. This prepared them for the day when one of them would be emperor, and the others his officials, and would have to accept and write imperial memorials at court. Memorials, written on scrolls, were the way in which officials from all over the country sent information and subtle advice to the emperor.

When the emperor moved from one part of the palace to another, it was a major expedition. Pu Yi described a walk in the garden in his autobiography: "At the head marched a eunuch, a herald whose function was like that of a car horn. He walked twenty or thirty yards in front of the others, constantly hissing 'chi, chi' to shoo away any other people in the vicinity. He was followed by two of the higher eunuchs walking like crabs on both sides of the path... If I was carried in my palanquin, two of the younger eunuchs walked at my side, ready to attend to my wishes at any time. If I was walking, they held me under the arms to support me. Behind me followed a eunuch with a great silken canopy. He was accompanied by a great crowd of eunuchs carrying all kinds of paraphernalia..." ❏

LEFT: an audience with the emperor.

lead down from the platform. In the middle of the stairs, along the former Imperial Way, lies a ramp hewn from a single block of marble weighing 250 tons and decorated with dragon motifs.

Map on page 126

THE INNER COURTYARD

The northern section of the Imperial Palace is entered through the **Gate of Heavenly Purity** (Qianqingmen), which leads to three large palaces: the Palace of Heavenly Purity , the Hall of Union and the Palace of Earthly Tranquillity . These palaces were the living and working quarters of the Ming and Qing emperors, and the scene of plots and intrigues between eunuchs and concubines in their manoeuverings for power and influence within the court.

Purity and peace

The **Palace of Heavenly Purity** (Qianqinggong) ❽ was the bedroom of the Ming emperors, but later in the Qing dynasty it was used for audiences with officials and foreign envoys, and also for state banquets. The inscription above the throne reads "just and honourable". The successor to the imperial throne was announced from here. Immediately to the north is the **Hall of Union** (Jiaotaian) ❾, where imperial concubines were officially approved. Within the hall are the imperial jade seals as well as a water clock dating back to 1745. The third palace, to the rear, is the **Palace of Earthly Tranquillity** (Kuninggong) ❿, the residence of the Ming empresses. The Qing rulers, following their religious traditions, also used the rear part of this hall for ritual sacrifices that entailed slaughtering pigs and cooking votive offerings. In the eastern wing is the bridal chamber of those Qing emperors who married after their accession, namely Kangxi, Tongzhi and Guangxu.

The last time the room was used for this purpose was in the winter of 1922, by the deposed last emperor Pu Yi. He later wrote: "After we had drunk the marriage cup at our wedding and eaten cakes to ensure children and children's children, we entered this dark, red chamber. I felt very uncomfortable. The bride sat on the *kang*, her head lowered. Sitting beside her, I looked about for a while and saw nothing but red: red bed curtains, red bedclothes, a red jacket, a red skirt, red flowers in her hair, a red face... everything seemed to be made of red wax. I felt most dissatisfied. I did not want to sit, but to stand was even less desirable. Yangxindiang (Hall of Mental Cultivation) was, after all, more comfortable. I opened the door and went back to my accustomed apartments."

To the sides of the Palace of Heavenly Purity lie the **East and West Palaces**, grouped like the constellations around the pole star. Here, the emperor was the only fecund adult male, surrounded by concubines, eunuchs, the empress, serving women and slaves. As late as 1900, there were still 10,000 people living in the palace.

The male palace servants were, without exception, eunuchs, therefore ensuring that after dark the emperor would be the only male capable of begetting a new generation. For many Chinese, especially for the poor, it was lucrative to enter the imperial service

BELOW: the Imperial Throne in the Palace of Heavenly Purity.

Incense was burned in bronze containers during official cere-monies. It is also said that the perfume served to obscure the smell of the eunuchs, who were not famed for their hygiene.

BELOW: gateways in the inner (rear) section of the Imperial Palace.

as a eunuch. Surgeons, called "knifers", stationed themselves at the gates to the Imperial City. Here, they would perform castrations at reasonable rates, but then sell the sexual organs back to the victims at a high price, for the organs had to be presented in a bottle for inspection at the Imperial Palace. The operations were not without complications. Many a young man lost his life during the process. As eunuchs were the only people who lived permanently in the Imperial Palace and were allowed to leave it and return they became not only well-informed, but also skilled at intrigue. Some of them became powerful people in their own right.

One of the most important buildings in the palace is the **Hall of Mental Cultivation** (Yangxindiang) ⓫ . This is where Emperor Qianlong (1736–96) and, a century later, the Empress Dowager Cixi lived. The last emperor, Pu Yi, also had his private apartments here. The working, living and sleeping rooms can be seen, as can the room where Cixi received audiences while hidden behind a screen. Strict Confucian protocol required that as a woman, and as an empress, she could not be seen by any Chinese of low birth or foreigners.

Dragons and longevity

To the southeast is the **Nine Dragon Screen** (Jiulongbi) ⓬, built out of 1,773 glazed bricks. The dragon is a symbol of heaven and, therefore, of the emperor, as is the number nine, the highest unit. It is no surprise that the dragon had, according to Chinese mythology, nine sons. Each of these nine dragons had different skills. Chao Feng, for instance, loves danger and is set on roofs to protect against fire – as seen in the Hall of Supreme Harmony.

Near the gate you pass through on your way to the Nine Dragon Screen there

PROLONGING THE DYNASTY

At night, the Forbidden City emptied of mandarins, and other royal relatives, leaving the emperor the sole mature male left within the walls. During the Qing dynasty, the emperor might have had over 120 empresses and concubines at his disposal. They were not all chosen for their beauty, however, but for their political ties to various Manchu noble houses. This perhaps explains why so many emperors found their way outside the walls in disguise, to the brothels not far outside the gates at Qianmen.

To prolong the dynasty, there were rules for insuring that the primary empress was impregnated. It was thought that the male life force *yang* (ie semen) was limited, while the female life force, *yin* (her bodily fluids), was inexhaustible. To build up sufficient potency to father a son of Heaven, the emperor required a great deal of *yin*. The best way for the female life force to transfer to the emperor was for him to engage in lots of sex with his concubines without achieving an orgasm. In this way he could store up lots of *yang* for his one monthly tryst with his empress. In practice, the emperors did not always restrain themselves. Most of them found one concubine that they liked, and ended up impregnating her. Cixi, for instance, got her start this way, providing the Emperor Xianfeng with his only male heir.

Map on page 126

is an interesting **clock museum** ⓭, filled with an array of timepieces collected by Qing emperors. As the temporal guardians of the harvest, emperors were responsible for predicting weather patterns, and were intensely interested in the scientific knowledge brought to China by visiting Jesuits.

Opposite the Nine Dragon Screen is the **Gate of Peace and Longevity** (Ningshoumen), which leads to the **Palace of Peace and Longevity** (Ningshougong) ⓮. The 18th-century Emperor Qianlong had this complex built for his old age. The **Imperial Treasury** ⓯, which gives some idea of the wealth and magnificence of the Qing emperors, is now housed in the adjoining halls to the north. On display are golden cutlery and table silver, jewellery, robes, porcelain, cloisonné, hunting equipment, and golden religious objects (many of the Qing emperors were followers of Tibetan Buddhism), as well as pictures made of precious and semi-precious stones, usually depicting animals and landscapes – symbols of longevity, health and good fortune.

The northern exit

On the way to the northeastern exit is a small well, the **Well of the Concubine Zhen** (Zhenfeijing) ⓰. Rumours were reported in the Western press, and passed down by historians who had no other record, that Cixi ordered the concubine Zhen Fei to be thrown to her death down this well before the imperial family fled to Xi'an in the wake of the Boxer Rebellion.

It was said that Zhen Fei, a supposed favourite of Guangxu, had supported the emperor in his ill-fated reforms of 1898, and that she begged Cixi to let her stay with him in Beijing to continue the fight. Cixi, the story goes, disapproved of Guangxu's efforts at reform. She ordered Zhen Fei to be executed and forced Guangxu to accompany her to Xi'an.

Perhaps Zhen Fei did support the emperor's reforms, but there is no evidence to suggest that Guangxu had any interest in his empress or his concubines. Nor was the emperor on bad terms with Cixi. It is possible that she supported his reforms up until she was forced by conservative elements in the palace to resume her regency. Besides, the well in question is also very small – too small for someone to squeeze into. Perhaps the legend has more to do with reports from foreign armies entering the Imperial Palace, who found frightened concubines hiding in wells for fear of being raped.

Follow the red palace walls to the west. Before leaving the palace it's worth taking time to see the **Imperial Flower Garden** (Yuhuayuan) ⓱. Laid out during the Ming period, it exemplifies the traditional Chinese skill at landscape gardening. The artificial rocks, pavilions, pines, cypresses, flowers and bamboo work together to produce a harmonious whole. This garden was the only chance for many of the people who lived in the palace to catch a glimpse of nature.

Leave the Imperial Palace by way of the **Gate of the Divine Warrior** (Shenwumen) ⓲, built in 1420 and erected during the Kangxi era. There is a great panoramic view of the Imperial Palace from Coal Hill (Jingshan), across the street (*see page 160*). ❑

BELOW: lily pond in the Imperial Flower Garden.

SOUTH OF TIANANMEN

Map on page 136

One of the liveliest parts of Beijing, the Qianmen area has retained the feel of the old Chinese city. Further out are the Muslim (Hui) district, Buddhist and Daoist temples, and the city's oldest church

Just to the south of Tiananmen Square, beyond the Qianmen Gate, is the area referred to as **Qianmen**, which used to be one of the busier sections of town near the gates in the wall linking the inner (Tartar) city with the outer (Chinese) city. In earlier times, officials came from the south and had to leave their horses outside Qianmen, or when they reached the side gates of Tiananmen (these were demolished in 1912 in order to open up the square). They then passed through the gates into the Forbidden City.

To the north of Qianmen Gate were the spacious estates of the imperial household, and tranquil temples set aside for ancestral and godly worship. To the south was the bustling mass of everyday life, where the pursuit of more earthly delights was also allowed. Brothels and opium dens were mixed in among shops and restaurants along what is now Qianmen Dajie. This is where the "old China hands" continued to meet in the 1920s and 1930s. A stroll from Qianmen into this district is well worthwhile. Here you will find interesting shops and restaurants, and it is still possible to get a feel of the old city of Peking.

PRECEDING PAGES: well-organized bicycle park. **LEFT:** Chinese Muslim (*Hui*). **BELOW:** shopfront on Dazhalan Jie.

The Qianmen area

Even today, Qianmen is noticeably more ebullient than other parts of the city. However, modernity has moved in and the little theatres are no longer the exclusive preserve of acrobats and the brilliantly-painted and costumed performers of Beijing opera. Kung fu films and trite film romances bring in more money.

Dazhalan ❶ is a small hutong heading west from Qianmen Dajie that is famous for its old shops and businesses, which draw customers from the suburbs and even from the provinces. It has recently undergone a complete renovation and become a pedestrianised zone. Dazhalan literally means "big stockades", and is an echo of Ming times when the streets were closed off at the evening curfew.

Not that any curfew could keep people from frequenting the many restaurants, shops, theatres and – most importantly – brothels in this area. It was in the so-called "Eight Big Hutongs" southwest of Dazhalan that Manchu officials and even emperors in disguise would come to taste forbidden pleasures. The Emperor Tongzhi, son of Cixi, was not especially diligent at the Confucian classics, or even at ruling, but he did start frequenting the brothels here at the age of fourteen. Most probably this is why he succumbed to syphilis when he was nineteen, leaving his mother to again preside over the country during the succeeding Guangxu's minority.

After 1949, prostitution was officially made illegal and the area was completely emptied of its more

Liulichang is a good place to purchase traditional Chinese watercolours.

lowly inhabitants, whose houses were given to working-class families – a population that still prevails in this area. But the shops remain. One of these is the **Tongrentang Pharmacy**, which hoards secret recipes of the Qing court and is reputed to be the oldest Chinese medicine shop in the entire country. This area is also a good place to buy silk and musical instruments.

Following the hutong further west you will find **Liulichang ②**, literally meaning "glazed tile factory", a shopping street restored in the 1980s to its original style, which offers a wide range of Chinese arts and crafts with a generous helping of kitsch. Its name derives from the five kilns established nearby during the Ming dynasty that were set up to provide glazed tiles for the palaces and halls being built in the new Imperial Palace. Later, during the Qing dynasty, the area was inhabited by Chinese officials serving a Manchu government who were not permitted to live in the Tartar City to the north. A thriving economy grew up around the community, catering to the mostly male officials, young men studying for their civil service exams and the many itinerant merchants who passed through here.

There are many long-established companies on Liulichang. On the eastern stretch are most of the antique (or purported antique) shops. Here you can also find **Zhongguo** (at No. 115), with its collection of old books, while **Yidege** (No. 67) has been selling artists' and calligraphers' supplies since 1865. **Diayuexuan** (No. 73) is the place to go for quality paintbrushes, which it has been selling since 1916. The western branch of the street has bookshops and art galleries as well as more calligraphic supplies. An interesting shop to visit is **Wen Sheng Zhai**, formerly suppliers to the palace and imperial officials of the ubiquitous red lanterns and fans. The shop's lanterns are still hung on

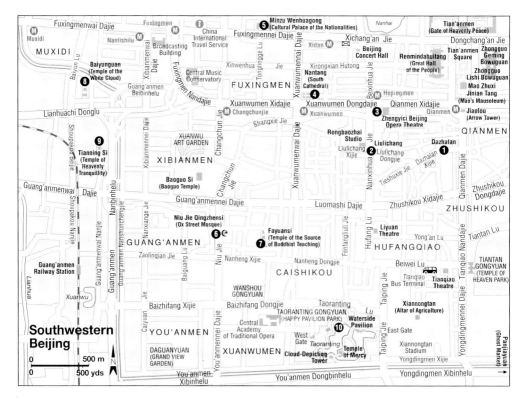

Tiananmen Gate for Chinese New Year. Another shop to visit is the **China Book Store**, on Xinhua Nanjie, where new and used scholarly books in Chinese and English can be found.

A short distance to the north is the **Zhengyici Beijing Opera Theatre ❸** (performances last from 7.30 to 9.15pm; entrance fee), the oldest Beijing Opera theatre constructed entirely of wood. The theatre was built in the 18th century but was later converted into a hotel, which eventually closed in 1949. Through much effort, the theatre finally reopened in 1995 and is a beautiful setting in which to see vintage Beijing Opera performed.

Christianity in China

Across Qianmen Xidajie is Beijing's oldest extant church, **South Cathedral ❹** (Nantang; open daily). The church was founded in the period around the end of the Ming dynasty and the beginning of the Qing dynasty, when Christianity began to establish itself with the arrival of Matteo Ricci (1552–1610) and Johann Adam Schall von Bell (1592–1666). Schall von Bell was responsible for the original structure which burned down in 1775. Money from Emperor Qianlong helped rebuild it, but it was later destroyed by the xenophobic Boxers in 1900.

The spires of missionary churches that seemed so breathtaking to Westerners were considered to be bad *feng shui* by the Chinese, and blamed for many current evils. It did not take much to encourage people to destroy the foreign building that was held responsible for the bad harvests of the previous few years. The current structure dates from 1904, but this in turn was heavily damaged during the Cultural Revolution. The building has been open to the faithful again since the early 1980s.

BELOW: locally made old-fashioned toys.

Mural on the Cultural Palace of the Nationalities. There are over 50 officially recognised minority groups in China.

BELOW: children of various tribes.

The cathedral also serves as the seat of the Patriotic Society of Chinese Catholics, an organisation that helps Catholics to practise their beliefs openly. The Patriotic Church is tolerated by the government in part because it does not officially recognize the Pope as a religious leader, and insists on its own autonomy. Catholic churches in Beijing belong to this denomination. Roman Catholics who remain true to the papacy have to practise their religion in secret. The Protestant churches are united under the Chinese Christian Council. The church is open daily, but of course the most interesting time to visit is on Sundays during mass.

Minority cultures

To the north on Fuxingmennei Dajie, is the **Cultural Palace of the Nationalities** ❺ (Minzu Wenhuagong; open daily, 9am–4pm; entrance fee). Two great bronze doors, adorned with the Chinese ideographs for solidarity and progress, form the entrance to this building, the ground plan of which is based on the Chinese character *shan* (mountain). The cultural centre is divided into six sections: museum, library, auditorium, dance hall, restaurant and guest house. The colours used in the building are striking: the earth-gold of the granite base, the white of the unglazed tiles and the blue of the roof tiles of the pagoda-shaped tower, which is exactly the same height as the White Dagoba in nearby Beihai Park.

Beyond them is the central hall, four storeys high, in white and green marble. A bronze chandelier hangs from the octagonal ceiling, and reliefs on the walls depict the many ethnic minorities of China. The relief on the southwestern wall portrays Tibetan, Miao and Buyi people in springtime. The southeastern wall

depicts people of the Zhuang, Li and Yao working on the rice harvest. On the northwestern wall a herd of sheep can be seen, together with Hui and Uighurs harvesting wheat, cotton and grapes. On the northeastern relief people in colourful clothing are grouped around a range of industrial products.

The museum in the northern part of the building has five exhibition halls and 35 smaller exhibition rooms. The library, with 600,000 volumes, is situated on the ground floor and is the basic source of information for studies of the 55 minorities of China.

The eastern wing of the Cultural Palace contains the auditorium with 1,500 seats, each fitted with headphones for eight channels. There are also facilities for radio and TV programmes, as well as a recording studio. The western wing with the dance hall, restaurant and music rooms is devoted to entertainment. Here you can get very good Russian food, among other dishes.

The Niu Jie Mosque

There are more than 200,000 Chinese Muslims living in Beijing today. Known as the Hui minority, they have 6 million members throughout China. Many of them are no longer orthodox Muslims, but, whether believers or not, they share one custom important to all Muslims: they don't eat pork. For this reason, there are in Beijing, as in many other Chinese cities, *Huimin Fandian*, or Hui restaurants, in which ritual-clean hands prepare snacks and meals, substituting mutton for pork. If you should be invited home by a Hui family in Beijing and served *jiaozi* (dumplings), these too, will be filled with mutton.

The Hui are known as Chinese Muslims because they use the Chinese language and can hardly be distinguished from Han Chinese. However, if you

Map on page 136

BELOW: inside the Niu Jie Mosque.

A Muslim bread stall on Niu Jie.

have the opportunity to visit a mosque in Beijing during prayers, or to take a stroll along Niu Jie, you will see many non-Han faces.

The largest concentration of Hui in Beijing – an estimated 10,000 or more – is along Niu Jie and in its many little side streets and hutong. Even the name points to the association with the Hui community: Niu Jie means "Ox Street". Walking down Niu Jie you pass Hui butchers, Hui shops and a Hui elementary school before arriving at a mosque on the east side of the street. At present, however, this area is undergoing massive reconstruction, with entire neighborhoods being knocked down to make way for new apartment buildings, and the widening of roads.

The **Niu Jie Mosque** ❻ (Niu Jie Qingzhensi; open daily, 9am–9pm; entrance fee), with its curved eaves and colourfully painted support and cross beams, looks more like a Chinese temple than a Muslim place of worship. On the outside, many Chinese mosques are built in the Chinese palace style, with main and side buildings laid out symmetrically. The buildings are wooden with roofs of glazed tiles, and the roof arches and posts are often adorned with texts from the Koran or other Islamic motifs.

The mosque was built in 966 in the style of a Buddhist temple, after the Islamic faith had entered China during the rule of the Tang dynasty (618–907). It was renovated under Emperor Kangxi (1662–1722). On a stone tablet is the following inscription: "Tell the provinces of the country that the governor will have anyone who spreads false tales about the Muslims executed and then bring a report to me. All Hui shall follow Islam and may not disobey my commands."

The proclamation was the reaction to a report that the preparations and celebrations leading up to a day of fasting were the beginnings of a rebellion.

BELOW: street scenes on Niu Jie.

The emperor did not believe the story. He visited Niu Jie and the mosque in disguise, and discovered that the accusation was quite groundless.

Right behind the entrance to the mosque is a hexagonal building, the **Tower for Observing the Moon** (Wangyuelou). Every year, at the beginning and at the end of the fasting month of Ramadan, the imam climbs the tower to observe the waxing and waning of the moon and to determine the exact length of the period of fasting.

Beyond the tower is the **main prayer hall**. This is where the faithful come for religious ceremonies, after ritually cleansing themselves in the washrooms. Like all mosque prayer halls, this one has no adornment or pictures inside. Since Islamic tradition dictates that Muslims have to pray facing Mecca, the front of the hall faces west. At the front is the pulpit for the imam. Women can only take part in the prayers in a niche screened off with curtains. They also have to cleanse themselves ritually beforehand and put on a white robe and a white head covering.

Beyond the prayer hall are a few smaller religious buildings and steles, while the minaret is positioned in the centre of the complex. In the little courtyard garden that runs east is the tombstone – with an Arabic inscription – of the founder of the mosque. During the Cultural Revolution, the faithful managed to save this by burying it next to the wall.

Also in the Niu Jie Mosque is a Koran school. As there is no religious instruction in Chinese schools, Hui children, if their parents insist on it, have to come here to learn about Islam. During the Cultural Revolution, this was strongly forbidden and the mosque was closed to the public. With state support, the mosque has been restored in recent years and today it is once more a

Map on page 136

TIP

The Niu Jie Mosque is open to non-Muslims (including women), but it is important to dress respectfully – no shorts or sleeveless tops.

BELOW: Chinese Muslims outside the Niu Jie Mosque.

meeting place for Muslims. The Hui are not the only ones who come here; so do the staff of the embassies of Islamic countries and the Uighurs from Xinjiang who are living in Beijing.

Buddhist Beijing

Just to the east, on Fayuansi Qianjie (a hutong leading off Niu Jie), is what is thought to be the oldest temple in the inner city of Beijing, the **Temple of the Source of Buddhist Teaching** ❼ (Fayuansi; open Tues–Thurs, 8.30am–3pm; entrance fee). It was built on the orders of the Tang emperor, Li Shimin, in honour of soldiers killed in battle in the unsuccessful Korean campaign, and took over 40 years to construct. It was completed in 696 and named Minzhongsi, but since 1734 it has been known as Fayuansi. Almost the entire structure has been renewed over the centuries, mostly during the Qing dynasty. The temple houses the **Buddhist Academy**, formed in 1956 by the Chinese Buddhist Society. The Academy is devoted to the teaching and study of Buddhism, and trains young monks for four to five years before they can enter other monasteries in China. The Fayuansi Temple also contains a library of more than 100,000 valuable books.

Although the Buddhist religion and its temples suffered during the Cultural Revolution (1966–76), many of these buildings were reopened to the public in the early 1980s. Even those destroyed by the Red Guards are being rebuilt, and most of them are filled with an increasing number of monks, priests and worshippers.

BELOW: relaxing in the park.

This vast complex has six halls to visit. Enter through Shanmen, the Mountain Gate, which is guarded by two stone lions. In the first temple courtyard are

LITERARY LANDSCAPES

To the southwest of The Temple of the Source of Buddhist Teaching are the Grand View Gardens (Daguanyuan) which may look at first sight as it they had been there for centuries but which in fact were laid out only recently as a backdrop for a TV series based on the popular Qing era classic, *Hongloumeng* (*The Dream of the Red Chamber*). The novel describes the downfall of the aristocratic Jia family through their ambition, decadent lifestyle, and their remarkable capacity for family intrigue. The story centres on the tragic love between the highly sensitive and poetically talented Jia Baoyu, the younger brother of the imperial concubine, and his fragile cousin, Lin Daiyu, whom he worships.

The layout of the park faithfully recreates the landscapes described in the novel. There is a lake with elegant pavilions, colourful walkways, zigzagging bridges, jetties and a temple. To the northwest of the entrance is the Court of Red Fortune, the residence of the hero of the novel, Baoyu. To the northeast is the Bamboo Pavilion, home of his beloved Daiyu. The gardens' bamboo plantation is a rarity in Beijing, given the harsh climate. But the plant is there for a reason – as a symbol of the loneliness, pride and sadness of the heroine.

two bronze lions in front of the **Tianwangdian** (Hall of the Celestial Kings). The Celestial Kings rule the four points of the compass and can keep away all evil spirits and the enemies of Buddhism. Enthroned in the middle of the hall is a Milefo, a laughing, fat-bellied Buddha, who encourages the faithful to "come in, follow me on the way to release in nirvana".

Such Milefo Buddhas represent Maitreya, the Buddha of the Coming Age. The first of them were made about the year 800. They can be seen at the entrance to almost all Chinese Buddhist temples and are always flanked – as here in Fayuansi – by the four celestial kings. These five statues are Ming dynasty bronzes, a rarity in Chinese Buddhist temples. In the popular conception of Buddhism, the Buddha's belly and his laughter seem to promise the Chinese peasants the good life in nirvana. In fact, his belly represents an enlarged centre of life, achieved by deep meditation and an ascetic life.

Behind the Milefo Buddha is the Guardian of Buddhism, with his face turned to the main hall of the temple, the **Hall of Heroes** (Daxiongbaodian). This is reached by leaving the first hall and crossing a garden with a bronze cauldron and stone steles. Within the hall is a Buddha flanked by two Bodhisattvas and surrounded by 18 Lohan, or saints, the lowest rank in the Buddhist divine hierarchy. The Lohan are still alive on earth, but each individual has achieved salvation, which is why they seem marvellous to the observer. The second rank is formed by the Bodhisattvas, who have rejected nirvana to help humanity, while Buddha, the Enlightened One, has already achieved nirvana and is, in his many forms and appearances, the embodiment of Buddhist wisdom itself.

Leaving the main hall, you will pass a small hall with stone tablets and come to the **Hall of a Thousand Buddhas**. Here, on a stone base, is a 5-metre (15-ft)

Map on page 136

The Temple of the Source of Buddhist Teaching is thought to be the oldest temple in inner Beijing.

LEFT: incense burner at Fayuansi.
BELOW: Buddhist monk.

high sculpture dating back to the Ming dynasty. showing the Buddhas of the five points of the compass; towering over all of them is the Dharma Buddha.

In the last hall there is a Reclining Buddha, and an excellent exhibition of Buddhist sculpture, with some pieces dating back to the Han dynasty (206 BC–AD 220). The most recent examples are bronze figures dating from the Ming and Qing periods (14th–20th centuries). A splendid Guanyin Bodhisattva with 1,000 arms is also on display.

Temple of the White Cloud

To the northwest, near the western railway station (Guang'anmen), is one of the few Daoist temples left in Beijing, the **Temple of the White Cloud ❸** (Baiyunguan; open daily 8.30am–4.30pm; entrance fee). Used as a factory during the Cultural Revolution, the temple was restored to its original purpose some years ago. By the end of 1988, it housed some 50 Daoist priests, mostly younger men. The temple site dates from the Tang dynasty (although the building itself dates from the Ming) and is the centre of the Daoist Dragon Gate sect. Daoist temples on the grand scale were not built until the Yuan dynasty and the reign of Kublai Khan. The latter appointed a priest named Qiu Chuji as "National Teacher", who took up residence in the temple. From that time on the temple has been the centre of Daoism in northern China.

The temple complex contains several courtyards. The overall design is similar to Buddhist temples in that the following elements lie one behind the other along a straight line: the memorial arch, the main gate, the pond, a bridge, the **Hall of the Officials of Celestial Censorship** (which is equivalent to the Hall of Celestial Kings in Buddhist temples), the **Hall of the Jade Emperor** and the

BELOW:
a Daoist procession in the Temple of the White Cloud.

Hall of Religious Law (equivalent to the rear halls found in a Buddhist temple).

In the centre of the furthest courtyard is the **Hall of the Four Celestial Emperors**, and on its upper floor is the **Hall of the Three Purities**. Daoist manuscripts are kept here in a compendium similar to those found in Buddhist temples. In a hall off one of the side courtyards of the western section there are old bronze guardian figures, and in a building behind this are 60 relatively newly-made figures of Daoist divinities, each one appointed to a year of the traditional 60-year Chinese calendar. Visitors can find their personal Daoist divinities according to this calendar. The Daoist priests who reside there will be pleased to help.

Daoist temples use obvious symbolic motifs more frequently in their decoration than Buddhist temples. Common designs include the Lingzhi mushroom (which is supposed to prolong life), Daoist immortals, cranes and the eight trigrams from the Book of Changes. In this temple, there is also a stele with calligraphy by Emperor Qianlong, telling the history of the temple and its founder.

Other sights

Situated a short distance to the south of Baiyunguan, is the **Temple of Heavenly Tranquillity** (Tianning Si) , thought to be the oldest building in Beijing. All that remains of the original building is the 58-metre (190-ft) hexagonal pagoda. This was one of the few tall buildings in the city at the time it was built in the 12th century, towards the end of the Liao dynasty – of which its style is thought to be typical. Times have changed, however, and the pagoda now courageously peers out from behind a threatening overpass. The pagoda rises in 13 storeys from a richly decorated podium that symbolises the mountain of the gods, Sumeru. The first level has windows and doors but is otherwise unadorned.

Another temple in the area, to the east of Tianning Si, just south of Xuanwu Park is **Baoguo Si**. To the east of Fayuansi, meanwhile, is the Qianmen Hotel, whose **Liyuan Theatre** is a good place to see performances of Beijing Opera.

Taoranting Park (Happy Pavilion Park) , to the south, was originally popular with scholars and common people, who did not have access to the imperial parks. The hill upon which the park stands afforded normal people a rare view from above the city, as buildings were not allowed to be higher than those of the Imperial Palace. Near the southern entrance to the park is the **Temple of Mercy**, built in the Yuan dynasty. There are two stone pillars in the courtyard, one erected in the Liao dynasty, the other in the Jin dynasty. In 1695 a three room wing west of the old temple was built, from which the park gets its name. Li Dazhao rented one of these rooms while he was in Beijing working to further the revolution and held many meetings here. There are also two *pailou* (gates of honour) which once stood on Chang'an Jie. Today there is a swimming pool complete with slides, an open-air dance floor and a cinema in the park. The park is very popular with Beijingers, particularly in the summer months. ❑

Map on page 136

This feature at the Temple of the White Cloud is found in many Daoist temples; throwing a coin at the bell brings good luck.

BELOW: Tianning Si.

THE TEMPLE OF HEAVEN

This peaceful complex was historically used for imperial ancestor worship. It has now been transformed into the popular Tiantan Park. Outside the temple is Beijing's fascinating pearl market

Map on page 150

The Temple of Heaven (Tiantan, park open daily, 6am–9pm; temple open 8am–5pm; entrance fee) is one of the city's most visited parks, popular among Beijing residents and foreign tourists. It is easy to get here from the Inner City by bus or by taxi; the park can be entered through several gates. The temple complex covers a total area of 273 hectares (675 acres). The buildings are divided into two main groups: northern and southern. The northern group, built to a semi-circular layout representing Heaven, gathers around one of the most impressive buildings in China, the Hall of Prayer for Good Harvests. The southern group, meanwhile, has a square layout that symbolises Earth.

A place of ritual

Built in 1420, the Temple of Heaven served as a place of ritual for Ming and Qing emperors. Every year at the time of the winter solstice the emperor would come here in a magnificent procession lasting several days, in order to honour his ancestors and to pray for a good harvest in the season to come. In the middle of the first lunar calendar month, the emperor prayed once more in the Temple of Heaven, this time in the Hall of Prayer for Good Harvests. This ceremony was last carried out in 1914 by the self-proclaimed emperor Yuan Shikai.

The observation of such ritual was more than a mere formality. The sacred nature of the emperor's rule had been established in the 3rd century BC: as the Son of Heaven, he administered heavenly authority on earth. According to the Chinese, natural catastrophes, bad farming practices, failing harvests, and increasing corruption were all signs that the emperor had lost the favour of Heaven and of his ancestors. In such circumstances, it was considered a legitimate act to overthrow him and invest another emperor with the mandate of Heaven. Exact attention to the practice of the sacrificial rites in the Temple of Heaven was therefore given the appropriate importance by the ever-wary emperor.

Ceremonies of the solstice

The procession for the winter solstice began at the Qianmen Gate at the southern edge of the Forbidden City. When it arrived at the Temple of Heaven the emperor changed his robes in the **Hall of Heaven** (Huangqiongyu) ❶. Built in 1530 and restored in 1730, this hall has a round, pointed roof with a golden spire. The ancestor tablets of the emperors were stored inside. Ancestor tablets were introduced some 2,000 years ago, and were based on the idea that during the religious ceremony the spirit of the dead person would be present in the tablet, which was engraved with his or her name, birthday and date of death. Originally,

PRECEDING PAGES: ornate incense burners outside the Temple of Heaven. **LEFT:** the Hall of Prayer for Good Harvests. **BELOW:** temple gate.

Dragon detail from a circular roof tile at the Temple of Heaven.

only the emperor honoured his ancestors in such ways but due to the spread of Confucianism ancestor worship became common among the general population in the first century BC.

A brick wall surrounding the courtyard of the Hall of Heaven has become famous as the **Echo Wall** ❷. If you stand facing the wall and speak to someone who is also standing by it, he or she will be able to hear every word at every point anywhere along the wall. Of course, it is necessary to wait until only a few people are present, which, unfortunately, is very rarely the case.

The three stone slabs in front of the stairs to the main temple are the **Echo Stones** (Sanyinshi), which produce another peculiar effect. If you stand on the first slab and clap your hands, you will hear a single echo. On the second step you will hear a double echo, and on the third, a triple. The secret of this ingenious phenomenon has to do with the different distances at which each stone slab is placed from the wall.

Before the winter solstice ritual, the emperor would fast in the **Hall of Abstinence** (Zhaigong) ❸, which stands in the west of the temple complex. Then, by the first rays of the sun on the day of the solstice, he would offer sacrifices and prayers at the **Altar of Heaven** (Yuanqiu) ❹, a stone terrace of three levels surrounded by two walls – an inner round one and an outer square one.

The lowest level of the altar symbolises the Earth, the second, the world of human beings, and the last, Heaven. The altar is built from stone slabs and its construction is based on the number nine and its multiples. In earlier times, odd numbers were considered the attribute of Heaven or *yang*. Nine, as the highest odd unit, was the most important number of all, and therefore became associated with the emperor. The innermost circle on the top level consists of nine

BELOW: Echo Wall.

slabs, the second of 18, the third of 27 and so on until the final ring on the lowest level, which, as the 27th circle, contains 243 slabs.

Here another odd sound effect can be heard. If you stand in the middle of the upper level on the round stone slab and speak in a normal voice, your voice is heard more loudly than those of any other people around you. This effect is caused by the echo retained by the balustrades, and by a hollow space within the stone slab that functions as a resonating cavity. This stone in the centre was considered by the Chinese to be the most holy place in the Chinese empire, indeed the centre of the Earth.

Prayers for the harvest

The most striking building of the Temple of Heaven complex is undoubtedly the **Hall of Prayer for Good Harvests** (Qiniandian) ❺, which is built on a three-level marble terrace. Each level is surrounded by a balustrade. First constructed in 1420, the hall was struck by lightning in 1889 and burned to the ground. It was rebuilt according to the original plans.

The pointed roof, with its three levels, its 50,000 blue glazed tiles – blue symbolises heaven – and its golden point, was constructed without using a single nail and has no spars or beams. It is supported by 28 wooden pillars; the central four, the Dragon Fountain Pillars, are almost 20 metres (66 ft) tall and represent the four seasons. The first ring of pillars surrounding them represents the 12 months; the outer ring, also of 12 pillars, the 12 divisions of the day. The wood for the pillars came from the southwestern Chinese province of Yunnan. In the centre of the floor is a marble plaque with veining showing a dragon and a phoenix (symbolizing the emperor and the empress).

Map on page 150

BELOW: inside the Hall of Prayer for Good Harvests.

Family portrait on a frigid winter day.

The eight altars

Leave the Temple of Heaven via the west gate, and follow Tianqiao Nandajie. Tianqiao means "Heavenly Bridge"; however, the bridge has not been in existence for a long time. Before 1949, this was a meeting place of acrobats, fortune tellers, sellers of miraculous elixirs, and other shady characters. Even today, the markets around the Temple of Heaven still bustle with life, and the residents of this district are considered a separate breed.

A sports park on this street marks the site of the **Altar of Agriculture** (Xiannongtan) ❻, which stood symmetrically opposite the Temple of Heaven and was dedicated to the legendary Emperor Shennong, the "first farmer" in China. This was one of the eight altars which, in addition to the Temple of Heaven, were central to the ritual life of Ming and Qing emperors. Another altar, The Altar of the Gods of Heaven (Tianshentan) stood in its grounds.

The other five altars are in different parts of the city, mostly in public parks. The Altar of the Land and Harvests (Shejitan) is in what is now Sun Yat-sen Park, next to the Imperial Palace. The Altar of the Silkworm (Xiancantan) stands at the north end of Beihai Park. Ditan Park, near the Lama Temple in the north of the city, incorporates the Altar of the Earth (Ditan). The Altar of the Sun (Ritan) also stands in a park, this time in the Jianguomen diplomatic quarter, not far from the Friendship Store. To the west of the city centre is the Altar of the Moon (Yuetan), adjacent to a telecommunications tower.

Palaeontology and pearls

Beijing's **Natural History Museum** ❼ (Ziyan Bowuguan; Tianqiao Street; open Tues–Sun, 8.30am–5pm; entrance fee), is in an unattractive building oppo-

Map
on page
150

site a department store in the Yongdingmen district, just to the west of the Temple of Heaven. The museum has an exhibition of more than 5,000 species in palaeontology, zoology and botany.

In the hall of palaeontology, you can see fossils from the Palaeozoic, Mesozoic and Cenozoic periods, such as a piece of ochre-coloured marble with a cloud pattern formed by fossilised seaweed – a silent record of life in prehistoric times, about 500 to 100 million years ago. There are also plenty of dinosaurs: in the centre of the hall is the skeleton of the high-nosed Qingdaosaurus, which had a horn on its nose. The skeleton of Mamenchisaurus, which is twice the size, was dug up in the village of Mamenxi in Sichuan Province. In contrast to these giants, there are the remains of a Lufengsaurus – 2 metres (6½ ft) high and 6 metres (20 ft long) – from Yunnan Province, and of a parrot-beaked dinosaur that was no bigger than a cat. Other notable displays include the Yangzi River sturgeon, a freshwater species that grows to more than 5 metres (16 feet) in length.

Just across the street from the Temple of Heaven's east gate is the popular **Hong Qiao Market ⑥**, a pearl market whose name means "red bridge". There is a live seafood market in the basement; clothes and sundries are sold on the first and second floors; and antique and pearl treasures on the third. The many stalls are densely packed and manned by merchants from the pearl producing provinces who vie for customers' attention. Bargaining usually brings good results. As an added enticement, one proprietor has put up pictures of herself with an array of visiting presidents and prime ministers.

Most of the pearls on sale are of the freshwater type that China has been producing for around 3,000 years. These are not the most highly prized variety, which accounts for the relatively good prices. ❑

BELOW: exhibit in the Natural History Museum.

BEIJING'S BICYCLES AND TRICYCLES

Cycles have ruled the roads of Beijing for more than 50 years, but they face an uncertain future in a city that has been promoting motor vehicles

Despite the building of multi-lane ring roads and boulevards to accommodate the growing number of cars, most Beijingers still rely on pedal power to get to work, go shopping, and take the children to school. Affluent youngsters ride expensive mountain bikes, while older and poorer people make do with classic black Flying Pigeon and Forever designs. People selling pancakes and kebabs cooked on small grills the size of a bicycle rack are the most prominent of tens of thousands who do business by bicycle or tricycle.

China has some 500 million bicycles, more than half the world's total. Greater affluence has brought not only private cars, but also an unprecedented number of cycles. Today, 8½ million bikes glide around the flat roads of Beijing, almost triple the 1980 total. Bicycles are still used for more than 50 percent of all journeys in the capital, though this figure is slowly falling.

BICYCLE "POLLUTION"

In 1995, the World Bank concluded that Chinese cities, including Beijing, were "mainly dominated motor vehicle traffic." As a showpiece capital, Beijing is image conscious; cars are a key part of its modernisation drive. Planners' and architects' drawings have a conspicuous absence of bicycles, and some officials even discuss the problem of bicycle "pollution."

▽ **FAMILY TRICYCLE**
Many families ride single cycles, though most now own an average of one bicycle per person.

▷ **STEEDS FOR SALE**
China produces around 30 million bicycles per year for export and domestic markets. Quality has improved over the years. Prices now range from 200 to 2,000 yuan.

△ **TAKING A BREAK**
People who cycle for a living work up to 12 hours per day, in all weather. Most are self-sufficient, carrying all their own equipment and spares.

△ **SEA OF COMMUTERS**
Traffic police try to keep order as 20,000 cyclists per hour pass major intersections at peak times. Cyclists face on-the-spot fines if caught breaking the rules.

▷ **OILING THE WHEELS**
Bicycle repairers eke out a living on street corners across the capital. Tough competition between mechanics means repair prices are minimal.

THREE-WHEELING: TRICYCLE CARTS

Recycling is just one of the industries that relies on the people who pedal "flatbacks" around the city carrying anything it is possible to carry. The flatbacks, tricycle carts with wooden slats on the back, circle the ring roads loaded with cardboard, plastic, metal and other waste. Most of Beijing's waste is still transported this way.

Tricycle mounted pigswill barrels collect waste food from restaurants. More flatbacks wait near large markets and furniture stores, often providing the most convenient way to deliver wardrobes and settees, or large orders of computers and clothing. Other tricycle drivers specialise in carrying gas bottles or beer crates on smaller, sturdy models.

Migrant workers play a vital role in recycling: Some pedal around the city in search of reusable items, some collect from regular pick-up points, while others work as sifters at large waste sites.

▷ **NIGHT SHIFT**
Some farmers cycle overnight from the outlying suburbs to bring fruit and vegetables to Beijing's early morning markets, often risking arrest by police or tax officers.

▽ **STOP, RED FLAG**
Armed with flags and whistles, traffic wardens, usually pensioners or unemployed youngsters, control the bicycle lanes that flank most main streets.

▷ **AT YOUR SERVICE**
Tricycle rickshaws, often known as trishaws or pedicabs, ply many of Beijing's main streets, train and bus stations, and tourist areas. Most are licensed, but all prices are negotiable.

THE LAKE DISTRICT

Part of the former lakeside pleasure grounds of the imperial family has been turned into the attractive Beihai Park. To the north are the famous Bell and Drum towers

Map on page 158

In the 15th century, the large lake in the middle of Beijing was divided in two parts. Today, the area around the Northern Lake, **Beihai Park** ❶ (open daily, 6am–9pm; entrance fee) is one of the most beautiful and popular places to spend a day out in the Inner City. In summer, the lake is used for boating, and in winter, for skating. The very youngest enjoy themselves on ice sledges – daring constructions consisting of a wooden chair, or sometimes just a large plank, fastened on to two runners. For imperial ice celebrations the ice was smoothed with glowing irons.

The other part of the lake, **Zhongnanhai** (literally "Central and Southern Lake") ❷, and its surroundings were a pleasure garden for the court. Right next to the Imperial Palace, this is where horse races and hunts, birthday receptions, and celebrations of the Lantern Festival took place. After 1949, Mao, Zhou Enlai, Liu Shaoqi and other prominent comrades lived here. Mao's private library is still there today. Surrounded by a thick wall, Zhongnanhai has been the seat of the Politbureau and the State Council since 1949: the communications centre of the political leadership . Foreign visitors are not admitted to the seat of government unless they are invited to an audience. It is not infrequently whispered that Zhongnanhai is the new "Forbidden City".

LEFT: the White Dagoba towers over lush Beihai Park.
BELOW: early-morning Qi Gong session.

Islands in the lake

The location of the park – west of Coal Hill (Jing-shan) and northwest of the Imperial Palace – marks the centre of Kublai Khan's Mongol capital, Khan-baliq (Dadu in Chinese). In the south of the park, with a separate entrance, is the **Round Town** ❸ (Tu-ancheng; open Tues–Sun, 8.30am–5pm; entrance fee), one of three islands in the Northern Lake. The khan had this island landscaped, along with the surrounding area, and from this spot, according to Marco Polo, he ruled in inimitable splendour. However, only the trees remain from that time, all the architecture of the Mongol Yuan dynasty having been destroyed.

An exquisite 1.5-metre (5-ft) wide nephrite container, in which Kublai Khan kept his wine, also survives; it stands next to the entrance of a pavilion with white marble pillars and a blue roof. In the 18th century, a poem by the Emperor Qianlong praising the beauty of this work of art, was engraved on the inside of the vessel. A second jewel in the Round Town is a 1.5-metre (5-ft) tall, white jade statue of Buddha with inlaid jewels. It can be seen in the **Receiving Light Hall** (Chengguandian).

Hortensia Island (Jade Island/Qionghuadao) ❹ is the most impressive part of the park as far as scenery and history are concerned. Going from the main south gate leads to a bridge more than 600 years old, across

A tourist poses in imperial costume on Hortensia Island.

which is the **Temple of Eternal Peace** (Yong'ansi) ❺, and beyond it, the **Hall of the Wheel of Law** (Falundian). From here, a twisting path leads up uneven steps to the 35-metre (115-ft) high **White Dagoba** ❻, an onion-shaped shrine in the Tibetan style, built on the ruins of a Ming palace in honour of the fifth Dalai Lama on the occasion of his visit to Beijing in 1651. It was this onion-shape that led foreigners living in Beijing during the Republican era to refer to it as "the peppermint bottle". In 1679, and again in 1731, the dagoba was destroyed by earthquakes, but was rebuilt on both occasions. It suffered only cracks during the 1976 Tangshan earthquake, and during restoration a golden reliquary containing two small bone fragments, probably of prominent lamas, was found. The view from here of the Imperial Palace, Beihai and Zhongnanhai, and the numerous hutong of the Inner City of Beijing, is only surpassed by the view from the peak of Coal Hill.

On the northern side of the dagoba, the path leads through a labyrinth of stairs, corridors, pavilions and bizarre rock formations carved into grottos

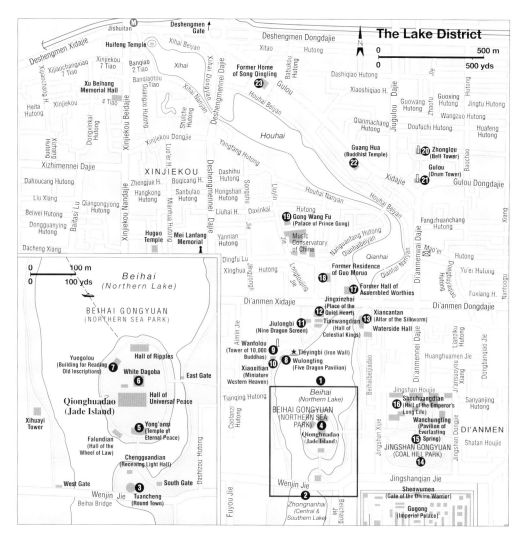

Map
on page
158

intended to resemble the houses of Daoist saints, and goes steeply down to the lake shore, which is bordered by a long, semi-circular covered walkway. Halfway up the northwestern slope of the island is a nearly 4-metre (13-ft) tall statue called the **Plate for Gathering Dew** (Cheng Lu Pan) which was placed here by Emperor Qianlong. It is thought to represent one of the Eight Immortals and records a legend from the life of the Emperor Wudi, who ruled early in the first century. When Wudi heard that drinking dewdrops would make him immortal he commanded a slave to sit outdoors overnight with a bowl and catch the dewdrops falling from Heaven, and bring the drops to him so that he could refresh himself with them and become immortal.

Right below this statue is the **Building for Reading Old Inscriptions** (Yuegolou) ❼. A collection of 495 stone tablets, engraved with the work of famous Chinese calligraphers, dating mostly from the 18th century, is kept here. Some of the inscriptions, however, go back 1,500 years. Rubbings were taken from the tablets – one of the earliest forms of printing.

Next door, in the Hall of Ripples, is the **Fangshan Restaurant**, established in 1926 by chefs of the imperial household who were suddenly left unemployed when Pu Yi was forced out of the Imperial Palace in 1924. With its stylish interior and its menus based on imperial cuisine, it was for a long time one of the best and most expensive restaurants in Beijing. But with the recent explosion of restaurant choice and quality in the city, Fangshan is now better known for its beautiful lakeside location than its food.

By the lake shore

From here, a ferry takes visitors to the **Five Dragon Pavilion** (Wulongting) ❽, on the northwest lake shore. These buildings from the Ming era are built in a zigzagging line over the water and connected by walkways. The largest pavilion, with its double-stepped, curved roof, forms the head of a curving dragon when seen from above. Emperors used to fish from this point. Beside the quay where the boats tie up is the 700-year-old, 4-metre (13-ft) wide **Iron Wall** (Tieyingbi), although it is not iron at all, but igneous rock. It was originally placed in front of a Buddhist convent, which had been a bell foundry in the Ming dynasty: hence the idea that it was made of iron. It was saved from a marauding foreigner, and brought here in 1947.

The path leads west from the waterfront to the **Tower of 10,000 Buddhas** (Wanfolou) ❾, built by the Emperor Qianlong in the 18th century on the occasion of his mother's 80th birthday. The pure gold statuettes of Buddha that filled the niches inside the tower were stolen – like so many other treasures – by European troops in 1900.

To the south stands what is probably the biggest pavilion in China, the **Miniature Western Heaven** (Xiaoxitian) ❿, which was built in 1770 as a shrine to Guanyin, the Goddess of Mercy. In the Mahayana Buddhist tradition that established itself in China, the idea of the "Western Heaven" is similar to Christian concepts of Paradise. Inside, Buddhist paintings are exhibited. The **Nine Dragon Screen** (Jiulongbi) ⓫

BELOW: peaceful Beihai Lake.

originally served to ward off the God of Fire from a workshop for translating and printing Lamaist scriptures that Qianlong had built in honour of his mother. When, in an ironic twist of fate, that building succumbed to fire in 1919, a gymnasium was built in its place, and the screen was moved here. A few steps to the east of the Dragon Screen, is the **Hall of the Celestial Kings** (Tianwangdian), a Ming dynasty workshop for the translation and woodblock-printing of Buddhist scriptures.

The **Place of the Quiet Heart** (Jingxinzhai) ⓬, just beyond, invites walkers to rest and pause in contemplation. It is a delightful garden within a garden laid out by Qianlong, interspersed with lotus pools, halls, pavilions and living quarters. Empress Cixi often used to lunch here. At other times Manchu princes used these peaceful surroundings to wrestle with Confucian classics. Another Manchu prince, the last emperor, Pu Yi, used this space to write his memoirs, *From Emperor to Citizen*.

On the other side of the bridge is the **Altar of the Silkworm** (Xiancantan) ⓭, one of the eight altars that played a large part in the ritual life of Ming and Qing emperors (*see page 152*). Here the empress would come to perform a ceremony honouring the goddess of silkworms – the wife of the mythical Yellow Emperor, who supposedly discovered the secret of the silkworm – and to pray for a good harvest. Turned into a tea house during the Republican era, it presently serves as a nursery school for children of high level officials.

Coal Hill

BELOW: the Nine Dragon Screen.

The so-called **Coal Hill** ⓮ (Jingshan; open daily, 6am–9pm; entrance fee), came into existence at the beginning of the 15th century, when the Ming emperor

Yongle had moats dug all around the Imperial Palace. *Feng shui* – Chinese geomancy – probably played a decisive part in the choice of a suitable spot to tip the spoil. The aim of feng shui is to site buildings in harmony with the natural topography and, by this means, to influence them positively. Coal Hill served to protect the Imperial Palace from malignant influences from the north. Pragmatism must also have played a role in the choice, as any approaching enemy could be seen at a distance by a lookout placed at such a height.

Map
on page
158

Its five crests – the middle one being the highest – make Coal Hill look from a distance like a Chinese scholar's brush holder. Five pavilions, dating from the 16th century, crown the chain of hills and emphasise their zigzagging lines. Each pavilion once housed a bronze figure of Buddha, but four of these were plundered by European troops in 1900.

The surrounding park was not opened to the public until 1928. Before this, it was a private imperial garden, and eunuchs, palace ladies and the imperial family members spent their leisure hours strolling in its picturesque scenery.

Here is where Chongzheng, the last Ming emperor, committed suicide in 1644, after the rebellious peasant armies walked into Beijing through the treacherously left-open gates. Upon hearing the terrible news, Chongzheng rang a bell to call his advisors, but nobody appeared. Sensing the end, he walked to the garden just outside the walls of the Imperial Palace and hanged himself. The tree he used was uprooted by Red Guards during the Cultural Revolution, but was replaced with a new one in 1981.

Skyscrapers have taken over from the hill as the highest point in Beijing. Yet the view from the **Pavilion of Everlasting Spring** (Wanchungting) ⓰, on the middle of the five peaks is superb. Looking straight along the north-south axis

BELOW:
view across the
city from Coal Hill.

Beihai Park is a popular place for weddings. Cars are often hired for the happy occasion and adorned with dolls and other decorations.

BELOW:
bird fanciers
discuss their pets.

of Beijing, one can see to the south the sea of curved golden roofs that is the Imperial Palace, with the White Dagoba towering over the picturesque Beihai Lake to the west. To the north are the massive Drum and Bell Towers; and on a clear day you can see, on the horizon to the northwest, the silhouette of the Western Mountains.

In the north of the park is the **Hall of the Emperor's Long Life** (Shouhuang-dian) ⑯, where the corpses of empresses and dowager empresses were laid before being removed to tombs outside the city. It now houses a children's cultural centre where courses in music, dance, theatre and painting are available.

North of Beihai Park

The **Sea of the Ten Buddhist Temples** (Shichahai) is a complex of lakes north of Beihai Park. Historically, this area has harboured many beautiful courtyard palaces of Manchu princes and Qing dynasty officials. More recently, the area has been undergoing extensive development, which so far has included destroying old homes, and widening of roads. Still, it is hard for this beautiful lake and winding hutong area to lose its charm.

Southwest of the lakes, after passing through the Lotus Flower Market, is the former **Hall of Assembled Worthies** (Hui Xiantang) ⑰, a popular gathering place during the Republican era. Weddings were often held here, and Mei Lanfang, the famous opera performer (*see page 186*), who only lived a short distance away, was often summoned to perform.

Nearby, in Qianhai Xijie, is the former **residence of Guo Moruo** ⑱ (open daily, 8.30am–5pm; entrance fee), an influential figure in the rise of communism in China. Guo was born in Sichuan province in 1892, the son of a wealthy land-

lord. Following a spell in Japan, where he studied at Kyushu Imperial University, he returned to China in 1921 and became known as a respected author as well as a proponent of change, having been profoundly influenced by the Russian October Revolution of 1917. He soon became an early adherent of the fledgling Chinese Communist party, meeting with Mao in 1926. Although exiled to Japan for ten years by the Guomindang government (having written an article criticising Chiang Kai-shek), he again returned to China in 1937, and later held several posts in the new Communist state. Guo was one of the first people to be attacked by the Red Guards during the Cultural Revolution.

Also nearby is the **Palace of Prince Gong** ⑲ (Gong Wang Fu; open daily 8am–4.30pm; entrance fee), the world's largest extant courtyard house. Prince Gong, the brother of Emperor Xian Feng, virtually ran the country during the minorities of the Emperors Tongzhi and Guangxu, from 1861 to 1884. His home and their 5.7-hectare (14-acre) grounds, including lush gardens, are now occupied by the China Conservatory of Music. The historic structures in the complex include Beijing's only preserved Qing dynasty theatre. Here, guests are served by women wearing traditional costumes of the period and treated to a sample of Beijing opera.

The Bell and Drum towers

On the east side of the Shichahai lakes are two towers dating from the rule of Kublai Khan. They have survived so many twists and turns of history that surviving the wars and revolutions of the twentieth century seems relatively unremarkable. Both the towers stand at the northern end of Di'anmenwai Dajie and once formed the northernmost point of the city. However, during the period of

Map
on page
158

BELOW: boating on Beihai Lake.

It is possible to climb up the 55-m (180-ft) wooden tower to admire the drum inside the Drum Tower.

BELOW: the Bell Tower as seen from the Drum Tower.

Mongol rule, they stood in the centre of the contemporary capital city of Dadu. Under the Ming emperor Yongle, the towers were rebuilt in 1420, somewhat to the east of their original position.

After the original wooden **Bell Tower ⓴** (Zhonglou; open daily, 8.30am–4pm; entrance fee) was destroyed in a fire, the present tower, 33 metres (108 ft) high, was built in 1747. The **Drum Tower ㉑** (Gulou; open daily, 8.30am–4pm; entrance fee) was last restored in 1800. In earlier years, 24 big drums were kept inside – only one has survived – which were struck 13 times every evening at 7pm to signal the start of the night hours and also the closing of the city gates. The drums were struck again every two hours, the last time being at 5am. By that hour, the officials to be present at the imperial morning audience were supposed to have taken up their kneeling positions just in front of the Hall of Supreme Harmony – failure to do so brought heavy penalties.

The day officially began at 7am with the ringing of the huge iron bell of the Bell Tower. When this proved too quiet, an even bigger bronze bell was installed in the tower, which could be heard 20 km (12 miles) away. The bronze bell has now disappeared, but the iron bell is on display behind the tower. The building is so sturdy it survived the serious earthquake of 1976 without serious damage: only one stone ornamental figure on the roof is said to have fallen down.

Inside the recently refurbished Drum Tower is the one remaining original drum, damaged during the opium wars of the 19th century, now flanked by two brightly-painted replicas. Climb the steep staircase of 69 steps for an unmatched view of a rapidly disappearing old-style neighbourhood. Looking down upon the grey and often grass-covered tile roofs, separated into a variety of geometric shapes by the walls of the hutong, you can get a sense of how each *siheyuan* is

a community in itself. Meanwhile, in the distance, tall, gleaming structures, and an ungodly number of construction cranes, are a reminder that Beijing is in a constant process of change.

Beyond the Silver Ingot bridge, on the east bank of Houhai, is the **Guang Hua Buddhist Temple ㉒** (open daily, 8.30am–5pm; entrance fee). Constructed during the Yuan dynasty, this active temple is now home to the Beijing Buddhist Society. While it is only medium sized in relation to some temples, it is well-preserved and stocked with the usual colourful array of Buddhist statues and artefacts.

Song Qingling's house

The **former home of Song Qingling ㉓** (open Tues–Sun, 9am–4.30pm; entrance fee), honorary president of the People's Republic of China, and wife of Sun Yat-sen, is nearby at No. 46 Beiheyan Jie, on the western bank of Houhai. The grounds were formerly part of the palace of Prince Chun, Pu Yi's father. The house where Pu Yi was born is just south of here, and occupied by the Ministry of Health.

Song Qingling moved into the house in 1963 and lived there until her death in 1981. The guest room contains an exhibition of photographs, documents, and objects from her life: her pampered Shanghai childhood as a daughter of one of China's most prominent families; her years as a student; her marriage to Sun Yatsen; her political activities; her work for the Society for the Protection of the Rights of the Chinese People; and her support for the resistance to Japanese occupation. An extract from her most famous speech, the essay, *Sun Yat-sen and his cooperation with the Communist Party*, is also on display.   ❏

Map on page 158

LEFT: golden evening light on Houhai.
BELOW: outside the former home of Song Qingling.

EASTERN BEIJING

Map on page 170

The West meets the Orient in this area of Beijing, which may seem at first sight brashly modern but which conceals several unmissable sights dating from the days of ancient China

What to outsiders might seem a shame, to the Chinese signals progress. Preservationists lost the battle to save the city walls and many of the ancient buildings within them when Mao himself dictated that rather than creating a new city somewhere in the suburbs, the existing city should be adapted to the modern age. The eastern sections of town, in particular the Chaoyang district between the second and third ring roads, are still steadily losing their more Chinese characteristics. Modern highrises are shooting up almost overnight, replacing the traditional single storey, grey-walled northern-style house.

The last big push of redevelopment was for the 50th anniversary celebrations, when the main arteries of the eastern district, Jianguomennei, Chang'An, and Fuxingmennei, were transformed into a stage for the grand parade. Traditional buildings – including those on some neighbouring hutongs – were flattened by the wrecking ball, as this was not the picture of a modern China that the government wanted to present to the world.

The eastern part of the city is also a centre for international business, and this is where you will find a concentration of foreigners, and all things foreign – especially hotels and restaurants that cater to a Western palate. Nevertheless, mixed in with all this modernity there are still some wonderful nuggets of ancient Chinese culture.

PRECEDING PAGES: Beijing's brave new world. **LEFT:** a Wangfujing shopping centre. **BELOW:** cleaning up Wangfujing in preparation for the 50th anniversary celebrations.

Wangfujing and around

A short distance to the east of the Imperial Palace is **Wangfujing ❶**. This street was originally called Shiwangfu, or "Ten Imperial Brothers Street". It was supposedly given this name when a Ming emperor ordered his ten brothers to take up residence here, so that he could keep an eye on them. It used to be referred to as "Morrison Street" by foreigners living in the Legation Quarter to the south, after the famous *Times* correspondent, George Morrison, who lived here at No. 98.

Always a smart address, in recent times Wangfujing has established itself as Beijing's premier shopping street. Over the past few years practically every building has been rebuilt, with the assistance of huge amounts of Hong Kong capital. This is the place to come to browse in upmarket Western-style shopping malls and department stores, both above and below street level. After much local debate and scandal that resulted in the imprisonment of the Beijing mayor on corruption charges, the flagship McDonald's on the southeast corner of the street, at the junction with Chang'an Jie, was knocked down in 1996 to make way for Li Kai-shing's enormous residential and commercial Oriental Plaza.

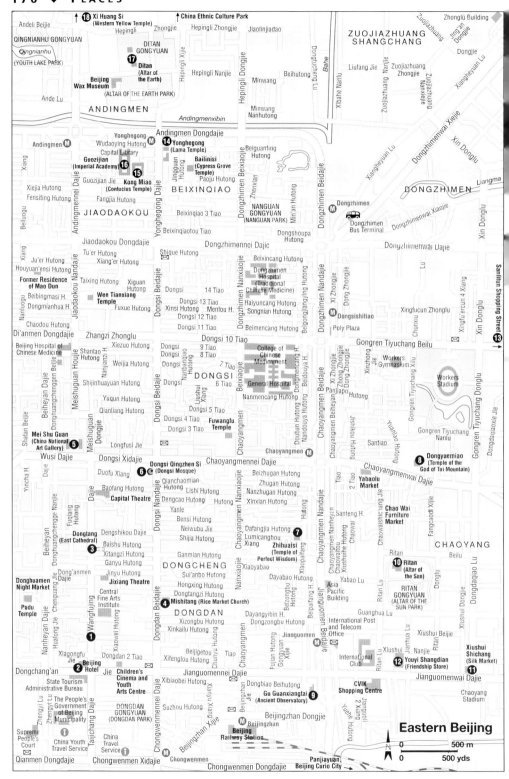

Eastern Beijing

Map
on page
170

The huge **Beijing Hotel** ❷, once the only place where foreigners could stay in the capital, is on the corner of Wangfujing and Dong Chang'an Jie. It was built in four stages. The earliest part of the building is the centre, dating from 1917, where ornate French-style vaulted ceilings and a sweeping staircase evoke the decadent days of the 1920s. The hotel was extended in 1954, and this section reflects the optimism of the early years of the People's Republic. The East Wing, added in 1974 towards the end of the Cultural Revolution, is, not surprisingly, somewhat bleak. The western section was added in 1989 and is a tribute to the financial freedoms of the Deng era. To the north is the Sun Dong An Mall, a pedestrian area renovated for the PRC's 50th anniversary.

This may be China's Brave New World, but mixed among the commercial highrises are remnants of times past. **East Cathedral** (Dongtang) ❸, also known as St. Joseph's, was burned to the ground in 1900, and had to be rebuilt. Prior to that the site was occupied by part of the house of Schall von Bell (*see page 137*), who died here in 1666. The cathedral has an active congregation, and masses are held here on Sundays in English and Chinese.

The **Rice Market Church** (Mishitang) ❹ at 21 Dongdan Bei Jie (previously known as Rice Market Street) is an important Protestant church. The grey brick building , with its Chinese roof and double wooden eaves, dates from the 1920s. At that time, this was the seat of the Bible Society; today it is home to the Beijing branch of the Chinese Christian Council

The Beijing Hotel is a well-known land-mark, and reflects four different periods of recent history.

At the northern end of Wangfujing is the **China National Art Gallery** ❺ (Mei Shu Guan; open Tues–Sun, 9am–4pm; entrance fee). The building was completed in 1959 and is still considered to be one of modern China's most impressive architectural creations. It has 14 halls for changing exhibitions and can be a good place to discover new as well as old trends in Chinese art. Some artists have studios in the gallery, and work can be bought from them directly.

BELOW: Wangfujing, Beijing's premier shopping street.

The **Dongsi Mosque** ❻ is not open to the general public, so an appointment must be made for a visit. From the street (after which the mosque is named), one would hardly notice that there is a mosque at all. It was built in 1447, and in 1450, the Ming emperor Jiangtai gave it the title Qingzhensi (meaning "Temple of Purity and Light"), which is how all mosques are now referred to in Chinese. While the front part of the main hall is built of wood in the Chinese fashion, the rear has a vault-like roof of tiles. In the front is a tablet with an Arabic inscription. The mosque can hold over 500 people and has a women's "corner".

Since 1949, the Dongsi Mosque has been the seat of the Islamic Society, where training courses for imams are held. Restored in the early 1950s but closed during the Cultural Revolution, the mosque is now self-financing. Its library contains many valuable Islamic manuscripts, among them a Koran manuscript that is almost 700 years old.

The Hui (Chinese Muslims) also have their own cemetery in Beijing. However, non-Muslims are not allowed to enter it. Cremation is the general rule for funerals in China, but the Hui have special exemption.

The Bronze Wonder Donkey at the Temple of the God of Tai Mountain. Touching the donkey brings health and good fortune.

BELOW: the stylish China Club, owned by Hong Kong tycoon David Tang.

East from Wangfujing

Located to the east of Wangfujing, not far from the second ring road, is the **Temple of Perfect Wisdom** ❼ (Zhihuaisi; open daily, 9am–4pm; entrance fee). It was built as a family shrine by a eunuch named Wang Zhen in 1443, during the Ming dynasty, but closed six years later when Wang was executed. The shrine then became imperial property. Laid out according to strict Buddhist rules, it is composed of three compounds. Wood blocks used for printing the "Grand Collection of Buddhist Scriptures" are kept here. They are the only officially carved blocks in Chinese.

On the other side of the second ring road, the **Temple of the God of Tai Mountain** ❽ (Dongyuemiao; open daily, 9am–4pm; entrance fee) is one of the few Daoist temples in the city – this is less to do with a lack of Daoism in Beijing than the fact that Daoists traditionally shun urban areas. The temple was built to honour the highest celestial ruler of the Tai mountain, one of the five Daoist holy mountains in China. Founded by Zhang Daoling during the Yuan dynasty, this was once the largest Daoist temple in northern China and belonged to the Zhengyi sect of the religion. All the extant buildings date from the Qing dynasty. After 1949 the temple was converted into schools and administrative offices, but in 1995 the neighbourhood of Chaoyang won the right to restore it and put it to its present use as the **Beijing Folklore Museum**.

The temple complex consists of three courtyards. Off the main courtyard are the Hall of Tai Mountain (Daizongbaodian) – in the centre of which is a statue of the god of Tai Mountain, surrounded by his high-ranking servants – and the Hall of Moral Perfection (Yudedian). The temple possesses more than 100 stone tablets that date from the Yuan, Ming and Qing dynasties.

The Observatory

At the junction of Jianguomennei and the second ring road, is the **Ancient Observatory** ❾ (Gu Guanxiangtai; open Wed–Sun, 9–11am and 1–4pm; entrance fee). Originally constructed in 1279 north of its present-day site, the observatory that you see today was built in the mid-15th century and sits atop a watchtower that was once a part of the city walls. It served both the Ming and Qing dynasties in making predictions based on astrology, as well as helping navigators who were about to go to sea. Its name has been changed several times. In the Yuan period it was known as the Terrace to Bring Down the Heavens, while in Ming times it was the Terrace for Watching the Stars. This was the workplace of, among others, the famous astronomer, hydraulics engineer and mathematician, Guo Shoujing.

Northeast of the observatory, in the Jianguomen diplomatic quarter and not far from the Friendship Store, is **the Altar of the Sun** ❿ (Ritan; open daily 6am–9pm; entrance fee), one of the eight altars which, along with the Temple of Heaven, played a great role in the ritual life of the Ming and Qing emperors. It is now a public park.

Gone shopping

No trip to Beijing would be complete without some shopping. One of the best places to hunt for bargains – frequented by both foreigners and Chinese – is the **Silk Market** ⓫, in a little alley of Jianguomenwai, east of the Friendship Store. Here you will find a multitude of products made in China for export only but which have somehow "fallen out of the container" before they were embarked. It is essential to bargain here as you never know exactly what you are getting,

Map on page 170

BELOW: the old observatory.

READING THE STARS

In the 13th century, astronomers at the Yuan dynasty imperial observatory fixed the length of the year at 365.2424 days – within one thousandth of a day according to modern calculations. They achieved such precision with the aid of bronze astronomical instruments such as those on display in the Ancient Observatory. The three armillary spheres, quadrant for finding stars, celestial globe, equatorial theodolite for determining horizontal angles and angles of elevation, altazimuth for determining the height of stars in the sky, and sextant on display today are all testament to the skill of Chinese scientists.

Such astonishing accuracy benefited astrology as much as astronomy. The casting of horoscopes earned the scientists the fortune and patronage they needed to develop their instruments and observatories.

The *luo pan* (net tablet), a wooden or brass disc covered in hundreds of characters, was the most complicated astrological instrument. Seventeen concentric rings surround a small compass, which represents the *tai qi* (Great Origin or Ultimate Cause). The *luo pan,* backed up by the consultation of charts, was used in complex forms of divination based on calculating changes in the position of the stars and planets.

Goods for sale in the Silk Market. Vendors here sell all kinds of silk items at low prices.

BELOW:
Mao memorabilia for sale.

and if you do get ripped off you will feel better if you only paid a few dollars for it. Rugs and souvenirs are also sold here. However, a recent law has been passed to force all outdoor market stalls to be put under a roof and the Silk Market may one day soon lose some of its charm. The nearby **Russian Market** (Yao Ba Lu Market) has already suffered this fate, and is now located in a huge canopied area further north on Chaoyangmenwai. This has not resulted in a drop in business. Russian traders still go in droves to buy large quantities of furs and clothing to take back north. It is difficult here to buy just one of anything.

For more traditional Chinese souvenirs, the **Friendship Store** ⓬ is always a good source, if a bit more pricey. In the 1970s and 1980s this was just about the only place in town where foreigners could purchase such luxuries as wine and other Western goods. Bargaining is not countenanced here. The newly opened Starbucks cafe in the same complex is another reason to visit. Not too far north is the **Chaowai Furniture Market**, where merchants will be more than happy to ship things home for you.

Further north still is **Sanlitun** ⓭ a street carrying similar goods to the Silk Market. At night this turns into a street of bars, where expats and Chinese come to drink and listen to music. It is especially pleasant during the summer when the bars put out tables and chairs on the pavement. In 1996 there was only one bar here, but in true Beijing style it was not long before copycat bars emerged hoping to cash in on the obvious success. This had been a mostly residential neighbourhood and when local residents complained of the noise a law was passed that all tables had to be brought inside at 11pm. Nevertheless the proliferation of bars has continued apace and there are rumours that the bars will soon be forced to relocate elsewhere.

Map on page 170

For the early risers, in southeastern Beijing to the east of Longtan Park is the **Ghost Market** (Panjiayuan; Huawei Lu Dajie), otherwise known as the Dirt Market. Formerly a small gathering of merchants selling goods of variable quality, it has expanded because of the numbers of foreign visitors it receives, and now warrants an enclosure. It is brimming at the seams with Chinese kitsch and Cultural Revolution memorabilia here. Most merchants are packed up by noon, so it is best to get there early.

While in the area, you can stop by the **Beijing Curio City** (Dongsanhuan Nan Lu, west of Huawei Bridge): four floors filled with higher quality antiques, paintings, jewellery and furniture. It also has a duty free shop, but remember to bring your passport, or you will not be allowed to buy anything.

The Lama Temple

In the northeastern part of the city is the largest, best-known, and certainly one of the city's most beautiful and interesting temples – the **Lama Temple** ⓮ (Yonghegong; open Tues–Sun, 9am–4pm; entrance fee). A visit here can easily be combined with a walk in Ditan Park (*see page 179*), on the other side of the second ring road, or a tour of the Confucius Temple and the Imperial Academy, to the west.

At first glance, you might think it odd that a Tibetan Buddhist temple enjoys such prominence in the capital, given Beijing's high profile squabbles with the Tibetan government in exile. But China's relationship with Tibet and its religion goes back further than the contemporary clashes. The presence of a Lamaist temple has been part of a centuries-long policy of pacifying the fractious "Land of the Snows", as well as other Lamaist states, such as Mongolia.

BELOW: monk at the Lama Temple.

The name Yonghegong ("Palace of Eternal Harmony") points to the courtly and imperial origins of the temple. Built in 1694, when it formed part of the city wall, it served as a residence for Yongzheng, the fourth son of Emperor Kangxi, before he ascended to the throne in 1722. Traditionally, the home of an heir to the throne would be turned into a temple after he had become ruler or even after his reign, and so Yongzheng's successor, his son Qianlong, sent for 300 Tibetan monks and 200 Chinese pupils and installed them in his father's old palace.

The palace served as a temple-cum-monastery from 1744 to 1960, and was considered one of the most notable centres of Lamaist Buddhism outside Tibet. During the Qing dynasty, the temple was closed to the public except for the annual performance of the "devil dance", which was staged as a warning against succumbing to human weaknesses – anger, greed, wine, sex and so on. The dance can still be seen today during the Spring Festival.

It is no coincidence that the Manchu emperors favoured a Tibetan monastery. Although many of them were officially followers of Confucius they were privately attracted to Tibetan Buddhism, perhaps because Buddhism attempted to deal with the unsettling idea of an afterlife. Unlike Confucianism, which places its emphasis on the present and does not deal with what its founder said he could not claim to know, Buddhists spend their whole lives preparing for the hereafter, in the hope of reaching nirvana. Lamaism, however, the variety of Buddhism practised in Tibet, Mongolia, Sikkim and Bhutan, was not widely observed in China, and unlike Mahayana Buddhism, does not exhibit many Chinese characteristics. Not even the main Lamaist scriptures have been translated from the Tibetan into Chinese.

During the Cultural Revolution, the monastery was closed. At first, groups of Red Guards took over the complex, but they were forbidden to destroy or plunder it by order of the president, Zhou Enlai. Many monks were ill-treated in spite of this and sent away to do manual labour in the countryside. In the early 1980s, the monastery was reopened and completely restored. More than 70 monks now live here in the rear part of the complex (bordering the second ring road) and now enjoy the use of washing machines and TV sets.

Study and training in the monastery are thorough. According to an often-told anecdote, one of the young novices, who work by day as supervisors in the temple halls, was asked, "How long do you have to study?"; he replied, "I don't have to at all. Learning lasts a lifetime." A philosopher, indeed.

The Lama Temple belongs to the Yellow Hat or Gelugpa sect of Buddhism, predominant in Tibet, whose spiritual head is the Dalai Lama. Whilst the Dalai Lama lives in exile, the second spiritual head of Tibetan Buddhism, the Panchen Lama, resides in Beijing. In contrast to the Dalai Lamas, the Panchen Lamas have recognised Chinese authority since the beginning of the 20th century. However, they have also defied the Chinese on at least one occasion. Following the death of the 10th Panchen Lama in 1989, the Chinese government assembled a group of lamas known to be sympathetic to their wishes, and asked

BELOW:
the Lama Temple.

Map on page 170

them to find a successor – a boy reincarnation of the previous Panchen Lama. But in 1995 it was revealed that the abbot in charge of the search committee had quietly asked for the Dalai Lama's approval of the chosen boy. When they discovered this, the Chinese authorities had the abbot arrested and put the boy and his parents under detention. They then announced that a new boy would be selected by the old method of drawing ivory lots from a golden urn. A new Panchen Lama was thus proclaimed in November 1995, but his validity is contested by Tibetans in exile.

Coming from the south, you enter the temple grounds through a gate. After crossing the gardens, you pass into the inner courtyard with its bell and drum towers and two pavilions with steles in them. To the north is the **Hall of the Celestial Kings** (Tianwangdian), with statues of the Maitreya Buddha and two guardian divinities.

Beyond the pavilion is a stone representation of the World Mountain, Sumeru. In the **Hall of Eternal Harmony** (Yonghedian) there are three statues of Buddha surrounded by 18 Lohan. The buildings to the left and right of this inner courtyard house a mandala and valuable *thangka* – figures representing the founder of the Yellow Hat sect, Tsongkhapa. Crossing the next courtyard, you come to the **Hall of Eternal Protection** (Yongyoudian), with statues of the Buddhas of longevity and medicine.

The halls to the left and right of the following courtyard contain, among other items, statues of Yab-Yum, a male and a female divinity whose intimate sexual connection symbolises the cosmic unity of all opposites. This courtyard is bounded by the **Hall of the Wheel of Dharma** (Falundian), in the middle of which is a 6-metre (20-ft) high statue of Tsongkhapa. Behind this statue is the monastery's treasure: a miniature mountain of sandalwood, and with 500 Lohan figures of gold, silver, copper, iron and tin. The fifth inner courtyard ends at the **Pavilion of Ten Thousand Happinesses** (Wanfuge). This contains an 25-metre (80-ft) high Maitreya Buddha made from a single piece of sandalwood. The three-storey pavilion is linked by bridges to the two-storey side buildings that flank it.

This inscription at the Lama Temple reads in Manchu, Tibetan, Chinese and Mongolian scripts.

BELOW:
an artist selling his calligraphy.

The Confucius Temple and the Imperial Academy

Across the street to the west, on a street graced by two of only a few existing *pailous* or decorative gates left standing in Beijing, are two important landmarks, although no longer serving their original functions.

The **Confucius Temple** ⓑ (Kong Miao; open daily, 9am–4pm, entrance fee) is now the Capital Museum, which has a permanent display of artefacts related to the history and culture of Beijing.

Confucianism has not fared well under the current government, which sees it as an embodiment of the feudal ways that communism was trying to eradicate. Hence, most Confucian temples throughout China have been converted to other uses or simply abandoned. The Beijing temple remains one of the largest outside of Qufu, the birthplace of Confucius.

Before the wide staircase leading up to the main

hall, look out for a cedar tree. It is said that a branch came loose from this tree and brushed off the head of a disloyal officer as it fell to the ground. In the main hall, the **Hall of Great Achievements** (Dachengdian), there are some of the musical instruments which were so important in Confucian ceremonies.

Confucian thought is the basic underpinning of traditional Chinese society. The philosophy was especially apparent in the system of choosing mandarins for the civil service which endured for 2,000 years. Each candidate was locked up for three days in a tiny cubicle, and required to undertake a test (*jinshi*) to prove his word perfect knowledge of the Confucian classics. This type of test encouraged the cultivation of a good memory and the ability to write formulaic essays following in the tradition of those who had gone before. Practical knowledge was not valued.

One of the most impressive sights in the temple today is the 198 stone tablets recording the names and hometowns of 51,624 candidates who successfully passed such tests held during the Yuan, Ming and Qing dynasties. These can be seen in the pavilions around the **Gate of the First Teacher** (Xianshimen).

Tradition dictated that on the right of a temple there should be an academy. So in the year 1306, during the Yuan dynasty, the **Imperial Academy** ⓰ (Guozijian: open daily, 9am–4pm; entrance fee) was founded as a school to teach the Chinese language to Mongol boys and Mongol to Chinese boys, and all martial arts to all pupils. Later it became a university which, in 1462, had 13,000 students. In total, the academy was responsible for producing 48,900 successful *jinshi* scholars. The building has now been turned into the Capital Library, housing books on the social sciences and Beijing local history.

BELOW: bronze statue in the courtyard of the Confucius Temple.

North of the Lama Temple

North of the Lama Temple is **Ditan Park** (open daily, 6am–9pm; entrance fee) which spreads around the **Altar of the Earth** (Ditan) ⓱, one of the original eight altars, along with the Temple of Heaven, that played a great role in the ritual life of the Ming and Qing emperors (*see page 152*). Not much remains of the original altar structure.

To the northwest is the **Western Yellow Temple** (Xi Huang Si) ⓲, among the best extant examples of Lamaist architecture in Beijing. Originally two temples, Eastern and Western, stood here, but they were destroyed in 1958 during the Great Leap Forward. The Eastern Temple was built by the Qing emperor Shunzhi, in 1652, for the fifth Dalai Lama on the occasion of his visit to the imperial court. A year later, the Western Temple was built to house his retinue. The only remarkable surviving structure is the White Pagoda, which Qianlong had built in 1780 to honour the sixth Panchen Lama, who died of smallpox while visiting Beijing. Subsequent Chief Lamas at the Lama Temple were required to have had smallpox and recovered (and be therefore immune) so that they could avoid similar fates.

If Beijing is your only stop in China, you may want to check out the **China Ethnic Culture Park** (open daily, performances on Fri and Sat, 8am–10pm; entrance fee), which is located next to the National Olympic Centre on the fourth ring road. China has some 56 minorities, and their homes, lifestyles, crafts, and traditions are extremely varied. The park contains replicas of the typical buildings made by each minority. Their traditional songs and dances are performed here, and you can see their crafts being made with traditional methods. Contrived, perhaps, but reflective of China's diverse lifestyles. ❑

Map on page 170

Sanlitun nightlife; many of the city's livelier bars and clubs are in this area.

BELOW: a young (and cold) audience at the opera, New Year, Ditan Park.

WESTERN BEIJING

Map on page 184

The university, breeding ground of revolutionaries, sets the tone for this fascinating section of the city, where you'll also find the zoo and its giant pandas, one of the famous draws of Beijing

Because of the presence of the university, located in the Haidian district of the city, the western areas of Beijing are historically associated with students and intellectual pursuits. Students occupy a sacred place in Chinese society. They are looked upon as the guarantors of the future and, to some people, as bearers of the revolution. Perhaps it is fitting that this part of town also harbours the former homes of some of China's best-known writers, revolutionaries and martyrs.

Besieged by Boxers

Situated not far to the west of Beihai Park, in a side hutong, is the imposing Gothic-style **North Cathedral ❶** (Beitang, also known as Xishiku; open daily; mass on Sunday), built by Jesuits in 1889. It is best known for its role in the frenzied Boxer Rebellion of 1900; when the Boxers' frustration with foreign missionaries reached fever pitch they lay siege to the cathedral, in which about 3,000 converted Chinese Christians had taken refuge under the protection of the French Bishop Favier. Although most of the other Boxers were rounded up, incorporated into imperial militias and marched off to face the approaching Allied troops, the Qing court allowed this one group to continue attacking the cathedral for seven weeks. resulting in the deaths of numerous Chinese converts. The siege was finally ended by the intervention of Japanese soldiers. The church survived, only to be shut down and looted during the Great Leap Forward, and again during the Cultural Revolution. It was restored in 1986, and today has a sizeable congregation made up of Catholics of the Patriotic Church.

PRECEDING PAGES: Beitang, the North Cathedral. **LEFT:** artist at work. **BELOW:** Guangjisi altar.

Two temples

At the eastern end of Fuchengmennei, wedged in between apartment blocks and warehouses, stands the **Temple of Universal Rescue ❷** (Guangjisi; open daily, 6.30am–8pm; entrance fee). This is currently the headquarters for the Buddhist Association of China, and visits are generally restricted to Buddhist groups or scholars. But it may happen that the doorkeepers at the entrance will be friendly and permit a chance passer-by to take a quick look inside. The temple is also a stop on the popular "Hutong Tour" which you can take in a pedicab from the north gate of Beihai Park.

Under the Ming Emperor Tianshun, an existing Jin dynasty temple on the site was renovated. This was in turn restored and extended in 1669, under Emperor Kangxi. In Qing times it acquired a 3-metre (10-ft) high sandalwood statue of Buddha but this was destroyed by fire in 1931. In 1935, the temple was

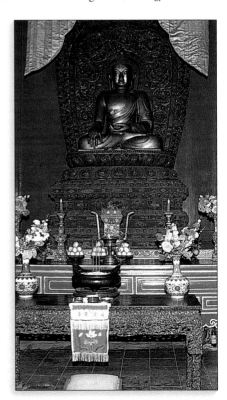

rebuilt. In 1952 it was restored again, although it was kept closed during the Cultural Revolution. The design of the temple follows the classic Buddhist architectural plan. In the third hall, the **Hall of Guanyin**, is a thousand-armed statue of the goddess of mercy, Guanyin, gilded during the Qing period. A copper Guanyin figure and a Guanyin on a lotus blossom dating from the Ming period are also on view in the hall. Stored in the library of the monastery are valuable handwritten sutras from the Tang dynasty, along with more than 30,000 old rubbings of stone inscriptions.

A 10-minute walk west from Guangjisi, towards the zoo, is the **Temple of the White Pagoda** ❸ (Baitasi; open daily, 9am–4.30pm; entrance fee), which was built in 1096 during the rule of the Liao dynasty. Kublai Khan restored it in Tibetan style in 1271 but it was destroyed by fire shortly afterwards. The monastery was rebuilt in 1457 and at the same time received its official name of Miaoyingsi (Temple of Divine Justice).

Porcelain jar from the Temple of the White Pagoda.

The temple is well known for its white dagoba (a Tibetan-style shrine). Its top is adorned by an engraved copper canopy, from which little bells hang, moving in the wind in order to drive away evil spirits. In the fourth hall there are sculptures of the three Buddhas and two Buddha pupils, as well as some *thangka*, or Tibetan scroll pictures. The temple and grounds were restored after 1978, when valuable objects were found in the dagoba, including Buddhist manuscripts and calligraphy by Emperor Qianlong, as well as jewellery and coins from various dynasties.

In the three other halls, there is an exhibition about the city of Dadu (Beijing's name during the Mongol Yuan dynasty). There are models showing the layout of the city, and of the canals and other water works that existed at that time. The

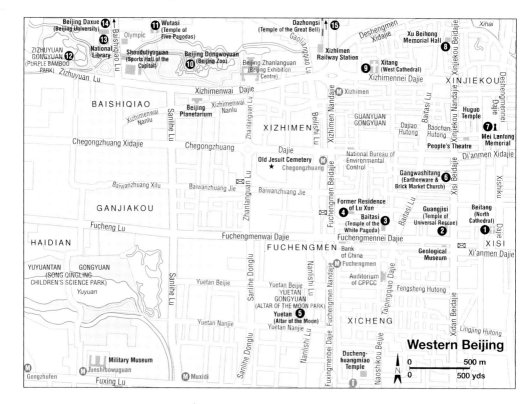

Western Beijing

social, economic and political systems of Mongol rule, meanwhile, are described on display boards and posters. Marco Polo is, of course, mentioned.

Beijing of the artists

Map on page 184

A short distance north on a side street is the **Former Residence of Lu Xun ❹** (open Tues–Sun, 9am–4pm; entrance fee). Lu Xun (1881–1936), one of the greatest Chinese writers of the twentieth century, lived in Beijing from 1923 to 1925. The typical Chinese courtyard house – which he bought with borrowed money – is situated near **Fuchengmen**, an old imperial gate due west of Beihai Park. The most eastern room in the northern part of the courtyard belonged to Lu Xun's mother; the western room to his wife. The rooms to the south served as living quarters and a library. The small room added on to the north side was the study and bedroom that Lu Xun called the "Tiger's Tail". Here he wrote the two stories, *The Tomb* and *Wild Grasses*. On the 20th anniversary of Lu Xun's death, the house opened as a museum. Photographs, unpublished manuscripts, letters and a copy of the entry he made in his diary on the day of his death are all on display.

Situated symmetrically opposite the Altar of the Sun (Ritan) in the plan of the imperial city is another of the eight altars that played such a great role in the ritual life of the Ming and Qing emperors (*see page 152*). The **Altar of the Moon ❺** (Yuetan; open daily, 6am–8pm; entrance fee), stands in a public park in which a telecommunications tower was built in 1969.

The **Earthenware and Brick Market Church** (Gangwashitang) ❻, in Xisi Beidajie, is one of the two most important Protestant churches in Beijing (the other is the Mishitang Church east of the Imperial Palace, *see page 171*). It was built at the beginning of the twentieth century for the London Bible Society.

BELOW: the Lu Xun Memorial.

Another Christian monument is the old **Jesuit cemetery**, in the courtyard of a Communist Party school on Maweigoulu, in the Fuchengmen district. Here the first Christian missionaries (who reached China under the Yuan dynasty) and 61 other Jesuits lie buried.

At No. 9 Huguosi Jie is the **Mei Lanfang Memorial** ❼ (open Tues–Sat, 9am–noon and 1–4pm; entrance fee), dedicated to the man who was most famous for making people think he was a woman. Just as historically in Western theatre women could not perform on stage, so it was with Beijing opera. As a consequence, certain players specialised in playing female roles exclusively. Mei Lanfang was considered to be the best such performer in the history of Beijing opera (*see box below*).

Further north is the **Xu Beihong Memorial Hall** ❽ (open Tues–Sun, 9am–noon and 1–4.30pm; entrance fee). Xu Beihong (1895–1953) was one of China's most famous modern artists, well known for his numerous paintings of horses. A Xu Beihong Memorial Hall was first established in the house he lived in. When she died, his widow, Liao Jingwen, left this house, along this with his books, calligraphy and other work, to the People's Republic and a memorial to Xu was built in the grounds. Later, when the house had to be demolished because of the building of the Beijing underground railway network, the Memorial Hall was moved here to No. 53 Xinjiekou Beidajie.

Xu's studio was rebuilt in the new Hall, exactly as it was shortly before his death. Hanging on the walls are a copy of his painting, *Rich Harvest*, works by Ren Bonian and Qi Baishi, and a photograph of Xu taken in 1913 by Rabindranath Tagore, the Indian poet and Nobel Prize winner.

The works of art exhibited in the Memorial Hall were almost all collected by

BELOW:
Mei Lanfang,
star of the opera.

HITTING THE HIGH NOTES

The most celebrated Beijing opera performer, Mei Lanfang (1894–1961), was a master of the *dan* role, a central female character traditionally played by a man. Mei was born into a family of performers. He began studying opera as a child, making his stage debut at eleven. By the time he was 20, he was already a household name. In fifty years as a *dan* performer, Mei played more than 100 female roles, including concubines, generals and goddesses. He was also an innovator, designing new dances and other routines to enhance his roles. He added a sword dance to the opera *Conqueror Xiang Yu Parts with His Concubine*, and a ribbon dance, based on drawings in ancient Buddhist frescoes, to *The Fairy Scattering Flowers*.

Mei was an ambassador abroad for his ancient art form, visiting Japan, Russia and the United States – which he toured in 1929 – and making many friends, including actor Charlie Chaplin and singer Paul Robeson. Berthold Brecht was among those who admired Mei's performance in Moscow in 1935.

Today, Mei's son, Mui Bo-kau, continues the family tradition in Hong Kong. Mui was the star of a week of classical Beijing opera staged during the Hong Kong handover celebrations in 1997.

Map on page 184

the artist himself during his lifetime. They include more than 1,200 examples from the Tang, Song, Yuan, Ming and Qing dynasties, as well as works from the time of the May Fourth Movement (1919). One of the most valuable items is a cartoon of the Tang painting, *The Scroll of the 87 Immortals*, by Wu Daozi. (*See box on page 219* for details on the tomb of Xu Beihong.)

Not far from Xizhimen stands another Catholic church, the **West Cathedral** (Xitang) ❾. Built in the 18th century, it was destroyed during the persecution of Christians in 1811. A second church, built in 1867, was, in turn, a victim of the Boxer Rebellion. The present building dates from the beginning of the 20th century.

Nearby there is a **bird market** – one of many in the city – which is particularly large and active at weekends. Birds are among the few pets that Beijingers are allowed to own. They are especially popular with older men, who you will see wandering through parks in the morning and afternoon, swinging their bird cages back and forth, so as to give the birds some air.

Cicadas for sale at the Bird Market.

Pandas and pagodas

Further to the west, past the second ring road, is **Beijing Zoo** ❿ (Beijing Dongwuyuan; open daily, 7.30am–5.30pm; entrance fee). Around the year 1900, a Manchu high official returned from a long journey abroad bringing a special gift for the Empress Dowager Cixi: a great number of animals, especially birds, which he had mainly bought in Germany. To accommodate them, Cixi had a decaying park transformed into the "Park of Ten Thousand Creatures". In time this became the present-day zoo. But be warned before you make a visit here: standards are not up to those of most Western zoos.

BELOW: souvenirs at Beijing zoo.
LEFT: giant pandas are the top attraction at the zoo.

The Temple of Five Pagodas (Wutasi) is modelled on the Indian Buddhist temple of Bodh Gaya.

The main attractions of the zoo, of course, are the giant pandas, whose quarters are right by the entrance. Next door, in the souvenir shop, you can buy everything panda: cuddly pandas; panda handbags, panda stickers, panda thermometers, red lacquer sticks with panda motifs, the unavoidable silhouettes, watercolours of pandas, T-shirts with panda designs, silk embroideries framed in brocade, and wall hangings showing archetypal pandas – not unlike the Stag At Bay so popular in European living rooms.

Just behind the zoo, to the north of the Shoudutiyuguan sports hall, is the **Temple of Five Pagodas ⓫** (Wutasi; open daily, 8.30am–4.20pm; entrance fee). In earlier years, when driving towards the Summer Palaces, it used to be possible to see the tops of the pagodas on the right-hand side, but now the area has been built up with new apartment blocks. A path behind the sports hall leads to this temple, which, until 1980, was closed and falling into ruin.

The temple, which dates back to the 15th-century reign of the Ming Emperor Yongle, was restored during Qianlong's reign but devastated by European troops in 1860 and again in 1900. The building, with five small pagodas standing on a massive square base, is in what is known in Buddhism as the "Diamond Throne Pagoda" style. Worth seeing above all else are the bas-reliefs on the outside which depict Buddha figures, symbolic animals, lotus flowers, heavenly guardians, the wheel of Buddhist teaching, and other Buddhist symbols.

Go up two flights of stairs to the terrace where the bases of the pagodas are also adorned with reliefs. In the cloisters down below, visitors can study the various styles of pagoda architecture in China through an exhibition of photographs. An impressive collection of steles also awaits in this courtyard. The temple does not get as crowded as most others in the city.

Across Baishiqiao to the west is the **Purple Bamboo Park** ⓬ (Zizhuyuan Gongyuan; open daily, 6am–8pm; entrance fee), which is mainly frequented by families with small children because it has an amusement park and playground. Around its three lakes, 10 different varieties of bamboo – a rare plant in northern China – can be seen growing. A total of 160,000 individual bamboo shoots are supposed to have been planted.

Every Sunday morning at a spot in the park known as "**English Corner**", hundreds of people mostly young adults and especially students – gather to practise their English with one another, since there are not enough native speakers to go around. Unsuspecting foreigners taking a walk here will soon be surrounded by a large crowd of talkative and curious Beijing Anglophiles. With ever more Chinese wanting to learn English, this activity is becoming increasingly popular, and "English Corners" may be found on weekday evenings in various other locations, especially around the universities.

Student days

Just north of the park is a massive complex housing the **National Library** ⓭ (open Sun–Fri, 8am–5pm). Established in 1909, this is the largest library in Asia and the fifth-largest in the world with some 21 million items. The library has an unrivalled collection of ancient Chinese texts. From here you can go north to the **People's University** (Renmindaxue), not far from the Friendship Hotel, which is home to foreign experts from all over the world. This takes you into Zhongguancun, which has been dubbed Beijing's "silicon valley".

Further north is **Beijing University** (Beijing Daxue, or "Beida") ⓮. The university was founded in 1898, but its first campus was in the city centre, in

Map on page 184

BELOW: a lecture at Beijing University.

Cyber cafés, like this one near the University, are increasingly popular in Beijing.

BELOW: Beida students calling for a boycott of Japanese goods after the May Fourth Movement of 1919.

the eastern part of the old Imperial City. The present campus, in the western district of Haidian, was previously the site of the American-founded **Yanjing University**, which joined with Beijing University in 1953.

Today, more than 10,000 students are studying at Beida, many of them foreigners, who are mainly from Third World countries. (In early 1989, attacks on African students gained world-wide attention.) The **Shaoyuan Guesthouse** of Beida has long been an international meeting place. The campus has park-like grounds with a quiet lake, on the shores of which students spend their free time, and a classical Chinese pagoda with pavilions and stone figures. Beida also numbers many famous politicians among its graduates.

The students of Beida have formed the political avant garde in most of the political upheavals of the 20th century, from the May Fourth Movement of 1919 to the Cultural Revolution. In the two years before the Marco Polo Bridge incident (1937) they staged massive anti-Japanese demonstrations. In more recent years, their demands for more democracy have resulted in the demonstrations and wall newspapers of 1979, and tragically the Tiananmen massacre of 1989.

Naturally, you should avoid visiting the campus at times of political unrest. In the aftermath of the Tiananmen violence, it was hard to get on to the campus; and student protests at the NATO bombing of the Chinese embassy in Belgrade kept even many students away. The 50th anniversary preparations also made it difficult to visit the university.

The remains of the old Beijing University – the so-called **Red Building** (Honglou; open daily, 8.30am–5.30pm; entrance fee), at the eastern end of Shatan Jie, in the northeastern part of town – can still be seen. Here, Li Dazhao,

one of the founders of the Chinese Communist Party, used to teach, and Mao Zedong used to work in the library. Chen Duxiu, the first General Secretary of the Chinese Communist Party, also taught at the old Beida.

Map on page 184

The Great Bell

Around two km (1½ miles) to the east of the modern Beida on the third ring road, squeezed in among the new buildings and the factories, is the **Temple of the Great Bell** ⑮ (Dazhongsi; open daily, 8am–5.30pm; entrance fee). This temple, built in 743, was much damaged during the Cultural Revolution but has now been restored and is used as a museum. On display are some 160 ancient bells, from tiny 150-gram (6-oz) specimens to the bronze giant that gives the temple its name. This is housed in the further part of the grounds, in a 17-metre (56-ft) high tower.

The Great Bell was made in 1406 on the orders of the Ming emperor Yongle. It is 7 metres (23 ft) high, has a diameter of 3 metres (10 ft) and weighs 46½ tonnes. Inscribed on the bell – which is one of the oldest in the world – is the entire text of the Huayan Sutra, consisting of some 200,000 characters.

The Huayan sect has had great influence in the Far East, influencing the Asian attitude to nature and for inspiring many artists. It was founded in 630 and endured until about 1000. Its teaching states that all creatures and things are imbued with a cosmic principle, that everything exists in harmony with everything else, and that every grain of dust contains all the wealth of Buddha. This teaching does not preach the need to influence the cosmic powers or to use magic, as is the case with Tantric (Tibetan) Buddhism. It relies, instead, on contemplation and observation. ❑

BELOW: the 7-metre (23-ft) bell at the Temple of the Great Bell (Dazhongsi).

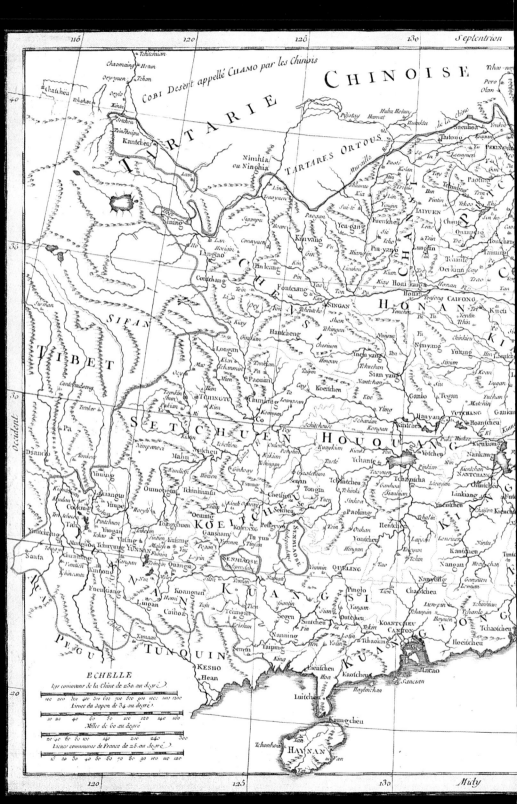

THE SUMMER PALACES

The great landscaped gardens and lavish palaces built outside Beijing for the pleasure of the emperor and his court are now available to anyone who wants to escape the bustle of the city

Map on page 198

Awe and fascination were the usual reactions of the few foreign visitors to observe the life of the Qing emperors in their various palaces firsthand. But they rarely understood much of what they saw. Hindered by their ignorance of the language, and the arch secrecy of the Qing court, foreigners in 18th and 19th century China mistakenly called the imperial residence outside Beijing the Summer Palace. In fact, the court spent most months of the year here, remaining in the city only in the depths of winter.

There were two "summer palaces", one built after the other; little remains of the first one, which was set fire to by foreign troops in 1860 at the end of the Second Opium War. The Count d'Herrison, secretary to the commander of the French forces on that occasion, remembers that perusing the grounds: "involuntarily we spoke in low tones, and began to walk on tiptoe on seeing before us such a profusion of riches for the possession of which mortals fight and die..."

The existing "New" Summer Palace was built by the Empress Dowager Cixi at the end of the 19th century; but it too was plundered by foreign troops, this time in 1900 during the Boxer Rebellion.

Between them, the two palaces were used by the Qing emperors for more than 150 years. During this time dozens of palaces, pavilions and temples were built in contrived idyllic landscapes of artificial hills, lakes and canals. Not all of this grandeur has survived but there is still plenty to be seen during a visit.

PRECEDING PAGES: the Mongshan mountains; Qing dynasty map of the empire.
LEFT: Pagoda of the Incense Buddha.
BELOW: musician in the park grounds.

THE OLD SUMMER PALACE

Little remains of the original Summer Palace, **Yuanmingyuan ❶** (open daily, 7am–7pm; entrance fee), but its large grounds are now a park providing a quiet retreat from the city and are a popular place for weekend picnics. Its northern entrance is guarded by two stone lions. Beyond them, unassuming little paths make their way through an overgrown park. Past a wide depression in the terrain is a broad field of ruins, where the remains of ornate pillars and frescoes are more reminiscent of European baroque buildings than the architecture of imperial China.

The magnificent complex of park and palace that once stood here was the creation of the Emperor Qianlong (1736–95). He called it Yuanmingyuan: the Garden of Perfect Purity. Qianlong was an enthusiastic admirer of southern Chinese landscape gardening. Six times he set out on the long and difficult journey to the southern and central regions of China in order to delight in its fascinating landscapes: the quiet beauty of the West Lake in Hangzhou, or the bizarre gardens and canals of Suzhou.

The court artists who accompanied him made innumerable sketches that were then used to transform

the surroundings of the new Summer Palace into a gigantic masterpiece of landscape gardening. Here, natural and artificial landscapes were merged into a perfect whole.

In the first phase of the construction, the southern and western parts of the grounds were laid out and refined in accordance with Qianlong's aesthetic ideas. Once the work was finished, the court artists had to capture 40 spots of scenic beauty and grace in Yuanmingyuan on their rice paper, while Qianlong composed a poem for every one of these landscapes. The island of Penglai (Home of the Immortals), in **Fu Hai Lake** (the Lake of Fortunate Life), was compared by Qianlong to a "jade palace in an elfin kingdom". On the eastern shore of the lake stood the Hut of the Beautiful View, long since destroyed. From here, Qianlong could see the Western Hills and enjoy the peace, surrounded by pines and bamboo – the "old friends" mentioned in one of his poems.

A vision of Europe in China

But that wasn't enough. Inspired by pictures of princely French and Italian palaces, Qianlong gave orders for buildings in the European style to be constructed in the northeastern part of the park. The architect was a Jesuit missionary and artist, Guiseppe Castiglione, from Genoa, Italy, later to be the confidant and teacher of Qianlong.

In an area comprising only 2 percent of the Garden of Perfect Purity, a complex of buildings unique in China was created between 1747 and 1759. There were little rococo palaces with horseshoe-shaped staircases, marble halls, fountains and even a maze – a bit of Versailles in the Middle Kingdom, the counterpoint to the Chinoiserie of European princes.

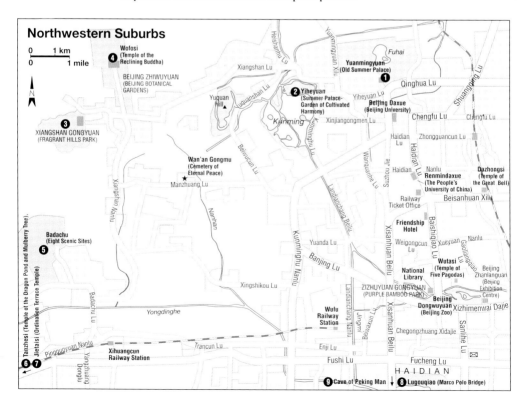

Northwestern Suburbs

The rooms in these unique buildings were equipped with European furniture, and there were even European toys for the children. Qianlong and his court listened to Western music and ate Western food, making him feel like the "Emperor in Rome". During the Mid-Autumn Festival, he sat in a raised pavilion in the centre of his maze. His court ladies, with torches in their hands, had to find their way to him, the first to do so being rewarded with a present.

Qianlong was particularly fond of European fountains, simple or elaborate. The remains of some of these can still be seen just south of the present palace museum. The fountains were composed of several levels of water-spouting figures; water sprayed from stone lion's heads, dogs' mouths and stag's antlers.

An interesting symbiosis of Chinese thought and European architecture was the water clock, designed by the French Jesuit, Benoit. Close to the Palace of the Quiet Sea, the ruins can be seen between the museum and the restored maze. Traditionally, the Chinese divided the 24-hour day into 12 segments, with every segment attributed to an animal. Benoit designed a construction with 12 stone animals, each of them spouting water for two hours.

In Qianlong's time, the French court contributed to the decoration of the buildings "in the Western style" and sent rare gifts. Ironically, roughly 100 years later, it would be French troops, together with the British, who destroyed these very palaces in Yuanmingyuan.

Map on page 198

The destruction of Qianlong's palace

During the Second Opium War (1858–60), when China vastly overestimated its strength and tried to permanently expel the unscrupulous foreign merchants, the Europeans took brutal revenge. The imperial house was considered person-

BELOW: ruins of the Old Summer Palace.

A Boxer rebel is executed; the already badly damaged Old Summer Palace was further plundered by foreign troops engaged in fighting the Boxers.

ally responsible for the xenophobic policies, and Lord Elgin, the commander-in-chief of the British forces, ordered the destruction of Yuanmingyuan. It was said that he wanted to spare the common people and only punish the court. Before the troops stormed the Old Summer Palace in October 1860, the emperor Xianfeng, together with his womenfolk (among them the concubine Cixi), managed to escape to the safety of Chengde.

The allied soldiers plundered the palace, taking away anything they could carry. Then they set fire to the buildings, and for three days the Summer Palace blazed. The wooden "Chinese" buildings were almost completely destroyed, and only a few of the Western-style structures survived. Attempts to restore Yuanmingyuan failed because of a chronic lack of finance. Its demise was complete when, following the Boxer Rebellion, peasants from the surrounding countryside took away valuable ceramic tiles and marble to build houses.

The Old Summer Palace today

For modern Beijingers, what was once the exclusive haunt of emperors is now a place for a day out. They come especially to enjoy Fu Hai Lake. In the summer, hundreds of paddle and rowing boats bob in the water and, in the winter, skaters glide over the ice. Also popular is the eastern section, the Eternal Spring Garden (Changchunyuan), with the European fountain ruins (*see page 199*) – one of the more intact structures in the complex.

BELOW: palace hall in the Old Summer Palace.

Renovations of the Old Summer Palace are continuing, but at a slow pace, and it has not yet been decided how far they will proceed. Historians are trying to reconstruct the original appearance of the palace and its grounds with models. The results can be seen in the **museum**.

THE NEW SUMMER PALACE

Although the Old Summer Palace could not be recreated in all its legendary splendour, it was to be replaced by a new imperial residence, known as **Yiheyuan** (The Garden of Cultivated Harmony) ❷ (open daily, 6.30am–6pm; entrance fee) – the Summer Palace you see today.

In 1888, the Empress Dowager Cixi set about expanding the original park, her craftsmen and architects following the example of Qianlong as far as they were able. As in every Chinese garden, rocks and water feature prominently, while blossoming shrubs and a colourful arrangement of flowering plants in tubs has been preferred to European-style flower beds. There is also a conscious use of walls and buildings to screen sections of the gardens so that small pieces of the landscape appear like framed pictures through windows in chequered, rhomboid, fan, vase and peach shapes. Sometimes a sudden and dramatic change of scene is possible within only a few yards. A walk through the Summer Palace can be likened to the slow unrolling of a Chinese scroll painting.

Beautiful **Kunming Lake** ❹ covers about two-thirds of the area of the Yiheyuan complex. This large body of water is intended to convey a sense of serenity and silence – an effect which would not have been achieved by using fountains and waterfalls. In summer, the lake is covered with a carpet of huge, round green lotus leaves, while pale pink lotus flowers rise between them and turn the surface of the water into a flower bed. The three islands in the lake recall a 2,000-year-old Daoist myth of three islands in the eastern sea supposedly inhabited by immortals.

The great artificial hill about 60 metres (200 ft) in height which rises behind the palace was named **Longevity Hill** (Wanshoushan) ❸ by Qianlong, in hon-

Maps on pages 198 & 203

BELOW:
Kunming Lake.

Ceiling paintings in the Long Corridor.

our of his mother on her 60th birthday. It divides the grounds of the Summer Palace like a giant screen into two completely different landscapes. The southern section, with the broad lake in the foreground, is reminiscent of the idyll of the West Lake in Hangzhou; the northern section, with its romantic groves and canals, creates an atmosphere like that of Suzhou.

The power behind the throne

The main path into the Summer Palace leads through a mighty wooden *pailou*, a kind of Chinese triumphal arch, past the ghost wall that is supposed to ward off all evil influences, directly to the **Eastern Gate** (Donggongmen). Visible beyond this is the **Hall of Benevolence and Longevity** (Renshoudian) **❻**, with its opulent furnishings and decorative *objets d'art*. This is where young Emperor Guangxu dealt with state business when the imperial court resided in Yiheyuan during the summer months; here, grand audiences were held for imperial ministers, advisers, mandarins, and later for foreign diplomats as well. Popular myth has it that Cixi, rather than Guangxu, effectively ruled China "from behind a curtain". Although it is true that she was concealed, as etiquette at the time kept her from showing her female face, there is some debate as to how far she actually exercised control over her nephew (*see box below*).

It was in the nearby **Hall of Jade Ripples** (Yulantang) **❼** that Cixi supposedly kept Guangxu under house arrest for his folly at attempting to reform a crumbling dynasty by opening China to foreign ideas in 1898. It has been argued, however, that Cixi was in reality quite supportive of Guangxu's attempts at reform, as she wanted his reign to succeed. His reforms were not particularly extensive, but hinged on modernising the fusty old bureaucracy. He even

BELOW: portrait photograph of the Empress Dowager Cixi.

WHO WAS THE REAL CIXI?

The builder of the New Summer Palace, the apparently omnipotent Empress Dowager Cixi, began life as a concubine of the third rank. She only rose to prominence when appointed as one of the two regents who ruled during her son Tongzhi's minority, following the death of the Emperor Xianfeng in 1861. Historians have always viewed her as an evil schemer, bent on fulfilling her own ambitions, and removing anyone who stood in her way. However there is an alternative view which maintains that the Empress Dowager wasn't so bad after all.

The much reviled Cixi, the theory goes, was a puppet, put on the throne by the princes and officials who actually made policy so that they could hide behind her, and act as they pleased. As a woman in Confucian society she had little personal power, and was further handicapped by her inability to read or write. Cixi was unable to ever know what was really going on because the only people she had contact with were those inside the court – as a woman of imperial rank she was not allowed to venture beyond the confines of the imperial palaces. The only weapon she had to wield was her son the royal heir, and her ambition for him was merely a form of self-defence. Far from being a schemer, she was the one being schemed against.

Map below

appealed to young Chinese scholars and asked for their ideas. Emboldened, he invited the Japanese creator of the new Meiji constitution, Ito Hirobumi, to China to ask for his thoughts. Such hubris, especially asking a Japanese, upset a very powerful xenophobic faction at court, led by Prince Tuan. This influential lobby convinced Cixi that Guangxu was endangering the regime, and told her that if she did not resume her position as regent, the dynasty would collapse. Lacking other advisers to consult, she capitulated, and cancelled the reforms. China turned inward and the stage was set for what ultimately became the Boxer Rebellion, an outburst against anything foreign.

Guangxu, obviously crushed, put himself in seclusion for three days, but there is no evidence that he completely disappeared from court life as had been commonly reported. However, never a robust individual, he grew despondent, and was not influential at court again. The idea of his imprisonment was given further credence by exiled reformers who continued to heap vitriol on the personage of Cixi, believing her to be responsible for Guangxu's emasculation.

The 128-course lunch

Not far from here, on the southeastern slopes of Longevity Hill, were Cixi's private living and sleeping apartments, the **Hall of Happiness and Longevity** (Leshoutang) ❸. Served by a staff of 48, she did not want for much except privacy. Servants, most notably the eunuchs, were everywhere. Stripped of their manhood, and ensconced in a stifling atmosphere, the eunuchs were known for their conniving. One story goes that Cixi, who expected exactly 128 dishes for the midday and evening meals, was particularly fond of shark's fin soup, sea cucumbers, duck's feet, and steamed butterfly-shaped buns, and so she only

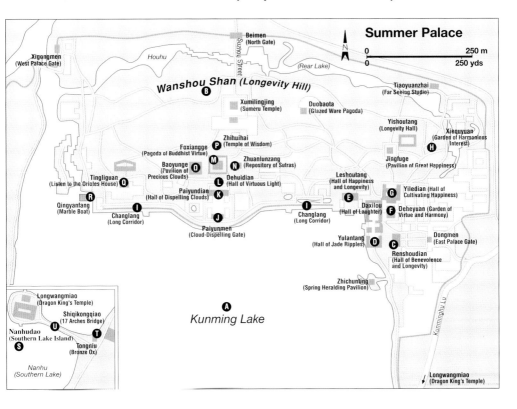

Cixi greatly enjoyed the performances of Beijing Opera at the Summer Palace.

ate from some of the dishes ordered and always the same ones. As time passed and this continued, her cooks used the food not favoured by Cixi on the table day after day, until the maggots crawling in them became too obvious.

A portrait of Cixi

Cixi was passionate about Beijing opera. There was an excellent ensemble at court, composed of 384 eunuchs. Cixi herself was supposed to have appeared in some operas as Guanyin, the goddess of mercy. She had an impressive open-air stage built in the **Garden of Virtue and Harmony** (Deheyuan) ❺. Its three stages, one above the other, were connected by trap doors, so that supernatural beings, saints and immortals could swoop down into the operatic scene and evil spirits could rise from the depths of the underworld. There was even an underground water reservoir for "wet" scenes.

Cixi observed these performances from the **Hall of Cultivating Happiness** (Yiledian) ❻, which was located opposite the theatre. She sat on a gold-coloured throne, a precious piece of lacquered furniture that portrayed a hundred birds doing homage to the phoenix – the symbol of the empress.

Today, the Deheyuan has been turned into a **theatre museum**. Costumes can be seen in glass cases, and the female museum attendants wear the clothes and hairstyles of the Qing dynasty. Under their Manchu shoes are high platforms, which gave women a swaying walk. Unlike the Han Chinese, the Manchu women – the palace elite of the Qing dynasty – did not have their feet bound. Apart from the theatre collection, there are also some of Cixi's private possessions on display. Some of her jewellery and cosmetic implements can be seen, as can the first automobile imported into China.

BELOW: springtime flowers at the Summer Palace.

Here, one can also see the famous portrait in oils painted by the British naturalized American artist Hubert Vos, painted when the Empress Dowager was seventy, but rendered to make her look as she would have appeared when she was twenty-five. The picture shows the "Old Buddha", as Cixi was respectfully known, in a Manchu silk robe of imperial yellow, covered with the ideogram *shou*, for longevity. In one hand she is holding a precious fan painted with peonies, and golden sheaths protect her outsize fingernails.

It is not necessarily a likeness. It was unheard of for Emperors or Empresses to model for a portrait during their lifetimes. Emperors were only allowed to be portrayed after their deaths. Artists never saw their model, either dead or alive, and had to ask the help of the mourners to point out the appropriate eyes, nose, mouth etc. from samples laid before them – much like building up an identity photo of a suspected criminal. Tradition demanded more of an idealized version of the subject, rather than a true-to-life rendition, and Vos was encouraged to err on the side of youth.

Fishing made simple

A highlight in the further eastern part of the palace gardens is the **Garden of Harmonious Interest** (Xiequyuan) **Ⓗ**, a complete, perfect and beautiful replica of a lotus pool from the Wuxi area in central China. When Cixi came here to fish, devoted eunuchs would dive under the water to hang a catch onto the old lady's hook, for she was impatient and given to outbreaks of temper. They not only attached fish, but sometimes put a precious piece of jewellery on the hook in order to keep her in a good mood. This is the spot where Bertolucci filmed the only Summer Palace scene in *The Last Emperor*.

Map on page 203

BELOW: the Garden of Harmonious Interest.

The Long Corridor

Covered walkways and galleries are established features of Chinese landscape gardening. These light, elegant, wooden structures link scattered individual buildings to make a composite whole. The **Long Corridor** (Changlang) ❶ is 728 metres (793 yards) long and runs along the foot of the hill parallel to the shore of Kunming Lake. The original walkway dated from the time of emperor Qianlong, but as with many other parts of the park, it was destroyed during the Second Opium War (1858–60) by French and British forces, and then rebuilt under Cixi.

The ceilings and rafters of the walkway are decorated with countless bird and flower motifs. If humans or human-like creatures appear in the pictures, they are either in scenes from famous legends, episodes of Chinese history, or scenes from classical novels such as *The Dream of the Red Chamber*, *The Bandits of Liangshan Moor* or *The Journey to the West*, with its hero, admired by old and young alike – the Monkey King, Sun Wukong.

To prevent the ceiling paintings from fading until they are unrecognisable, the colours have to be renewed every 12 years. Here, as in some other parts of the palace, it is unfortunate that the work of restoration has not been particularly sensitive. Many of the colours are somewhat gaudy, and much of the complexity and wealth of detail in the original paintings has been lost.

Buddhism and birds

BELOW: the Zhihuihai (Temple of Wisdom).

In the middle of the walkway, where the east-west axis of the palace park meets the north-south axis, the **Gate of Dispelling Clouds** (Paiyunmen) ❷ – a great triumphal arch, or *pailou* – marks the start of the climb up Longevity Hill. Next

Map on page 203

to 12 massive, bizarre-shaped stones symbolising the signs of the Chinese zodiac is an elegant pair of lions cast in bronze – perhaps the most beautiful in all of Beijing – guarding an imposing Buddhist temple complex, which is surrounded by a red wall. Go through two gates and over a bridge to reach the **Hall of Dispelling Clouds** (Paiyundian) **Ⓚ**.

A temple once stood on this site during the Ming dynasty. The Emperor Qianlong had it rebuilt and, on his mother's 60th birthday, renamed it the **Temple of Gratitude for a Long Life**. It was destroyed in 1860, and the present form of the complex dates from Cixi's time in 1892. This was where she celebrated her birthdays with extravagant and elaborate court ceremonies. Many of the presents given to her on these occasions are on exhibition in the rooms of the Paiyundian, often with the yellow paper labels attached, marked with words of adulation such as "Given in honour and respect by your true and loyal subject ..."

Go past the Hall of Dispelling Clouds, through the **Hall of Virtuous Light** (Dehuidian) **Ⓛ**, and up a steep stone staircase to reach the massive, 38-metre (125-ft) tall, octagonal **Pagoda of Buddhist Virtue** (Foxiangge) **Ⓜ**. This is the highest point of the palace. From here is a lovely panoramic view of the Summer Palace: the blue of Kunming Lake, the green of the trees, the red of the pillars and the grey-blue of the tiled roofs. Only the most important buildings have yellow roofs. There are hardly any stern, hard colours or symbols; a clear, elegant atmosphere predominates.

To the east is a group of buildings, the **Repository of Sutras** (Zhuanlunzang) **Ⓝ**, once used as the archives for copies of Confucian classics and Buddhist scrolls. To the west is a rare and quite extraordinary masterpiece of Chinese architecture – the **Pavilion of Precious Clouds** (Baoyunge) **Ⓞ**, framed on all four sides by smaller pavilions and walkways. In Cixi's day, Lamaist monks gathered here to pray on the 1st and 15th day of every lunar month. Its stepped roof, and its beams, columns and struts, make it look like a wooden building, yet they were all cast from bronze in 1750 with the help of wax moulds. This is why it is usually called the Bronze Pavilion (Tongting). It is one of the few buildings of the Summer Palace to have survived the wanton destruction of 1860 and 1900 relatively undamaged.

Behind the pagoda on Longevity Hill, a narrow path leads to the **Temple of Wisdom** (Zhihuihai) **Ⓟ**. There are countless little statues of Buddha in the niches of its greenish-yellow ceramic facade.

The emphasis on Buddhism in Yiheyuan may seem surprising – especially in view of the fact that temples and shrines of the ancestor cult are missing. But Cixi had no point of contact with the veneration of ancestors who prescribed a male succession and excluded women from ritual and political life. She felt attracted to Buddhism, and in particular to the goddess Guanyin, who played, and still plays, a role in the spiritual life of Chinese women, similar to that of the Virgin Mary among Catholics.

It was part of the Buddhist rites at court that Cixi had to release 10,000 birds every year on her birthday. This pious gesture would, she hoped, improve her chances when she was reborn into another life. She

The Summer Palace is popular with local as well as foreign tourists.

Kites for sale at the Summer Palace.

was inexpressibly happy when some of the freed birds refused to leave her and returned again and again to rest on her shoulders. Little did she suspect that this loyalty was not due to her charisma, but to the training skills of some of her eunuchs. Nor did she guess that these very eunuchs, once she had returned to her apartments, climbed into the trees to recapture the recently freed birds, then shut them into cages and sold them for a good price in the markets.

Make-believe market

On a fine summer Sunday, thousands, indeed tens of thousands, of people will walk along the shores of Kunming Lake or crowd around the buildings near the main eastern gate. Relatively few, however, will venture to the other side of Longevity Hill and the area around the **Northern Gate** (Beimen).

Near here, at the end of the 19th century, a market street was constructed. Something akin to a film set, this market was held especially for the imperial family. It was intended to recreate the lively southern atmosphere of Suzhou. Book and antique shops and tea houses were added to give the inhabitants of the palace – forbidden to take part in life outside the walls – the illusion of participation in everyday trade and exchange. When the imperial dignitaries approached, eunuchs dressed as traders busied themselves with spreading out their wares, and praising them with theatrical gestures.

Eating like an emperor

BELOW: bridge on the western part of Kunming Lake.

At the foot of Longevity Hill, almost at the end of the long walkway, is a restaurant serving imperial-style cuisine in traditional surroundings. This is the **Listen to the Orioles House** (Tingliguan) **Q**. Visitors can put on old Chinese

silken robes and have their photographs taken in an imperial pose. This pretty spot is called **Huazhongyou** – "As If Walking Through a Picture" – and the view into the distance does indeed create such an illusion.

"Borrowing a landscape from outside" is part of traditional Chinese landscape gardening, and means that attractive elements of the natural scenery outside the walls of the gardens are carefully incorporated into the view. From Huazhongyou, for example, the walls of the Summer Palace are invisible, and the distant Jade Spring Hill seems to have been delicately painted with watercolour and brush. In the picturesque buildings behind the restaurant, the Emperor Qianlong used to invite his friends to a cup of rice wine and demonstrate his poetic talents by reciting his verses.

Map on page 203

The Marble Boat

A little further to the west, in the waters of Kunming Lake, lies the famous **Marble Boat** (Qingyanfang) ® with its two stone wheels on either side. This is a reminder of the convoluted scheming that went on behind the scenes at the royal court. Commonly accused of squandering the money reserved for the Chinese navy on building this ship, Cixi may well have had no knowledge of where the money came from. Prince Chun, Guangxu's father, was in the habit of flattering Cixi as a way of encouraging her to support his policies, and squeezed funds from wealthy gentry and rich officials (who thought it was going to benefit the Empress Dowager) in order to pay for it.

As chairman of the Admiralty Board, Chun was also responsible for the build-up of the Chinese fleet. When the Chinese suffered a comprehensive and humiliating defeat during the Sino-Japanese war of 1895, the blame was put on the

BELOW: Cixi's Marble Boat.

Map on page 203

cost of Cixi's expensive pleasure garden, rather than the ineffective management of anybody involved with the Admiralty Board. It is also worth remembering that the ship was in fact originally built by Qianlong, badly damaged by marauding foreign troops in 1860, and later refurbished by Cixi.

The lake islands

From the Marble Boat, one can cross the lake by ferry, landing either on the **Nanhudao** (Southern Lake Island) ❺, or on the neighbouring mainland. Close to the bridge leading to Nanhudao crouches the **Bronze Ox** (Tongniu) ❼. Its task, as the characters engraved on its back make clear, is to pacify the water spirit and to protect the surrounding land from floods. The script also relates how Emperor Qianlong decided to enlarge the lake; in recording this on the statue, Qianlong was identifying with the legendary Emperor Yuan, a hero of Chinese mythology, who is described as having commanded the damming of a flood from the back of an ox.

Seventeen Arches Bridge (Shiqikongqiao) ❶ crosses the water in a suprememly graceful curve, linking Nanhudao with the mainland. Some 500 stone lions and other exotic creatures keep watch on the balustrades. On the little island itself is the **Longwangmiao** (Dragon King's Temple).

The Boxer Revolt and the demise of the palace

The destruction of Cixi's palace was a tragic irony. The Boxer groups and societies had sought to defend traditional Chinese values against the encroaching influences of the West. Instead they brought about the desecration of one of the greatest symbols of imperial China by the very foreigners they despised. The Boxer Revolt grew out of a disenchantment with the presence of missionaries in the outlying parts of China. A detached and ineffective government combined with a run of bad weather to produce poor harvests and hardship for the majority of the Chinese population. Foreigners provided a convenient scapegoat for imperial officials to sidestep their responsibility for the problems.

This dovetailed with a rise in Nationalism, and with it the desire to preserve Chinese traditions at all costs and to expel all things foreign. But the Boxers' plans blew up in their faces. Rather than being expelled from China, the foreigners ended up plundering the capital city, making off with untold cultural riches.

As the European powers plundered and partially destroyed the Summer Palace, Cixi fled to Xi'an. She is said to have become apoplectic with rage when she heard that her throne had been flung into Kunming Lake, her robes stolen, and the walls of her bedchamber scrawled with obscene words and drawings. When at last she returned to Beijing, she set about restoring the palace to its former glory with her typical energy. Some buildings, however, were not restored. The Lama Temple, on the far side of Longevity Hill, has only been partially rebuilt in the last few years. And, of course, following her death in 1908, imperial China itself was to survive only three more years. ❏

BELOW: paddling on Kunming Lake.

Chinese Inventions and Discoveries

Historically, China has been responsible for a number of the world's greatest inventions and discoveries.

A belief in the inter-relation of celestial and earthly events led to the early development of astronomical observation. In the 13th century, Beijing Observatory had 17 different astronomical instruments. Halley's Comet was first recorded in 467 BC. A 360-day calendar was in use in China by the 3rd century BC and in the 13th century, the length of the year was calculated to within less than a thousandth of the true figure (*see page 173*).

By the 3rd-century AD, the *Book of Mathematics* had explained the multiplication and division of fractions and the formation of square roots.

Imperial geographers knew about the deviation of magnetic north from true north even before Europeans were aware that the earth had a magnetic field. The Chinese compass originally consisted of a metal plate with a metal spoon on it, the handle of the spoon pointing to the south. Around the year 132, Zhang Heng built a seismograph that could show in which direction an earthquake had taken place.

Experimentation and observation led to other inventions. The so-called Archimedean Screw was pumping water in the 1st century, and the water wheel and block and tackle in use by the 5th century. The Clock Tower of Su Song, built in 1088, is an early example of the highly-developed art of the clockmaker. Chain-driven and powered by a water wheel, it is fitted with a kind of escapement to regulate the wheels to show astronomical movements very precisely.

Some inventions had a significant effect on Chinese industry. Around 1100, iron foundries in China were already producing quantities of iron and steel that would be unmatched in Europe until the 18th century.

Silk production was also an important industry. The cultivation of silkworms can be traced back to the 3rd century BC. Up until AD 200, the Chinese had a monopoly on silk, largely because passing on the secret of its source was classed as treason. It was not until the 6th century that the manufacturing of silk became possible in the West..

One of the best known Chinese inventions is gunpowder, which was first made in the 9th century by Daoist monks who mixed charcoal, saltpetre and sulphur in the search for the elixir of eternal life. Thereafter imperial troops had bombs and grenades at their disposal.

Paper is still made throughout the world in the same way as it was first made in China around AD 200: fibrous material is soaked, the fibres separated, and a pulp formed which is then thinned, pressed into pages, and dried and smoothed. Printing, however, was not developed in China until some eight centuries later. Stone rubbing and printing with stamps were the preferred methods of reproducing the written word, not least because Chinese script consists of thousands of characters. ❑

RIGHT: an ornate Qing-dynasty celestial globe maps the heavens.

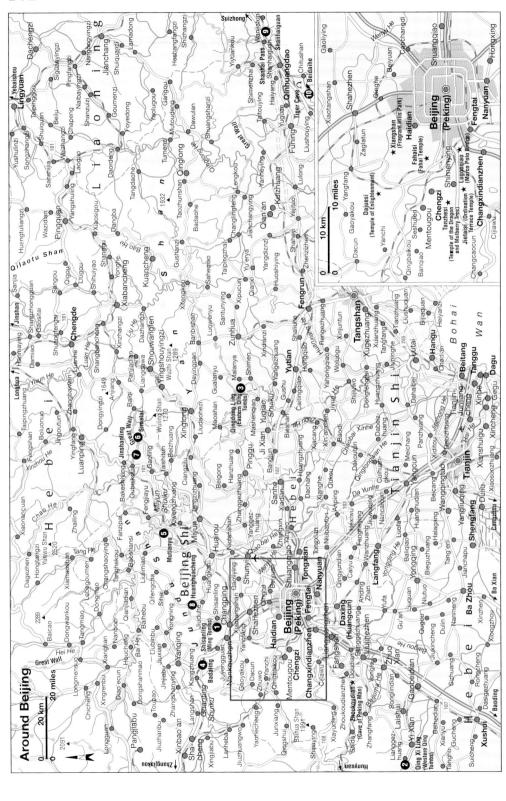

Around Beijing

WESTERN FRINGES

A short distance to the west of Beijing are many sites worth visiting,
including places of historical – and prehistorical – significance,
and temples set in steep forested hills

Maps
on pages
198 & 214

I f you're staying in Beijing for more than a few days, you may want to break up your sightseeing with a trip to the hills and valleys of the pleasant rural areas to the immediate west of the city. Not only will you get to see a China vastly different from that experienced in the urban sprawl, but you will also gain an insight into some important moments from the country's past.

The Fragrant Hills

Whether you're escaping the heat of a Beijing summer, or just the madding crowds, a trip to the **Fragrant Hills Park** (Xiangshan) ❸, only an hour's drive to the northwest (beyond the Summer Palaces), is a convenient way to get away from the metropolis for a day. When the sky is clear, you will be rewarded by an excellent view of the city you have left behind.

In the Liao dynasty (907–1125), noble and wealthy merchant families built elegant villas on the cool slopes of these hills, to which they could flee when temperatures in the city soared. Those that could not afford to buy or build their own property rented guest quarters in temples. The journey was undertaken on mule at an easy pace, travelling through the woodlands, enjoying the feeling of communion with nature, and staying overnight in Daoist or Buddhist shrines.

Later, the Ming emperors turned the area into an imperial game preserve. As recently as 300 years ago, the Qing Emperor Kangxi is supposed to have killed a tiger here. Qianlong turned it into a landscaped park, a complex of 28 scenic zones, named the Park of Tranquillity and Pleasure. This, however, was badly damaged by foreign troops in 1860, and again in 1900. Few of the buildings have survived.

The Fragrant Hills were opened to the public in 1957, and quickly became one of the most popular excursions for Beijing dwellers. No longer forcibly "sent down" to the countryside to work alongside their peasant brethren, this is as close to nature as some Beijing residents ever get. Bear in mind that on summer and autumn weekends the crowds are so large it can feel as if you are still in the city. The hills are particularly popular in late autumn because of the blazing red of the sycamore leaves. Tang dynasty, poets sang the praises of the frost-flecked red of the trees.

The English name of the peak after which the park is known, "Fragrant Hill", is an imprecise translation. On the 550-metre (1,830-ft) summit are two formations of rock that are often veiled in fog or cloud, so that from a distance the peak resembles a sacred incense burner with smoke rising out of it. As there is no semantic difference in Chinese between "incense" and "fragrance," the "incense burner hill" became known as the "fragrant hill".

BELOW:
preparations for
a souvenir photo
in the Fragrant
Hills Park.

The Glazed Tile Pagoda (Liulita) is a prominent landmark in the Fragrant Hills Park.

BELOW: the 600-year-old Temple of the Azure Clouds.

Turn right inside the main eastern gate to the park and you come to the **Temple of Clarity** (Zhaomiao) **A**, built in 1780 for the Panchen Lama, in the Tibetan style. In its grounds is the octagonal **Glazed Tile Pagoda** (Liulita) **B**, which has little bells hanging from the corners of its eaves, the lightest breeze making them chime delicately. The **Chamber of Introspection** (Jianxinhai) **C**, to the east of the pagoda, has a courtyard in the southern Chinese style with a semi-circular pond, as well as the usual walkways and pavilions. Only a few steps ahead lie two lakes separated by a jetty, and known, because of their shape, as the **Spectacles Lake** (Yanjinghu) **D**.

Beyond this is the northern gate, from which a chair lift will take you to the summit of the "Fragrant Hill". From here you can see over steep, thickly wooded slopes and deep ravines to the Temple of the Azure Clouds (in a side valley on the northeast side of the park). Further away, is the Jade Spring Hill, with its ancient pagoda, and beyond that the Summer Palace and Kunming Lake. In the far distance are the skyscrapers of the Haidian district of Beijing. On a clear day, you can get a good impression of the immensity of Beijing, with its ever growing population. If you're feeling fit you can climb the hill on foot instead of taking the chair lift, but you will need good shoes and at least a couple of hours to spare. The steepest part of the hill bears the name Guijianchou, which means "Even the devil is afraid of it!"

Near the eastern gate stands the **Xiangshan Hotel** **E**, probably the most beautifully situated hotel in the Beijing region. It was designed by the famous Chinese-American architect I. M. Pei. His attempt to translate the ancient Chinese court style into modern architecture has been much acclaimed.

The southern part of the park beyond the hotel is excellent for picnics. Yet

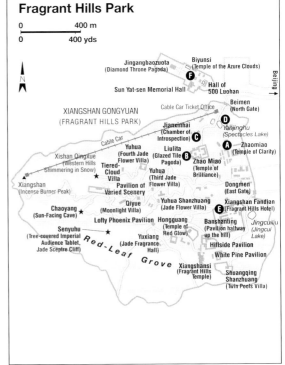

Fragrant Hills Park

0   400 m
0   400 yds

Jingangbaozuota (Diamond Throne Pagoda)
Biyunsi (Temple of the Azure Clouds) **F**
Sun Yat-sen Memorial Hall
Hall of 500 Luohan
Cable Car Ticket Office
Beimen (North Gate)
XIANGSHAN GONGYUAN (FRAGRANT HILLS PARK)
Jianxinhai (Chamber of Introspection) **C**
Yanjinghu (Spectacles Lake) **D**
Zhaomiao (Temple of Clarity) **A**
Cable Car
Yuhua (Fourth Jade Flower Villa)
Liulita (Glazed Tile Pagoda) **B**
Zhao Miao (Temple of Brilliance)
Xishan Qingxue (Western Hills Shimmering in Snow)
Tiered-Cloud Villa
Yuhua (Third Jade Flower Villa)
Xiangshan (Incense Burner Peak)
Pavilion of Varied Scenery
Dongmen (East Gate)
Xiangshan Fandian (Fragrant Hills Hotel) **E**
Qiyue (Moonlight Villa)
Yuhua Shanzhuang (Jade Flower Villa)
Chaoyang (Sun-Facing Cave)
Banshanting (Pavilion halfway up the hill)
Jingcuiliu (Jingcui Lake)
Lofty Phoenix Pavilion
Hongguang (Temple of Red Glow)
Senyuhu (Tree-covered Imperial Audience Tablet, Jade Sceptre Cliff)
Red-Leaf Grove
Yuxiang (Jade Fragrance Hall)
Hillside Pavilion
White Pine Pavilion
Xiangshansi (Fragrant Hills Temple)
Shuangqing Shanzhuang (Twin Pools Villa)

only a few visitors ever seem to find their way here. Past the remains of the once-massive **Xiangshan Temple** (destroyed at the end of the Second Opium War in 1860) that rose over six levels, you will reach the remote **Twin Peaks Villa** (Shuang Qing Shanzhuang), and the **Pavilion Halfway Up the Hill** (Banshanting). Here, a little tower has been restored, and from it you get a good view of the park.

Map on page 214

The Temple of the Azure Clouds

The **Memorial Hall for Sun Yat-sen** (1862–1925), founder of the National People's Party, the Guomindang, and charismatic leader of the middle-class democratic movement, is in the **Temple of the Azure Clouds** (Biyunsi) ❻, adjacent to Fragrant Hills Park. The Buddhist temple is about 600 years old and comprises four great halls, the innermost being the memorial hall for Sun Yat-sen. Here lies an empty coffin, a gift from the Soviet Union, which could not be used because it did not arrive until two weeks after the funeral .

To the left of the main entrance of the hall, letters and manuscripts left by Sun Yat-sen are on display. On the wall is an inscription in marble: a letter from Sun Yat-sen addressed to the Soviet Union. There are exhibition rooms on both sides of the memorial hall. The first shows photos from the great man's youth; the second contains photos from the period of his active involvement in the democratic revolution.

Beyond the memorial hall is the pagoda courtyard. The marble **Diamond Throne Pagoda** (Jingangbaozuota) was built in 1748 under the rule of Emperor Qianlong, and is modelled on the Temple of the Five Pagodas in northwest Beijing (*see page 188*). In March 1925, Sun Yat-sen's coffin lay in state in the

BELOW: the Temple of the Azure Clouds is set amongst the thickly wooded slopes of the Fragrant Hills.

Sun Yat-sen's empty coffin in the Temple of Azure Clouds. The coffin, a gift from the Soviet Union, was never used.

pagoda, before being moved in 1929 to Zhongshanling, the Sun Yat-sen mausoleum in Nanjing. His clothing and personal belongings, however, remained here. In front of the building is a stele with an inscription by Hu Hanmin, one of the older leaders of the Guomindang. The pagoda itself is 35 metres (114 ft) high, and its base is adorned with numerous statues of Buddha.

There are other places nearby worth seeking out. To the northeast, past the **Botanical Gardens**, is the **Temple of the Reclining Buddha** ❹ (Wofosi; open daily, 8am–5pm; entrance fee), dating from the Tang dynasty. The 5-metre (18-ft) Buddha is made of lacquered and painted bronze and of indeterminate age, although experts have expressed doubts that it is the original statue. Surrounding the Buddha are transcendental *bodhisattvas*. Beyond the temple is the **Cherry Ravine** (Yingtaogou), a romantic spot.

Eight Scenic Sites

On a hillside about 7 km (4½ miles) to the south of Fragrant Hills Park is a group of former temples and monasteries that can be visited together, the **Eight Scenic Sites** ❺ (Badachu; buildings open daily, 8am–5pm; park open 6am–9pm; entrance fee). In the pagoda of the second temple you come to, the **Temple of the Sacred Light** (Lingguangsi), there is a holy relic reputed to be a tooth of the Buddha.

The **Temple of Great Compassion** (Dabeisi) is renowned for its 18 Lohan statues. The temple below the peak, the **Cave of Precious Pearls**, is built around a cave in which a hermit is supposed to have lived for 40 years during the Qing dynasty. These temples used to be in a restricted military area and were only open to visitors with special passes, but the public now have full access.

BELOW:
Temple of the
Reclining Buddha.

Western Temples

The oldest Buddhist temple of Beijing is not in the city centre, but in the Mentougou district on Tanzheshan Hill, over an hour away by car. It is easy to combine a visit to the **Temple of the Dragon Pond and the Mulberry Tree ❻** (Tanzhesi; open daily, 8am–5pm) with a side trip to the Ordination Terrace Temple (*see page 218*). Both are delightful because of their rural settings and the sense of peaceful isolation which you can get on weekdays – at weekends they are more crowded. Tanzhesi is a good place to stop for lunch as there is a reasonably priced restaurant serving good and wholesome food.

The Tanzhesi Temple was built between 265 and 316 AD on terraces carved in dense woods. Both Buddhists and Daoists used to withdraw to such beautiful places where they could meditate undisturbed. Over the centuries, its name has changed several times, until finally Tanzhesi prevailed. *Tan* refers to the Dragon Pool above the temple, and *zhe* to the wild mulberries that grow in the hills. There is an old proverb that says, "First came Tanzhe, then came Youzhou" – as the Beijing region was known in the 6th century.

The temple is built in three parts along a north-south line across the hill slope. Enter following the central axis from the south, through the **Gate of Honour** (Pailou), and the adjoining **Mountain Gate** (Shanmen). The path is lined by many old pine trees, which are sometimes compared by the Chinese to flying dragons. Beyond the Mountain Gate, one behind the other, are the **Hall of the Celestial Kings** (Tianwangdian), the **Daxiongbaodian Hall** (the main hall), the **Zhaitang Hall**, and the **Piluge Pavilion**, which is dedicated to the Buddha Vairocana. Above the main hall are legendary beasts, sons of the Dragon King, who are supposed to have captured a monk and chained him to the roof. You can

Map on page 198

BELOW: the Western Mountains.

get the best view of Tanzhesi and the surrounding country from here, the highest point in the grounds. Beyond the Hall of Daxiongbaodian are two **gingko trees**, called the Emperor's Tree and the Emperor's Companion's Tree, which are supposed to date from the Liao dynasty (916–1125).

Take the western path from here and look into the **Temple of Guanyin,** where you can see the Paving Stone of Beizhuan, on which the nun Miaoyan, a daughter of the Mongol emperor Kublai Khan (1260–94), is supposed to have prayed to Buddha daily in penance for her father's misdeeds. The path continues to the Temple of the Dragon King and the Temple of the Founding Father of this monastery, all of which belong to the distinct Buddhist sect of Huayan.

In the eastern part of the grounds are a white dagoba dating from 1427, two groups of 12th-century pagodas, a bamboo grove and the **Pavilion of the Moving Cup** (Liubeige), where Qianlong stayed during his visits to the temple.

It was something of a tradition for the nobility of the city to meet at Tanzhesi on the third day of the Chinese New Year festival. The water of the mountain spring pours out of a lion's mouth into a twisting, dragon-shaped runnel and then flows away. Everyone would place his filled cup in the runnel. If a cup fell over, its owner had to drink a cup of wine and recite a poem.

Eight km (five miles) to the south, at the foot of Ma'anshan Hill, is the **Ordination Terrace Temple** ❼ (Jietaisi; open daily, 8am–5pm). This imposing temple dates from 622 and owes its name to the three-level stone terraces, which were surrounded by statues and upon which the dedication ceremony of monks took place. The Main Hall is the Daxiongbaodian, and beyond it is the Thousand Buddhas Pavilion. Steles with Buddhist inscriptions dating from the Liao and Yuan dynasties can be seen in front of the Mingwang Hall. There is no longer much to be seen inside the halls, but it is worthwhile taking a walk to enjoy the temple grounds with their old pine trees.

BELOW: traditional point of view.

In the western suburbs of Beijing is the **Temple of Enlightenment** (Dajuesi), at the foot of Yangtai Hill. It was founded in 1068, but the present buildings date from 1428, when the temple was rebuilt. It is known for its "six wonders" which include a 1,000-year-old stele, a millennial gingko tree and the beautifully clear Dragon Pool fed by a nearby spring.

To the south, in the district of Shijingshan, is the **Fahaisi Temple**, built by the eunuch Li Tong in 1439 and today visited chiefly for its murals dating from the Ming dynasty.

Marco Polo Bridge

The **Marco Polo Bridge** ❽ (Lugouqiao; open daily, 7am–7pm), is 15 km (9 miles) southeast of central Beijing. The bridge can be reached by bus from Guang'anmen, and can be comfortably combined with a trip to see the cave-home of Peking Man.

The Italian merchant Marco Polo, who stayed at the court of the Mongol emperor Kublai Khan in the 13th century, admired this bridge: "Ten miles past Cumbaluc (Khanbaliq) the traveller will reach the broad river Pulisanghin. Merchants travel on it with their wares down to the sea. A magnificent stone bridge crosses the river, and it has no equal anywhere in the world. The bridge is three hundred paces long and eight paces broad. Ten riders, flank to flank, could cross it with no difficulty. The twenty-four arches and the twenty-four pillars are of grey, finely dressed and well-placed marble blocks. Marble slabs and pillars form a balustrade on both sides. The first pillar is at the bridge head; it bears a marble lion, and at its base another lion can be seen. The next pillar is one and a half paces away, and it also bears two lions. The space between is closed by a grey marble slab, so that none can fall into the water. It is wonderful to see how the row of pillars and the slabs are so cleverly joined together."

Lugou means "Black Ditch", and is an earlier name for the **Yongding River**, which flows under the bridge. The first bridge was built here in 1189, and improved in 1444. When it was seriously damaged by a flood in 1698, during the reign of Emperor Kangxi (1662–1722), it was rebuilt exactly as it had been. It has 11 arches, each with a span of 7.5 metres (25 ft). On the balustrade on either side are 140 stone posts crowned with lions. The people of Beijing claim that these lion statues are too many to be counted. In fact, there are 485 lions, some only a few centimetres tall, others comparative giants; no two lions being exactly alike. At each end of the bridge is a 5-metre (15-ft) high stele. One of these records the rebuilding of the bridge in the 17th century; the other is inscribed: "The moon at daybreak over the Lugou Bridge", one of the eight wonders of old Beijing.

As the Yongding River was prone to flooding, the 11 arches of the bridge have been fastened with iron clamps to strengthen it (local people refer to these as "Swords for Beheading Dragons"). It has recently been closed to traffic. Upriver a dam has created an artificial lake, so that the river bed is usually dry

Maps
on pages
198 & 212

Stele at the Marco Polo Bridge.

BELOW: the tomb of Xu Beihong.

HEROES' CEMETERIES

The Heroes' Cemetery (Babaoshan) is located about 15 km (9 miles) west of Tiananmen, off Shijingshan Lu (the western extension of Chang'an Jie) next to the Babaoshan subway station. Most of the tombs date from the 1950s and 1960s and are those of dedicated or long-serving communists, but there are also some of famous people, such as the artist Xu Beihong.

To the north, the Cemetery of Eternal Peace (Wan'an Gongmu; *see map on page 198*) and the tomb of the much revered Li Dazhao. A noted activist of the May Fourth Movement of 1919, and a co-founder of the Chinese Communist Party, Li was part of an influential generation of scholars. After completing his studies at Waseda University in Tokyo, he was appointed chief librarian of Peking University in 1918, and in 1920 was promoted to professor of history. Inspired by the Russian Revolution, Li began to study and lecture on Marxism, and soon met and influenced the young Mao, who was working as a clerk in the library. In 1927 he sought refuge at the Soviet Embassy from Zhang Zuolin, the vehemently anti-leftist Manchurian warlord in charge of Beijing at the time. Zhang ordered his army to seize all the Chinese who were being protected by the embassy. Li was hanged with 19 of his comrades.

The Beijing Metro is an excellent way of reaching the western suburbs.

in summer, and sadly this has taken away some of the original charm. The river was navigable until the early twentieth century, and there was a landing place here from which travellers embarked on journeys to the south.

The bridge gained world-wide fame in the 1930s because of the "incident" which is seen as the start of the Japanese invasion of Asia during World War II. On 7 July 1937, Japanese troops of the Tianjin garrison attacked the Marco Polo Bridge, provoking the Chinese guards to fire at them. This retaliation provided a pretext for further aggression by the Japanese. By August, China and Japan were at war. A memorial **museum** at the bridge explains the background to these events in full.

Ancestral cave

The site of the discovery of Peking Man, *Sinanthropus pekinensis*, lies close to the small town of Zhoukoudian, about 50 km (30 miles) southwest of Beijing. The **Cave of Peking Man** ❾ (open daily, 9am–4pm; entrance fee) is on the northern slopes of Longushan (Dragon Bone Mountain).

About 450 million years ago, the site was underneath an ocean. As the waters receded, limestone caves gradually developed. Over 500,000 years ago early hominids settled in these caves; they were to inhabit them for the next 300,000 years. When this hominid race disappeared, the caves became naturally filled in, and the tools, food scraps and bones in them remained covered by deposits until modern times.

As early as the Ming dynasty, workers digging for lime found many animal fossils, which were believed to be the bones of dragons. By the beginning of the twentieth century, peasants were finding human teeth at this site.

BELOW: the Marco Polo Bridge.

In 1921, the Swede John Gunnar Andersson found a rich source of fossils that attracted many other scientists. More discoveries were made in the following years, until, in 1927, systematic excavations began. Two years later the complete upper skull of Peking Man was found. Java Man and Heidelberg Man were known at that time, yet the discovery of Peking Man was a surprise for science and caused a great sensation. Unfortunately, the skull was lost during World War II and today only copies of it exist.

Who found Peking Man? The Chinese say that it was a Chinese palaeoanthropologist, Pei Wenzhong. In other countries, however, the Jesuit priest and philosopher, Teilhard de Chardin, is often claimed to have discovered the skull. He certainly spent several years excavating here, during which time many fossils were discovered.

Up until the beginning of the Japanese invasion in 1937, fossil remains of more than 40 individuals of both sexes had been found. The men of this hominid race were some 1.5 metres (5 ft) tall, the women slightly smaller. They had skulls about a third smaller than people of today and, because they had broad shoulders and strong muscles, the could already walk upright. Their hands could use stone tools, and they understood the use of fire. Altogether, four caves have been discovered in Zhoukoudian. In the Upper Cave, the remains of *Homo sapiens,* who settled here some 18,000 years ago, were also discovered.

There is a small **museum** on the site, close to the Peking Man Cave and the Upper Cave. The exhibits are divided into three sections and provide information on evolution in general, of Peking Man in particular, and on the development of Chinese palaeontology. There are also displays of other fossils found in the area – ancient bears, tigers, elephants and rhinoceroses.   ❑

Maps on pages 198 & 212

LEFT: the Peking Man cave entrance.
BELOW: artist's impression of Peking Man.

IMPERIAL TOMBS

They craved immortality but, unable to cheat death, China's emperors built for themselves, their concubines and their wives monumental sepulchres by which they would be remembered

Maps on pages 212 & 225

A lthough Beijing was the capital of the Middle Kingdom for five dynasties, the tombs of the Ming emperors are the only ones in relatively close proximity to the city. The tombs of the Qing emperors, both the eastern and western sites, are further away, although still within reach. The burial places of the Liao dynasty (916–1125) are in distant northeast China; those of the Jin dynasty (1125–1234) were destroyed at the end of the Ming era; and the Mongol rulers of the Yuan dynasty (1279–1368) had no special burial rites and left no mausoleums behind them.

THE MING TOMBS

Thirteen of the 16 Ming emperors are buried in a valley to the south of the Tianshou Mountains, 50 km (30 miles) northwest of Beijing. The foothills of the Yanshan Mountains form a natural entrance to the 40-sq-km (15-sq-mile) basin, "defended" on both sides by the Dragon and Tiger Mountains, which are said to keep harmful winds away from the holy ground. With the completion of the eight-lane Badaling Expressway, the **Ming tombs ①** (Shisanling; open daily, 8am–5.30pm; entrance fee) have become more readily accessible. A visit here is usually combined with a trip to the Great Wall at Badaling.

Behind the **Great Palace Gate** (Dagongmen) **Ⓐ** at the entrance to the Ming necropolis is a square stele pavilion on which can be seen a great tortoise bearing a tall stele on its back. The gate marks the beginning of the **Avenue of Stone Figures Ⓑ**, also known as the Avenue of Ghosts. This 7-km (4-mile) road leading to the tomb of the Emperor Yongle is flanked by pairs of stone lions, elephants, camels, horses and mythological creatures, followed by 12 military and civil dignitaries representing the imperial court. Beyond these figures is the **Dragon and Phoenix Gate** (Longfengmen) **Ⓒ** with its three entrances which in earlier years were sealed off behind heavy doors.

Yongle's Tomb

The **Tomb of the Emperor Yongle** (Changling) **Ⓓ** is the biggest and best preserved of the 13 surviving Ming tombs. Built on a south-facing slope, its three courtyards are surrounded by a wall. The first courtyard stretches from the massive three-arched entrance gate to the **Gate of Eminent Favours** (Ling'enmen). In the east of this courtyard is a pavilion with a stone tablet, a stone camel and a stone dragon. The **Hall of Eminent Favours** (Ling'endian) is in the second courtyard. The central section of the stone steps leading up to the hall is adorned with sea monsters and dragons. In the east and west parts of the hall there are "fire basins", in which balls of silk and inscrip-

PRECEDING PAGES: the Avenue of Stone Figures at the Ming Tombs. **LEFT:** figure of a dignitary in front of the Tailing tomb.

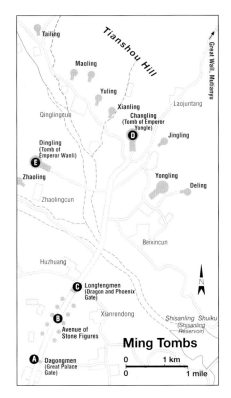

Ming Tombs

Posing for a photograph on the Avenue of Stone Figures.

BELOW:
an old sketch
showing the layout
of the Ming Tombs.

tions were burned as offerings to the imperial ancestors. Four mighty wooden pillars, each one made out of a single trunk of a nanmu tree, along with 28 smaller posts, support the construction.

In the third and last courtyard, a stele tower can be found, with an incense basin and other ritual objects in front of it – the so-called "nine stone utensils". On the stele is the inscription "Tomb of the Emperor Chengzu of the great Ming dynasty" (Chengzu was the temple name of Emperor Yongle). A wall with a circumference of about one km (half a mile), known as Precious City, was built to enclose the burial mound which is 31 metres (102 ft) long and 38 metres (125 ft) broad. To the east and west are the tombs of the 16 imperial concubines, who were buried alive to serve their emperor in the underworld.

Subterranean palace

The **Tomb of Emperor Wanli** (Dingling) ❺ lies to the southwest of Changling. The emperor Wanli (1573–1619) was buried here in 1620, together with his two wives, Xiaoduan and Xiaojing. About 30,000 workers took a total of six years (1584–90) to complete the tomb, which cost 8 million taels of silver (equivalent to the total land tax for two years).

A tunnel leads down to a depth of more than 7 metres (23 ft), to the first massive gate of a subterranean palace. The palace consists of five rooms with mighty marble vaulting and a floor of highly polished stones, known as golden stones. The 50,000 stones were specially prepared in Suzhou over a period of three years and were then transported 1,400 km (900 miles) to the north.

The marble thrones of the emperor and his wives stand in the central hall. An "eternal lamp" (an oil lamp with a floating wick that was believed to burn for-

ever) and five sacrificial offerings (an incense bowl, two candelabra, and two vases of yellow-glazed earthenware) can be seen in the room. Next to the central hall are two side chambers that contain pedestals for coffins. These platforms, which are covered with the "golden stones" and filled with yellow earth, are known as the Golden Fountains. No coffins were found in this chamber.

The rear hall is the largest and the most imposing in the subterranean palace. It is 9.5 metres (30 ft) high, 30 metres (100 ft) long and 9 metres (30 ft) wide. On pedestals in the middle of the hall are the coffins of the emperor Wanli and his empresses. Around the coffins are 26 lacquered chests filled with crowns, gold and jade pitchers, cups, bowls, earrings, and wine containers. There are also sacred objects of jade, and items of blue-and-white Ming porcelain. Among the more than 3,000 objects is an extraordinarily fine filigree crown of gold adorned with two dragons playing with a pearl. This crown, together with a valuable embroidery showing 100 playing children, and other exhibits of historical interest, can be viewed in the two exhibition halls within the complex.

The tombs of the other Ming emperors are not open to the public at present, but you can wander around the grounds for several miles, discovering the ruins of other tomb structures, and escaping from the crowds.

THE WESTERN QING TOMBS

The **Western Qing tombs ❷** (Qingxiling; open daily, 8am–5pm; entrance fee) lie in a hilly district on the southern slopes of the Yongning Mountains in Hebei Province, some 125 km (80 miles) southwest of Beijing. The area is bordered by the Zijing Pass to the west, the River Yi to the south and the site of the former second capital of the kingdom, Yan, to the east. The Qing emperors

Maps
on pages
212 & 225

BELOW: the Western Qing tombs.

Yongzheng, Jiaqing, Daoguang and Guangxu, along with three empresses, seven princes and many imperial concubines, are buried here.

Yongzheng stays away from his father

The biggest tomb in the complex is the **Tomb of Emperor Yongzheng** (Tailing). Yongzheng (1723–35) is not remembered kindly by history. In order to consolidate his rule, he did not hesitate to have his brothers and ministers imprisoned and executed. He was extremely suspicious and developed a network of spies who were supposed to observe the activities of his ministers. He rarely left his palace for any length of time, and only six years after ascending the throne, began to seek a suitable site for his tomb. Because he had gained the throne in an illegal manner, it is said that Yongzheng was afraid of being buried close to his father, Kangxi, in the Eastern Qing Tombs.

In 1730, his 13th younger brother, a respected geomancer, whom the emperor trusted, chose this favourable site. Yongzheng's tomb was built between 1730 and 1737. Yongzheng died unexpectedly in 1735, but was not buried here until 1737. His empress, Xiaojingxian, and his concubine, Dunsuhuang – both of whom had died before him – are also buried here.

Adjacent to the **Way of Souls** (Shendao), which leads to the tombs proper, is a series of carefully placed buildings. To the right, just beyond the **Great Palace Gate** (Dagongmen) – the main entrance to the grounds – is the **Hall of Robes**, where the priest presiding over the imperial funeral rites changed into his robes. The Way of Souls leads north across a bridge of seven arches, and is bordered by stone sculptures consisting of six animals, and two civil and two military dignitaries.

BELOW: the tomb of Emperor Guangxu.

Passing a natural protective wall, the so-called **Spider Hill**, you reach the **Dragon and Phoenix Gate** (Longfengmen). Continuing north, you then pass a small stele pavilion and three stone bridges, each comprising three arches, before coming to a large square, where the sacred kitchen and a well pavilion are to be found.

The **Gate of Eminent Favours** (Longenmen) as the entrance to the main part of the complex. Within the gate there are furnaces for burning the offerings of silk, and the former storehouses for paper offerings, which now serve as exhibition halls. Offerings were made in the **Hall of Eminent Favours** (Longendian), which contains the thrones of the emperor and the empress, together with an altar for offerings and gifts. Beyond the hall there are two gates, several stone receptacles for offerings, and a stele tower, below which lies the underground palace of the emperor.

According to a decree of the Emperor Qianlong, the emperors of subsequent reigns were to be interred alternately in the Eastern or the Western Qing Tombs. The Emperors Jiaqing and Daoguang were therefore buried in the Western Tombs, and Xianfeng and Tongzhi in the Eastern Tombs.

Not far away to the west of Yongzheng's tomb is the **Tomb of Emperor Jiaqing** (Changling). The number of buildings and their style are almost identical to that of the Tailing. The Changling tomb was completed in 1803, but Jiaqing was not buried here until March 1821. According to the customs of the Qing dynasty, the Empress Xiaosurui, who had died before Jiaqing, was buried here, but her successor, who died after the emperor, was laid in a tomb to the west of the Changling tomb.

Daoguang and Guangxu

Five km (3 miles) to the west of the Changling tomb is the **Mausoleum of Emperor Daoguang** (Muling), built between 1832 and 1836. After he had ascended the throne, Daoguang immediately began to have a mausoleum built in the Eastern Qing Tombs. One year after its completion, it was discovered that the subterranean palace was full of water. The enraged Daoguang is said to have blamed the builders of the tomb for driving several dragons from their homes, and in 1832, he personally visited the Western Qing Tombs to chose a new site.

When the new subterranean palace was being built, new homes had to be found for the displaced dragons. Hence, the unique work of art of the **Hall of Eminent Favours** (Longendian): on its coffered ceiling of nanmu wood, every panel bears a writhing dragon and the unpainted beams are carved in dragon forms.

The **Tomb of Emperor Guangxu** (Chongling) lies five km (three miles) to the east of the Tailing. It was built in 1909, and is the last of the imperial tombs, although Guangxu was not to be the last emperor of the Qing dynasty. That dubious honour is held by Pu Yi, who was made emperor at the age of six in 1909, but who died in 1967 as an ordinary mortal who could not therefore be buried beside his imperial ancestors.

The mausoleum of Emperor Guangxu was begun after his death and left incomplete after the fall of the

Map on page 212

BELOW: portrait of Emperor Guangxu.

Ritual urn at the entrance to Kangxi's tomb, used for burning incense and other offerings.

Qing dynasty. In 1915, the republican government had it finished off with money from treasury funds of the former Qing imperial household.

To the east of Guangxu's mausoleum is a mausoleum for his concubines, including Zhen Fei and her sister, Jinfei. Zhen Fei is popularly believed to have been the Emperor Guangxu's favourite concubine, who Cixi is supposed to have had executed and thrown down a well in the Imperial Palace (*see page 131*). Whatever the cause of Zhen Fei's death, her body was found in 1901 and first buried in Taincun, a small village outside Xizhimen, before being transferred here to the Western Qing Tombs in 1915.

THE EASTERN QING TOMBS

Among the largest and most beautiful tombs in China are the **Eastern Qing Tombs ❸** (Qingdongling; open daily, 8.30am–5pm; entrance fee), to the west of the village of Malanyu, in the Zunhua district of Hebei province, 125 km (80 miles) east of Beijing. Stretches of poor road can make the tombs a three or four-hour drive from the city. There is agreeable countryside to look at on the way and once you arrive the cobbled courtyards, stone bridges, streams and pathways make the stroll around the wooded tomb complex much more pleasant than the trudge around many tourist sites. The Jingxing mountain range, which resembles an upturned bell, borders the area to the south.

BELOW: policemen in relaxed mood.

Five Qing emperors are buried in an area covering more than 2,500 sq km (965 sq miles). Shunzi (1644–61) chose this broad valley for the site of his tomb while on a hunting expedition. Kangxi (1662–1722), Qianlong (1736–96), Xiangfeng (1851–61), and Tongzhi (1862–75) are also buried here, as well as the Empress Dowager Cixi (who died in 1908), and a total of 14 other empresses, 136 imperial concubines and various princesses.

The main entrance to the tombs is a great white marble gate, its rectangular surfaces covered with inscriptions and geometric designs. Pairs of lions and dragons form the base of the pillars.

Beyond this is the **Great Palace Gate** (Dagongmen), which served as the official entrance to the mausoleum complex. It has a tower in which a carved *bixi* (a tortoise-like animal) bears a tall stone tablet on its shell. Engraved on the tablet are the "sacred virtues and worthiness" of the Emperor Shunzi.

Passing a small hill to the north, you come to a *shenlu* (spirit way) with 18 pairs of stone figures, similar to the one at the Ming Tombs, but a little smaller. This road leads through the **Dragon and Phoenix Gate** (Longfengmen) and crossing a marble bridge with seven arches. This is the longest and most beautiful of nearly 100 bridges in the complex, and is known as the **Five Notes Bridge**. If you step on one of the 110 stone slabs, you will, it is said, hear the five notes of the pentatonic scale.

At the other end of the bridge is the **Gate of Eminent Favours** (Ling'enmen), the entrance to the **Tomb of Emperor Shunzi** (Xiaoling). Beyond the Gate of Eminent Favours is the **Hall of Eminent Favours** (Ling'endian), where the ancestor tablets and the offerings to the ancestors were kept. A stele tower rises behind the hall. The stele within is covered with red lacquer and bears the following inscription in Chinese, Manchu and Mongol: "Tomb of the emperor Shunzi". The underground tomb has yet to be excavated.

Map on page 212

Qianlong and Cixi

The **Tomb of the Emperor Qianlong** (Yuling) has been restored and is open to the public. The Qing dynasty flourished under Emperor Qianlong. He reigned for 60 years, longer than any of the other nine Qing emperors. In 1743, after eight years of rule, he began to plan his mausoleum, which was to cost a total of 1.8 million taels of silver. The three vaulted chambers of the subterranean palace, which is 20 metres (65 ft) underground, covers an area of 327 square metres (126 sq ft). A relief of the goddess of mercy, Guanyin, adorns the eight wings of the four double doors. Behind the doors are fine sculptures of the Tianwang, the four Celestial Kings. Other reliefs cover the vaulting and the walls of the tomb, including the Buddhas of the five points of the compass, and Buddhist inscriptions in Sanskrit and Tibetan.

The **Tomb of the Empress Dowager Cixi** (Dingdongling) can also be visited. The tomb lies about one km to the west of Yuling. Here, the two wives of Xianfeng lie buried: the eastern Empress Dowager Ci'an, and the infamous western Empress Dowager Cixi. The two tombs were originally symmetrical and built in the same style. But Cixi was not satisfied and had Ling'endian, the Hall of Eminent Favours, pulled down in 1895. The tomb that she then had built for 4,590 taels of gold is the most splendid and extravagant of all.

As Cixi died before the work on her tomb was completed, the underground part is relatively plain, and is outshone by the fine craftsmanship of the stonework between the steps in front of the tomb, and the balustrades in front of the hall. These show exquisite carvings of dragons in the waves and phoenixes in the clouds – traditional symbols of the emperor and empress. The Hall of Eminent Favours has an exhibition of Cixi's clothes, articles for daily use, and a number of other tomb offerings. Also on display is the Dharani, a robe of sacred verses, woven in pure silk and embroidered with more than 25,000 Chinese characters in gold thread.

BELOW: marble bridges span the moat in front of Emperor Kangxi's tomb.

Other tombs

The concubines of Emperor Qianlong occupy tombs under 38 burial mounds. The concubine Rongfei, who was buried here in 1788, lies under the first mound in the second row of tombs to the east of the stele tower. Better known as Xiangfei ("the Fragrant Concubine"), Rongfei was the daughter of a prince of the Uighur kingdom in Central Asia. Other small tombs worth seeing in the complex are the **tomb of the wife of Emperor Shunzi** (Xiaodongling), the **Changxiling** and the **Mudongling**. These tombs, recently excavated, had already been plundered.

The **Zhaoxiling** stands alone outside the Great Palace Gate. Although Zhaoxi, who was buried here in 1687, was a simple concubine, she was given the title of Empress Dowager because she had given birth to the future emperor Shunzi. ❏

THE GREAT WALL

The greatest fortification in human history was built to prevent invasion by nomadic tribes from the steppes of central Asia. Today it is one of the greatest tourist attractions in the world

Map on page 212

Beijing

The "Ten Thousand Li Great Wall" (Wan Li Chang Cheng) represents the pinnacle of 2,000 years of wall building in northern China. The construction visible today dates mostly from the 15th century and stretches for some 4,000 km (2,500 miles). It is a structure of overwhelming physical presence; a vast wall of earth, brick and stone topped by an endless procession of stout towers, rolling over craggy peaks, and across deep ravines and barren deserts. But the Great Wall is more than a remnant of history. It is massively symbolic of the tyranny of imperial rule; the application of mass labour; the ingenuity of engineers commissioned to work on the grandest scale; and the human desire to build for immortality.

It is, however, misleading to speak of one wall. Archaeologists have identified many walls, some of which date back to the 5th century BC. These fortifications came into being because the flourishing agricultural settlements on the fertile plains along the Yellow River and its tributaries had to protect themselves against constant plundering by nomadic tribes. Each settlement built its own "great wall" of rammed earth, the earliest probably being in the state of Qi, in modern Shandong province. The length of all such walls so far discovered totals some 50,000 km (30,000 miles).

PRECEDING PAGES: the Great Wall threads its way across the Western Hills. **LEFT:** the Wall at Mutianyu. **BELOW:** visitor and graffiti at Badaling.

The rise and fall of the Wall

It was Qin Shi Huangdi, considered to be the first Chinese emperor (221–210 BC), who conceived the idea of a single, protective Great Wall. He forced all the states of China to submit to his rule. After having removed internal threats in this way, he linked the northern walls into a single defensive bulwark against the nomads. Under the leadership of General Meng Tian, an army of 300,000 forced labourers is said to have constructed the Great Wall. In those days, the Wall began in the west of Lintao (to the south of Lanzhou) and ran east through Inner Mongolia, Shaanxi and Hebei provinces. It ended in the east of what is now Liaoning province.

The Great Wall did not always fulfil its purpose of keeping enemies out. It was breached regularly even before the Tang dynasty (618–907) extended the borders of its empire well beyond it. Sometimes it simply had no purpose at all. The Mongol conquerors who ruled northern China from 936 to 1368 had no need of the Wall, since it lay in the middle of their territory, and served neither as a boundary nor defence.

However, the overthrow of the Mongols by the first Ming emperor, Zhu Yuanchang (1368–98), changed the situation. The maintenance of the Great Wall became a matter of life or death for the new Ming dynasty, which had to defend itself against attacks

Tourist souvenirs for sale at Badaling, by far the most visited section of the Wall.

from the Mongols. For more than 200 years, work went on to strengthen the Wall. New sections were built, fortified towers were extended, and the logistics of defending and administering it were overhauled and improved.

The Wall was mostly left to decay after the middle of the eighteenth century. The Manchu rulers of the Qing dynasty were invaders from beyond the wall, and were intent on expanding rather than consolidating their empire. Wind and weather gradually eroded away some sections of the redundant walls. Peasants recycled bricks and stones to build farmhouses and stables. This process of deconstruction continued into modern times. During the Cultural Revolution, army units built whole barracks out of bricks taken from the Great Wall.

The Wall has since been given a new lease of life as one of the most familiar images of China at home and abroad. As a patriotic symbol, it now adorns the badges of China's public security officers. On the screen it has formed the background for Japanese children's choirs, American fashion shows, religious services, sporting events, and mobile phone advertisements. It is used as a brand name for everything from computers to wine. Plays have been staged in its towers, motorcyclists have jumped over it, and parachutists have landed on it. Illusionist David Copperfield once walked through it.

Where to see the Wall

BELOW: T-shirts for sale at Badaling.

Since Deng Xiaoping launched a campaign in 1984 to "Love China, Restore the Great Wall", many sections have been rebuilt and opened to tourists. The most convenient stretch to reach from Beijing – and consequently also the most crowded – is at **Badaling**. Despite the hordes of sightseers, Badaling does have great scenery, restored forts and exhibitions to see.

Map
on page
212

Slightly further out from Beijing is the restored section of Wall at **Mutianyu**. It has good facilities, but fewer groups visit here, making it easier to escape the crowds. To see the wall at its most spectacular, **Simatai** is the place to go. A two-hour drive northeast from Beijing, this section has fewer visitors than either Badaling or Mutianyu, although numbers are rising. Parts of the Wall are so steep, and so narrow, that good climbing shoes and a little courage are required.

Jinshanling, which adjoins Simatai to the west, is a well-restored but relatively quiet section. The unrestored Wall at **Huanghuacheng**, meanwhile, midway between Badaling and Mutianyu, attracts many hikers.

The Wall meets the sea at **Shanhaiguan**, 200 km (125 miles) east of Beijing. This is where it begins (or ends – depending how you look at it), though a less well-built part runs further east to the Yalu River in Liaoning province.

Allow a full day for a visit to the Wall – or three to four days for a round-trip from Beijing to Shanhaiguan. For a quick look, you could combine a trip to Badaling, Mutianyu or Huanghuacheng with a visit to the Ming Tombs.

Rambling on the ramparts

To truly experience the splendour of the Wall, you need to hike on it. Of old, parts of the Wall were used as routes for porters and itinerant traders. In this age of leisure walking many enthusiasts hope it will become the world's ultimate long-distance footpath.

Since so much of the Great Wall near Beijing is unrestored, seeing wilder sections need not be an endurance test. You will walk mostly on the Wall, so it is difficult to get lost, but the going is often slow. Take care on steep, crumbling sections in remote areas. In some places, you may have no alternative but to leave and rejoin the Wall; in others, rickety piles of fallen bricks may be your only climbing aid. And thorny scrub not unlike the Mediterranean maquis blocks some flat sections.

The best way to organise your own hiking trip is to book a taxi. Depending on departure and return times, this will cost 300–600 yuan for a full day or for dropping off and picking up on different days.

You can visit the Wall in all seasons. It looks as spectacular flanked by summer greenery as by winter snow, or by autumn oranges, yellows and browns. Spring and autumn are best for hiking, however, as summer heat and dense vegetation make an excursion more of an ordeal and in mid-winter snow and ice make the steep slopes dangerous. In any season, solid and comfortable footwear is advised.

Simatai, Jinshanling and Huanghuacheng are three of the more popular stretches for walkers. Jinshanling has easier hiking but is more difficult to access. Huanghuacheng is less developed, and sees fewer tourists. The most popular place – and the most challenging, if you traverse the whole ridge – is Simatai.

It is also possible to walk from Gubeikou, the once heavily fortified pass west of Jinshanling, all the way to Simatai. If you are very fit, and used to scrambling, you can do the whole 25-km (15-mile) walk in one day, but it is best to split it into two days, camping in one of the

BELOW: the Simatai section of the Great Wall has not been restored.

many towers en route. Walking this route from west to east is a good idea because it avoids saving the long, difficult, unrestored section from Gubeikou to Jinshanling for the second day, and because transportation back to the city is easier to find at Simatai. You may be asked to buy a ticket as you leave the wall at Simatai.

Camping is not officially allowed but, while numbers remain small, it seems to be tolerated. The views from your beacon tower at dusk and dawn more than compensate for a night on the bricks. The more remote your campsite, the less likely you are to be disturbed. You will need a sleeping bag, mat, and plenty of water. If you do sleep on the wall, enjoy the privilege of spending a night in this unique environment: do not light fires, and take all your litter with you.

T-shirts and karaoke in Badaling

The Great Wall at Badaling can easily be reached by the fast new road from Beijing or, more slowly, by train from Beijing Station. To get here by road you need to travel 60 km (40 miles) northwest to **Juyongguan fortress**, which is built in a narrow, 20-km (13-mile) long valley north of Nankou Pass.

Juyong means "dwelling place for labourers," an ancient reference to the Qin dynasty, when the pass was a wall-building depot. In the middle of the valley is a stone platform of white marble, the Cloud Terrace (Yuntai). Built in 1345, it once served as the foundation for a great gate with three stone pagodas. After the fall of the Yuan dynasty, the pagoda gate was destroyed and replaced years later with a temple, which burned down in 1702. In the vaulted passage of the gate there are splendid reliefs, mostly Buddhist motifs, among them the four Tianwang (Celestial Kings), and inscriptions of Buddhist sutras in six different languages: Sanskrit, Tibetan, Tangut, Uighur, Mongol and Chinese. The fortress

BELOW: tourist dressed up as a Mongol warrior. **RIGHT:** the Wall at Badaling is illuminated during the summer, and on special occasions at other times of the year.

is 10 km (6 miles) south of Badaling Pass. Tours normally include a short stop here before continuing on to the Wall.

The most popular, best preserved and most comprehensively restored section of the Great Wall is at **Badaling** ❹ (open daily, 6.30am–sunset; entrance fee; cable car extra). This section of wall was strategically important and heavily fortified by the Ming emperors. The gate facing west bears the inscription "The Bolt of the Northern Gate", while the one facing east states, "The First Line before Juyongguan". The towers are solidly built, with high arrow slits. The way up on both sides of the valley leads to high beacon towers, from which you can see the northern plain and the Wall snaking across faraway hills. The western side is a steeper climb.

The only drawback of Badaling is that it can seem unbearably crowded and commercialised. Vendors of tacky souvenirs and T-shirts compete for sales, not only as you approach but also on the Wall itself. In the evening, karaoke sessions and laser shows are sometimes held. Only by a brisk walk of an hour or so can you escape from the tour groups.

Along the ridge at Mutianyu

The Wall at **Mutianyu** ❺ (open daily, 7am–sunset; entrance fee; cable car extra) is equally spectacular but less crowded than Badaling. A long section of restored Wall follows a high ridge giving views over wooded ravines 90 km (55 miles) northeast of Beijing. The nearest point on the Wall is a steep one-hour climb from the car park, though a cable car offers a breathtaking alternative.

Mutianyu was not part of the main wall but a barrier wall shielding passes to the north towards Zhangjiakou. High parapets, crenelated on both sides, are

Map on page 212

Photo opportunity at Badaling.

BELOW: sunset near Mutianyu.

part of the major Ming dynasty renovations completed in 1569. As at Badaling, large blocks of granite were used in the foundations because of the strategic importance of the area, which became known as the North Gate of the Capital.

A pavilion for admiring the view at Mutianyu.

Simatai and the stairway to heaven

Rapidly becoming a magnet for hikers, **Simatai ❻** (open daily, 8am–5pm; entrance fee; cable car extra) shows the unrestored Great Wall at its most majestic, crowning a narrow ridge and sharp pinnacles. To get there by public transport, take a bus from Beijing's Donzhimen bus station to Miyun, then continue by taxi to Simatai, 120 km (75 miles) from Beijing. The whole journey takes two to three hours.

You can either take the cable car to a point 20 to 30-minutes' walk below the wall, or make a longer excursion on foot. If you opt for the latter, from the car park, you will see a small reservoir between two steep sections of wall. Go through the entrance gate and take the path to the right (east) leading to the higher section of Wall. This is the most spectacular stretch. Alternatively, turn left (west) for a quieter, easier walk towards Jinshanling.

The scramble to Viewing the Capital Tower (Wangjing Lou) via the ridge demands a good head for heights but rewards you with some of the best views and most exciting walking anywhere on the Wall. In places, you walk on wall just two bricks (40 cm) wide, which locals call the *tianti,* or "stairway to heaven." Yet even on the most inaccesible sections you may find someone waiting to sell you a soft drink. On the lower reaches, inscriptions on bricks give details like "made by the infantry camp of suppressing enemy troops in the sixth year of the Wanli reign."

BELOW: hikers at Simatai in winter.

Jinshanling and Gubeikou

First built by the Northern Qi dynasty in 555 AD, **Jinshanling ❼** (open daily, 7am–sunset; entrance fee), like Simatai, was part of a 3,000 *li* wall from Shanhaiguan to northern Shaanxi province. Nearby Gubeikou was considered a weak point in the defence of the capital. It occupies a broad valley among low mountains cut by streams and rivers, allowing many possible routes to Beijing. Tribes of Mongol and other nomads repeatedly forced their way through here. In 1554, the same group raided Beijing three times via Gubeikou. Heavy fortification followed in the late 16th century, including unique "arrow walls" inside steep sections of the main Wall (*see page 245*).

In the late 17th century, when emperor Kangxi built his summer resort in Chengde, the pass, which lies on the route to Chengde, was more heavily guarded. The 158 fortified towers are particularly remarkable for their variety of shapes: rectangular, round, oval and polygonal. Most of the towers on the section east of Gubeikou have been restored, but this is usually the quietest of all the tourist stretches. It makes a good choice for an easier walk with views east towards the more dramatic Simatai.

The yellow flowers of Huanghuacheng

Once one of the main garrison areas guarding the capital, **Huanghuacheng ❽** (always open), or Yellow Flower Wall, is the closest Great Wall to Beijing. It has few tourist facilities, other than a couple of restaurants that serve barbecued fish. Climb up on either side from a small reservoir to the east of the road. The more spectacular section begins across the reservoir – and across the narrow dam. If you are scared of heights, you will have to take a detour to cross the

Map on page 212

BELOW: the steep slopes of the Western Hills.

Map on page 212

On holiday at Beidaihe.

BELOW: Shanhaiguan. **RIGHT:** Beidaihe is one of China's most popular seaside resorts.

stream below the dam, leaving a steeper climb up to the wall. Several large towers along the ridge offer great views on both sides. A stone tablet lies on the floor of the largest tower. Further on, the Wall resembles a saw blade as it drops steeply into the valley to your right (south). To complete a circular route, descend to the valley on a path leading down from the large tower, which is the lowest point on the ridge. Once at the bottom, head west through orchards of apples, walnuts and apricots, until you reach the road back to the reservoir.

Shanhaiguan and the dragon's head

Ancient walls still enclose about half of the small market town and former garrison of **Shanhaiguan ❾**, in Hebei province. The East Gate, rebuilt in 1639, is known as the First Pass Under Heaven. Manchu troops rode through here to Beijing to replace the deposed Ming emperors in 1644. The Ming general, Wu Sangui, who was in command of Shanhaiguan, collaborated with the Manchu and surrendered without a struggle.

As a counterpoint to all the enthusiasm for the Wall, it is worth recalling the legend of Meng Jiangnu, whose temple lies 6 km (4 miles) from Shanhaiguan. Meng's husband was one of the hundreds of thousands of labourers forced to build the first Great Wall. After hearing no news for many months, Meng set off to look for her husband. She wandered the country until she reached Shanhaiguan, where she discovered that, like so many others, he had fallen victim to the murderous work regime. She wept so bitterly that part of the Wall collapsed, exposing her husband's body. While in Shanhaiguan on a tour of inspection, Emperor Qin Shi Huangdi heard her story and took a liking to Meng. She succumbed to the emperor's wooing only after being granted a state funeral for her husband. But once the funeral was over she threw herself into the sea in sight of the emperor.

As the Great Wall rises steeply inland from Shanhaiguan, two sheer drops have to be climbed by ladder. From the top, you get a fantastic view of the Wall dropping below you and then bounding over the plain towards the sea. In the opposite direction is the Old Dragon's Head, where bricks and earth crumble into golden sand at the edge of the Bohai Sea.

Party goers

Shanhaiguan is a favourite photo spot for the hordes of day-trippers who arrive from nearby **Beidaihe ❿**, a beach resort long favoured for company conferences and official junkets. China's top leaders meet here annually to discuss important policy issues and to enjoy a welcome respite from Beijing's polluted air. When Jiang Zemin and his entourage are in town, they hide away at a private beach to the south of Beidaihe. Their conferences usually start in late July or early August, which is also the peak time for groups of lesser officials and army officers. On the crowded, sandy beaches, you can watch paddlers in Mao suits and PLA uniforms.

Cheap seafood restaurants line a small boardwalk area on the 10-km (6-mile) main beach. From hills behind the town, old brick villas overlook the sea. Party officials and organisations now use many of the 700 villas built around Beidaihe before 1949. ❏

BUILDING THE WALL, GUARDING THE EMPIRE

Civil engineers organised millions of conscript labourers to bring the greatest fortification in history to its peak during the 17th century, 2,000 years after the astonishing project began

The Ming dynasty Ten Thousand Li Great Wall averages 8 metres (26 ft) high and 7 metres (21 ft) wide. Some sections are broad enough to allow five or six soldiers to ride side by side. Surveyors planned the route so that, where possible, the outer (generally north-facing) wall was higher. Countless parallel walls, fortified towers, beacon towers, moats, fortifications and garrisons completed a complex system. Local military units supervised construction. In a simple contract, officers and engineers detailed the time, materials and work required.

HIDDEN SENTRIES

Many sections of the wall around Beijing were built on granite blocks, with some foundation stones weighing more than one ton.

Elaborate wooden scaffolding, hoists and pulleys, and occasionally iron girders aided the builders. To speed up the construction process, prefabricated stone parts were used for beacon towers, including lintels, gate blocks and gullies.

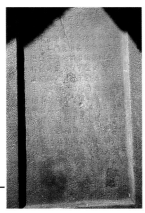

▷ **TAKING COMMAND**
Stone tablets, like this one at Huanghuacheng, were set into the wall to record what was built when and by whom, as well as listing command structures.

▷ **UNNATURAL BARRIER**
Surveyors often chose unlikely routes across near-vertical hillsides. Engineers coped by using stretches of "single" wall, bridges, viaducts, and incorporating natural features.

△ **COMMUNICATION LINE**
Towers in remote areas were built close enough to enable the beacon system devised in the Tang dynasty. Guards signalled the size of an enemy by lighting up to four torches.

△ **EARTH, RUBBLE, BONES**
Outer layers of brick and stone enclose an inner core of earth, rubble and, legends say, the bones of conscript labourers.

▷ **GIANT BRICKS**
Ming dynasty bricks were extremely heavy; pulleys, shoulder poles, handcarts, mules, and goats were used to move them.

LIFE ON THE EDGE: A GUARD'S STORY

△ DRY STONE WALL
Materials and construction techniques varied; in some areas, stone was quarried locally to build dry stone outer walls. Other sections used wood and compacted reeds.

▽ OVER THE TOP
In 1640 Manchu troops used ladders to scale the Great Wall near Jinzhou in the northeast. Other sections were destroyed with cannons. Four years later the Qing dynasty was founded.

▽ INNER DEFENCES
Arrow walls, which usually flank high towers, are a series of small walls built across the inside of the main wall to protect archers firing down onto the enemy.

▽ HOT WORK
Brick kilns were constructed as close to the wall as possible. To guarantee quality, brick makers recorded their names and the date of production on some bricks.

From their small rooftop sentry boxes, Great Wall guards, though they kept their weapons and torches primed, saw no enemies for months on end. If an assault came, the guards' main function was not to defend the wall but to alert the nearest garrison using a complex system of torch signals.

Most guards lived in remote watchtowers shared with five to ten others. During the day, those not on lookout tilled small patches of farmland on the hillside, collected firewood and dried cattle or wolf dung, and sometimes hunted. They carried out minor repairs to the wall and tower. They ground wheat flour and other food in stone mortars. To supplement food supplies brought by road, migration of farmers was encouraged or enforced, and guards helped them construct irrigation canals and farmhouses.

The guards' crowded living quarters also served as storage for grain and weapons. Doors and windows had heavy wooden shutters to keep out the winter cold, and often guards shared a *kang*, a heated brick bed.

CHENGDE: IMPERIAL RESORT

Once the summer playground of emperors, this lavish Qing dynasty retreat still offers perfect respite for anyone seeking to escape from the heat, dust, crowds and noise of the capital

Map on page 250

By the end of the 17th century the Qing emperors had established their capital at Beijing, and they began to look around for somewhere cool and green to retreat to when the dusty heat of summer set in. They found what they were looking for at Chengde, 250 km (150 miles) northeast of Beijing, beyond the Great Wall. Here they created a summer residence, exploiting mountains, woods and other existing natural features to which they added contrived landscapes to make settings for innumerable pavilions, palaces and temples.

Today, the idyllic landscapes of the **Imperial Resort** (open daily, 5.30am–6.30pm; entrance fee), bordering the northern edge of the town of Chengde, are open to the public. The name Chengde means "to inherit virtue" but the town used to be known as Jehol, which is derived from the name of the River Rehe (Warm River) which flows through it.

Probably the best way to get to the Imperial Resort from Beijing is by train. The journey takes four to five hours, so plan to stay for at least one night, two if you have time. Railway enthusiasts might also enjoy walking along the town's railway line, where steam trains still run.

PRECEDING PAGES: view of the Temple of Happiness, Chengde.
LEFT: the summer residence of the emperors.
BELOW: Emperor Qianlong.

The creation of the Imperial Resort

In 1703, Emperor Kangxi (1662–1722) ordered the building of a summer palace which was to be called Bishushanzhuang, or "Mountain Manor for Escaping the Heat". "Several times I have travelled to the shores of the Yangzi," he wrote, "and have seen the lush beauty of the south. Twice my way then led me on to Gansu and Shaanxi, and therefore I know the land in the west well. In the north I have crossed the Dragon Sands, and in the east I have wandered in the region of the White Mountains, where the peaks and the rivers are mighty, but the people and their lives have remained true to the simplicity of nature. I cannot count all the places I have seen, but I have chosen none of them, and here, in the valley of Rehe, is the only place in which I desire to live."

Chengde was chosen for its natural beauty and its agreeable mountain climate. The average mid-summer temperature here rarely exceeds 20°C (68°F).

Construction continued through most of the reign of Emperor Qianlong (1736–96), for a total of 87 years. The buildings and gardens that you can still see today cover an area of 560 hectares (1,400 acres), and are surrounded by a wall 10 km (6 miles) long. Chengde is the largest imperial residence in China that has survived in its original condition. Outside the palace walls, to the north and west, a total of 11 temples – mostly in the Tibetan style – were built. Seven of these can still be visited.

Chengde roof detail.

The road to Chengde

For nearly 150 years, beginning with Kangxi, the Qing emperors and their retinues moved to Chengde to pass the summer months. Apart from indulging in hunting excursions, equestrian games and other diversions, the emperors conducted state business from here, making Chengde the second political centre of the Qing dynasty after Beijing. Their presence here also helped nurture relationships with the people of the northern fringes of the empire.

Every summer the court would set off for Chengde. Before it did so, a flurry of building activity took place. Roads were improved, and 18 smaller palaces placed along the route from Beijing were prepared to serve as rest stations. But an accident in 1820 caused the abrupt decline of the Imperial Resort. In that year a bolt of lightning killed Emperor Jiaqing, who was in residence at Chengde. Fearing that fate might deal them a second blow, the court stayed away through the following decades and the buildings and gardens fell into ruin.

Xianfeng was the only emperor ever to stay at Chengde again. And he only did so when forced to flee Beijing during the Second Opium War in 1860. It was at the Imperial Resort that he was obliged to sign the Treaty of Peking, which granted far-reaching concessions to foreigners. A year later Xianfeng died.

Rooms with a view

BELOW:
Emperor Kangxi.

The **Bishushanzhuang palaces** (open daily, 8am–5pm; entrance fee) are in the south of the Imperial Resort. They consist of three great complexes reached by passing through the **Lizhengmen Gate ❶**, which has a tablet bearing inscriptions in Chinese, Mongol, Manchu, Tibetan and Uighur. The **Inner Gate** (Neiwumen) bears an inscription in Emperor Kangxi's hand, naming the resort.

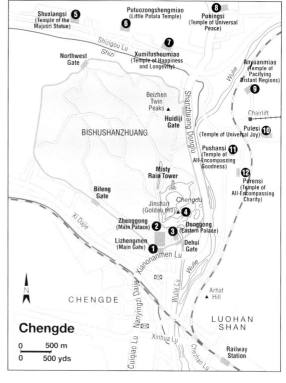

Shuxiangsi ❺ (Temple of the Majusri Statue)

Putuozongshengmiao ❻ (Little Potala Temple)

Puningsi ❽ (Temple of Universal Peace)

❼

Northwest Gate

Shizigou Lu Shizi

Xumifushoumiao (Temple of Happiness and Longevity)

Anyuanmiao (Temple of Pacifying Distant Regions) ❾

Beizhen Twin Peaks ▲

Huidiji Gate

Chairlift

BISHUSHANZHUANG

Shanzhuang Donglu

Pulesi ❿ (Temple of Universal Joy)

Pushansi ⓫ (Temple of All-Encompassing Goodness)

Misty Rain Tower

Purensi ⓬ (Temple of All-Encompassing Charity)

Bifeng Gate

Jinshan (Golden Hill) ▲

Chengdu

Zhenggong (Main Palace) ❷

Donggong (Eastern Palace) ❸

Xi Dajie

Lizhengmen (Main Gate) ❶

Dehui Gate

Xianonanmen Lu

Nanyingzi Dajie

Wulie Lu

Wulie Lu

Arhat ▲ Hill

CHENGDE

LUOHAN SHAN

Chengde

0   500 m
0   500 yds

Cuiqiao Lu

Xinhua Lu

Chezhan Lu

Railway Station

As in the Imperial Palace in Beijing, the first halls entered are those in which state business was conducted and ceremonies were held, with the private imperial apartments occupying the rear of the palace. The main hall of the **Main Palace** (Zhenggong) ❷ is built of precious nanmu hardwood from southwest China, and is therefore sometimes called the **Nanmu Hall**. This was the hall in which, in 1860, Emperor Xianfeng reluctantly signed the treaty dictated by the British and the French.

The **Hall of Pines and Cranes** (Songhezhai), to the east of the Main Palace, was the private residence of the emperor's mother. Beyond this is the **Hall of Ten Thousand Pine Valleys in the Wind** (Wanhesongfeng), from which you get a view of the magnificent scenery of the northern grounds. Here, the 12-year-old Qianlong was instructed by his grandfather, Kangxi, in the proper form of answering petitions, and in classical literature. In memory of Kangxi, he later named the hall, the **Hall for Remembering Kindness** (Ji'entang).

The **Eastern Palace** (Donggong) ❸ lies in the southeast corner of the resort – what little remains of it. In 1948 the last part standing, a three-storey theatre, completely burned down.

Gardens of China

The park adjoining the palaces to the north can be divided into three areas. Directly bordering the palaces to the north is the lake area; to the northwest is a plain; and to the west is a forested, hilly landscape with ravines and valleys.

About 55 hectares (135 acres) of the park area are covered with water. The **Lake of Pure Water** (Chengdu Lake) is divided by a number of dams into eight smaller lakes. Everywhere are little pavilions, tea houses and resting

Map on page 250

BELOW: overview of the Chengde complex, with Putuozongsheng in the background.

places, very reminiscent of the southern Chinese lakes, such as the area around the West Lake near Hangzhou. The lake is fed from the **Warm Spring** (Requan), so it does not even freeze in the frigid north Chinese winter. Smaller lakes and pools have clever features. One, for instance, offers a daytime reflection of the crescent moon – an effect created by rocks carefully placed above the water.

The artificial **Golden Hill** (Jinshan) ❹ acts as a belvedere. The hilltop Jinshan Pavilion is a replica of the Jinshan Tower in Jiangsu Province. Here, the Qing emperors made offerings to Daoist gods such as the Jade Emperor.

Further north lies a broad plain, which Emperor Qianlong named the **Park of Ten Thousand Trees** (Wanshuyuan). Pines, acacias, willows and old cypresses grow in abundance here, and Qianlong delighted in the many birds and in the plentiful red deer . The court met in Mongol yurts, feasting and watching or wrestling bouts, or enjoying displays of horse-riding or folk arts . To the west of the gardens was a great riding arena where the emperors chose their horses and had them broken in and trained for equestrian performances.

In the southwest of the plain stands one of the seven famous libraries of the Qing dynasty period, the **Siku Quanshu** (Collected Writings of the Four Categories of Literature). From 1772 to 1782, a team of 360 scholars collected all the available works and manuscripts that they could. They are said to have amassed more than 80,000 volumes, which were then copied by 15,000 scribes. This collection, containing the most valuable of old Chinese works, has been housed in the National Library (*see page 189*) since 1915.

In the northwest of the summer resort, the hilly and forested landscape forms a dramatic backdrop to the lakes. It is crossed by five deep valleys: Pine Cloud Valley (Songyunxia), Pear Tree Valley (Lishiyu), Pine Forest Valley

BELOW: dragon figure on a bell.

(Song'linyu), the Hazel Valley (Zhenziyu), and West Valley (Xiyu). The hills rise above the plain to 180 metres (590 ft) and were originally dotted with many little pavilions and halls. Of the four pavilions that stood on the summits, only the **Snowscape at Southern Hill Pavilion** (Nanshanjiuxe) remains. Some 44 gardens were laid out here during the reigns of Kangxi and Qianlong. A pavilion cast from 200 tonnes of copper once stood in the Zhuyuan temple grounds, but this was demolished and removed by the Japanese towards the end of World War II. A copper tablet and two copper plaques in the museum housed in the Main Palace are reminders of the magnificent temple grounds.

Map on page 250

Homage to Tibet

Many of the temples at Chengde were built in Tibetan style. This reveals much of the Qinq dynasty's route to power and the emperors' aspirations. For the Manchu, the path to victory had lain through the steppes. The first important victory was won when the Mongols from the eastern part of the Gobi desert allied themselves with the Manchu. However, this expansion also upset many nomadic peoples of the western steppes and in Central Asia. Conflict was brewing, made more extreme by religious differences. The Qing rulers had accepted Chinese culture even before their conquest of China, and had surrounded themselves with Confucian Chinese advisers. But the peoples of the steppe were mostly followers of Tibetan Buddhism, sometimes called Lamaism by the Chinese.

When the Mongols first conquered Tibet in the 13th century, they converted to Tibetan Buddhism in return for Tibetan acceptance of Mongol dominion. During the subsequent centuries, Tibetan Buddhism spread among nearly all the peoples of the eastern steppe, though Islam retained its influence further west.

BELOW: Xumitushou Temple is based on Tashilhunpo monastery, at Shigatse in Tibet.

The Sakyamuni Buddha is important in both Chinese and Tibetan Buddhism.

The Qing rulers may have believed they could emulate the Mongols, gaining control over Tibetan and Mongol territory by adopting the faith of the people. They declared themselves to be protectors of the Gelugpa school, the most influential in Tibetan Buddhism, and this action brought great political advantages. Under the emperors Kangxi and Qianlong diplomatic ties between China and Tibet were closer than they had ever been.

In 1651 the fifth Dalai Lama visited Beijing at the invitation of Qing emperor. The White Dagoba in Beihai Park in Beijing was built in his honour. As a consequence, many Buddhist writings were translated and printed in Beijing. Ties with Tibet were strengthened by these signs of favour bestowed by the Chinese emperors; after an army of Dsungars was driven out of Tibet in 1751, the country finally came under the control of Beijing. These same Dsungars were defeated again in the northwest, which was conquered in 1759 and renamed Xinjiang (the New Territories). The Chinese empire then covered about 11.5 million sq km (4½ million sq miles), an area that it would never match again.

The Eight Outer Temples

The Tibetan temples in Chengde were another sign of the favour shown to the Tibetan religion by the Qing emperors. Eleven such temples were built on the hills northwest of the Imperial Resort during the reigns of Kangxi and Qianlong. Divided into eight groups, they became known as the Eight Outer Temples. The main gates of these buildings pointed towards the palace, symbolising the unity of China's various ethnic groups under the central rule of the Qing emperors.

Seven temples remain, with halls modelled on famous Tibetan Buddhist buildings. In a kind of giant ancient Buddhist theme park, you can see replicas of the

Potala Palace in Lhasa; the Tashilhunpo and Samye monasteries elsewhere in Tibet; the Gu'erzha temple in Xinjiang; the Shuxiang temple in the Wutaishan Mountains of Shanxi province; and the Anguo temple in Zhejiang province.

In Qing times these were also living temples, not just copies of famous buildings. Today several temples again have small communities of monks living in them, allowed back in the 1980s after the religious repression of the Cultural Revolution had ceased. All temples are open daily from 8am to 5pm.

In the extreme northeast is **Temple of the Majusri Statue** (Shuxiangsi) **❺**, dating from 1774. A replica of the Shuxiang temple in the Wutaishan Mountains, it holds a Manchu translation of the Buddhist scriptures, the *Kanjur*.

Further west, due north of the Imperial Resort, is the **Putuozongsheng Temple ❻**, which bears the name of Putuo Shan, a sacred Buddhist mountain on an island in the East China Sea. It is modelled, however, on the Potala Palace, which was the residence of the Dalai Lama in Tibet until 1959; hence it is also known as the "Little Potala". Building started in 1767, and the temple was completed four years later. It served as a residence for high Tibetan dignitaries when they stayed at the Chinese imperial court.

Behind the entrance gate is a stele pavilion with three stone pillars bearing inscriptions that tell of the inclusion of many different peoples into the Qing empire. Beyond this pass the Indo-Tibetan-style Five Pagoda Gate and a Chinese-style gate of honour with glazed tiles to reach the "Little Potala" itself. It consists of a 17-metre (56-ft) high white fundament upon which the Red Palace is built. From the outside this palace appears to have seven floors, but actually it only has three. Above the Red Palace is a hall, Wanfaguiyidian. This contains many Bodhisattva figures.

Map on page 250

BELOW: Tibetan architectural styles at Puningsi.

Map on page 250

Detail from Putuo-zongsheng Temple.

BELOW:
the Mahayana
Hall at Puningsi.
RIGHT:
fur offers protection
from the harsh
northern winters.

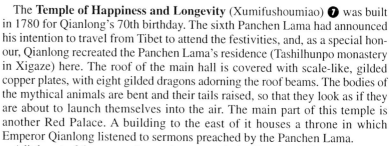

The **Temple of Happiness and Longevity** (Xumifushoumiao) ❼ was built in 1780 for Qianlong's 70th birthday. The sixth Panchen Lama had announced his intention to travel from Tibet to attend the festivities, and, as a special honour, Qianlong recreated the Panchen Lama's residence (Tashilhunpo monastery in Xigaze) here. The roof of the main hall is covered with scale-like, gilded copper plates, with eight gilded dragons adorning the roof beams. The bodies of the mythical animals are bent and their tails raised, so that they look as if they are about to launch themselves into the air. The main part of this temple is another Red Palace. A building to the east of it houses a throne in which Emperor Qianlong listened to sermons preached by the Panchen Lama.

A little out of the way to the northwest stands the **Temple of Universal Peace** (Puningsi) ❽, built in 1755. The model for the rear buildings of the temple was the Samye monastery in Tibet. The buildings in front of this are Chinese style. The Mahavira Hall, the main building to the front of the temple, houses three Buddha statues and 18 Luohan (Arhat) figures. The Mahayana Pavilion symbolises Meru Mountain (Kang Rinpoche, or Mount Kailash, in Tibet), the cosmic centre of the Buddhist world. The 37-metre (120-ft) high pavilion is China's tallest wooden pavilion. It is flanked by a Moon Hall and a Sun Hall, and surrounded by Tibetan stupas. Inside is a carved wooden statue of the Bodhisattva Avalokiteshvara, 22 metres (73 ft) tall, measuring 15 metres (49 ft) across, and weighing more than 120 tons. This statue is known as the Thousand Arm, Thousand Eye Guanyin Buddha, an incarnation of the Goddess of Mercy. Her 42 arms, each with an eye on the palm, symbolise her inexhaustible power of salvation. A statue of the Buddha Amitabha sits on the head of the goddess.

To the south of the Temple of Universal Peace is the **Temple of Pacifying Distant Regions** (Anyuanmiao) ❾, built in 1764 as a replica of the Gu'erzha temple in Ili, in Xinjiang. Only the Pududian (Hall of Universal Conversion) survives, with its statue of the Bodhisattva Ksitigarbha, the King of Hell, whom the Chinese know as Ludumu.

Further south lies the **Temple of Universal Joy** (Pulesi) ❿, built in 1766 in honour of Kazhak, Kirghiz and other nobles from northwest China. The building is similar in style to the main hall of Beijing's Temple of Heaven. Beyond the entrance gate, bell and drum towers stand on either side. The main building, Pavilion of Morning Light (Xuguangge), or Round Pavilion, rests on a square terrace, the combination symbolising Heaven and Earth according to ancient Chinese cosmology. The Temple of Universal Joy also contains bronze images of Tibetan deities conquering their enemies and in erotic embrace – fine examples of the simultaneously gorgeous and terrifying imagery of Tibetan Buddhism. Behind the temple you can hike or take a cable car to the bizarre eroded rock of Club Peak.

Adjoining the grounds of the Temple of Universal Joy to the south is the **Temple of All-Encompassing Goodness** (Pushansi) ⓫, which has fallen into ruin. And next to this, again to the south, is the **Temple of All-Encompassing Charity** (Purensi) ⓬. The southernmost of the Eight Outer Temples, it was built in 1713 to celebrate Emperor Kangxi's 60th birthday. ❑

TIANJIN

China's fourth-largest city is an historic port with an old town centre containing a wealth of 19th-century Western architecture and a renowned antiques market

Map on page 260

Only an hour and forty minutes by train from Beijing, Tianjin (literally, "the point where the Son of Heaven once forded the river") lives in the shadow cast by its big neighbour to the north. The city grew up as a trading post. It is the closest port to Beijing and in imperial times it also thrived on the vast amounts of tribute rice that wended its way north along the Grand Canal. The city became a pawn in the 19th-century trading disputes and wars between the imperial authorities and those European states – particularly the British – who wanted to "open up" China. Attempting to keep the foreigners at bay, while permitting limited and regulated trade, the Chinese allowed Tianjin to become part of the "Canton System" – a scattering of cities in which foreigners could live and trade.

Under this system the British were particularly successful. They profited mostly through the large trade in opium, which they brought in from their colonies in Southeast Asia, exporting Chinese tea in return. They were eventually able to use this lucrative trade as a wedge to force the Chinese to open more cities to trade. Once the Chinese government realised the size of the opium trade, and its detrimental effect on the population, they attempted to ban it. Thus began the First Opium War, which ended in 1842 with the Treaty of Nanjing, and the opening of more cities to foreign trade – most famously Hong Kong.

A further trade dispute blew up in 1858, as the Chinese attempted to regulate the sale of opium. This led to the Second Opium War, which was settled by the Treaty of Tianjin. China was forced to open Tianjin and other Chinese ports to foreign trade. Tianjin became another "concession" in which foreigners could live and work.

Haunts of the last emperor

Though the foreigners were eventually sent packing by the Communist government in 1950, Western buildings still dot the cityscape of Tianjin, testament to the period of foreign influence that many Chinese would prefer to forget.

Yet during its time as a "treaty port", as the coastal cities of the Canton system were known, Tianjin was far more cosmopolitan than Beijing. Not every Chinese person despised the presence of the Westerner. Many built themselves Western-style villas in and around the city. Pu Yi, the last emperor, lived in the Japanese concession from 1925 to 1931, fleeing the republican government who had thrown him out of the Forbidden City. **Zhang Garden**, the villa he lived in with his empress, Wan Rong, and his concubine, Wen Xiu, still stands. The house was named after the first owner, Zhang Biao, who built it in 1916.

LEFT: Xikai Cathedral is dwarfed by a modern tower block.
BELOW: market outside the Confucius Temple.

The Astor Hotel remains a Tianjin landmark.

Pu Yi was known to frequent another Tianjin landmark, the late 19th-century **Astor Hotel** (Lishunde Fandian) ❶, where he enjoyed many pleasant evenings in the ballroom. Due to unfortunate renovations in 1984, the hotel does not retain much of its old world charm, but it has an interesting array of historical photographs, including one of the future president of the United States, Herbert Hoover, and his wife Lou Henry Hoover. The couple were married here in 1899, when Hoover was working as an engineer in the city.

Downtown sights

Down Tai'an Dao, and then to the south on Zhejiang Lu, is another Tianjin institution, **Kiessling's Bakery** ❷, set up by an Austrian in 1911 to supply bread to foreigners living in the concession. This is in the same building as the Qishilin hotel. There is another Kiessling's in Beidaihe (*see page 242*).

Following Qufu Dao into Nanjing Lu toward the Friendship Hotel, there is the **Monument to the Tangshan earthquake** ❸, which struck on 28 July 1976,

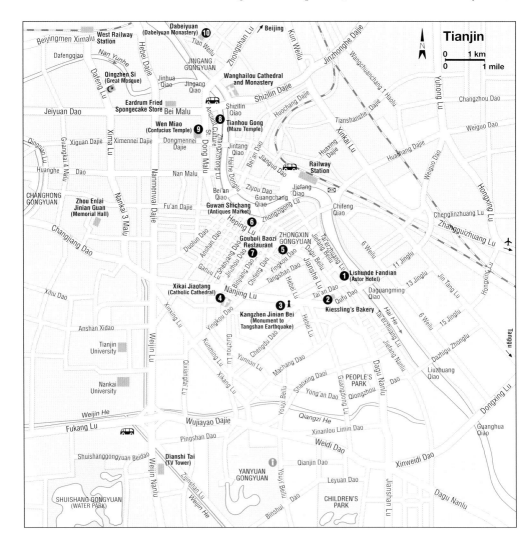

Map on page 260

just a few weeks before Mao's death. The epicentre was at Tangshan, 80 km (50 miles) to the northeast, but surrounding areas, including Tianjin and Beijing, felt the effects and suffered many collapsed buildings. An estimated 242,000 people died, although this figure went unreported by the government at the time.

Further west along on Nanjing Lu, close to the junction with the large shopping street of Binjiang Dao, is another relic of concession days, the **Xikai Cathedral ❹**, which was built by French Catholics in 1916. Today it has an active congregation of Catholics who have renounced any allegiance to the Pope in Rome – the government will not allow Catholics to worship if they recognise the Pope. On the Feast of the Immaculate Conception (December 8) the faithful come in droves to pay their respects to the Virgin Mary.

Another area evocative of concession days is **Zhongxin Park** (Zhongxin Gongyuan) **❺**, near the intersection of Heping Lu and Chifeng Dao. Within this attractive circular park surrounded as it is by old colonial-style buildings, it is easy to feel as if you are in Europe rather than China.

From the park it is just a short walk to the northwest to Shenyang Dao. On the section of this street closest to the river there is a well-known **antiques market** (Guwan Shichang) **❻**. If local lore is to be believed, the true antiques for sale here were confiscated from wealthy families during the Cultural Revolution, and stored in Tianjin. The government is now selling off these treasures to local merchants, who in turn sell them to tourists. Stickers occasionally appear on the merchandise, supposedly indicating from whom the piece was taken, as well as the time and place of the appropriation. The market is also a good place to buy old books and stamps as well as Cultural Revolution memorabilia. Opening hours are approximately 7am to 3pm.

BELOW: the decidedly un-Chinese Zhongxin Park.

Canine attitudes

Southwest of the antiques market, on Shandong Lu, is the **Goubuli Baozi Restaurant ❼**, famed throughout the region for its steamed bread dumplings. Literally translated, the name means "Even Dogs Will Ignore". It is said that this was the nickname of the original owner, who had either been down on his luck and therefore "ignored", or so ugly that "even dogs will ignore" him. Despite the name – or perhaps because of it – the restaurant flourished, and is still booming a century after opening. Former US President George Bush liked to frequent the restaurant when he was the US Ambassador to China.

Marine goddess

Further north, where Zhangzizhong Lu meets Dongmennei Dajie, is the **Ancient Culture Street** (Guwenhua Jie). Built to look like an old Chinese city, it is now filled with merchants hawking familiar Chinese souvenirs. On some public holidays, Chinese opera performances take place here. In the middle of the street is the **Mazu Temple ❽** (Tianhou; open daily, 8am–4pm; entrance fee), dedicated to the Goddess of the Sea. It was originally built in 1326 during the Yuan dynasty and is supposedly the oldest extant building complex in Tianjin.

Worshipped by seafaring people throughout China, the goddess is known as Matsu in Taiwan and Tin Hau in Hong Kong. Mazu's main temple is located on the Taiwanese island of Meizhou, where temple fairs are held every year. Tianjin, as the largest port city in northern China, had the largest Mazu temple in the area, and would hold an annual temple fair in her honour. The Emperor Qianlong once visited this fair, celebrated on Mazu's birthday, the 23rd day of the 3rd lunar month. The tradition lapsed for a time, but has been revived in recent years.

BELOW: Ancient Culture Street. **RIGHT:** burning incense at the Mazu Temple

Other sights

At the corner of Dongmennei and Dong Malu is the **Confucian Temple** ❾
(Wen Miao; open daily, 8.30am–5pm; entrance fee), dating from 1463, and renovated in 1993. Located in what is known as the old Chinese quarter, the temple is now surrounded by high rise malls and modern apartment buildings.
Though the strains of pop music tend to filter in from the large mall across the
street, the temple is still quiet and peaceful. No temple would be complete without a *cha guan* (tea room). You can stop in here and sip tea while listening to
Peking opera on Sunday afternoons.

Further north, across the river on Shizilin Dajie is **Wanghailou Cathedral**,
a Gothic-style Catholic church and monastery built in 1869, which is currently
occupied by 22 initiates. Still further north is the **Dabeiyuan Monastery** (open
daily, 9am–4pm; entrance fee) ❿, originally built in 1669 during the reign of
Emperor Shunzhi in the early Qing dyansty. It managed to survive the Cultural
Revolution intact, and was renovated in 1980. It houses 100.

The Hai River runs right through the middle of Tianjin, and in the city
centre there is a strip of parkland on both sides it. It is possible to take a
cruise on the river from the pier close to the Astor Hotel. The irresistibly-
named **Eardrum Fried Sponge Cake Store** is a short distance to the southwest, on the north side of Bei Malu. It takes its odd name from a nearby
hutong and not its speciality, which are innocuous cakes of rice powder,
sugar and bean paste fried in sesame oil.

Tianjin is noted for its carpet manufacture. Eight large factories produce the
carpets, although many of them are still made, at least partially, by hand. Visitors
can visit some of the factories to observe the process and buy a rug or two. ❑

*Cycling past Wang-
hailou Cathedral.*

BELOW:
chops for sale.
FOLLOWING PAGE:
detail from the
Imperial Palace.

INSIGHT GUIDES
Travel Tips

New Insight Maps

Maps in Insight Guides are tailored to complement the text. But when you're on the road you sometimes need the big picture that only a large-scale map can provide. This new range of durable Insight Fleximaps has been designed to meet just that need.

Detailed, clear cartography
makes the comprehensive route and city maps easy to follow, highlights all the major tourist sites and provides valuable motoring information plus a full index.

Informative and easy to use
with additional text and photographs covering a destination's top 10 essential sites, plus useful addresses, facts about the destination and handy tips on getting around.

Laminated finish
allows you to mark your route on the map using a non-permanent marker pen, and wipe it off. It makes the maps more durable and easier to fold than traditional maps.

The first titles
cover many popular destinations. They include Algarve, Amsterdam, Bangkok, California, Cyprus, Dominican Republic, Florence, Hong Kong, Ireland, London, Mallorca, Paris, Prague, Rome, San Francisco, Sydney, Thailand, Tuscany, USA Southwest, Venice, and Vienna.

☆ INSIGHT GUIDES
The world's largest collection of visual travel guides

CONTENTS

Getting Acquainted

The Place

Area: Beijing covers an area of 16,807 sq km (10,443 sq miles). The city is divided into 10 districts: Dongcheng, Xicheng, Xianwu and Chongwen in the city centre, surrounded by Chaoyang, Fengtai, Haidian, Shijingshan, Mentougou and Yanshan. In addition, there are nine areas outside the city: Daxing, Tongxian, Shunyi, Changping, Pinggu, Fangshan, Miyun, Huairou and Yanqing.

Geography: Beijing lies on the northern edge of the North Chinese plain at approximately the same latitude as Ankara, Madrid and New York: 39° 56' north; longitude 116° 20' east. The city centre is 44 metres (143 ft) above sea level. The land is hilly to the north and northwest, and opens out into a wide, level plain to the southeast. About 60 percent of the area of Beijing is hilly, but the city centre is flat. The Western Mountains (1,000–1,500 metres; 3,300–4,900 feet) lie to the northwest, with the Jundu Range (highest peak 2,000 metres or 6,560 feet) to the north. Two fairly large rivers flow north to south: the Yongding to the west of the city, and the Chaobai to the east.

Population: 11.7 million. This figure does not include an estimated 2–3 million migrant workers.

Language: Beijingers, in common with most of their countrymen, speak "Mandarin" Chinese, known as *putonghua*. English is spoken in many of the leading hotels, restaurants and shops. Street signs are usually written in both Chinese characters and *pinyin*, the standard system for writing Chinese in the Roman alphabet.

Religion: Since 1949, mainly atheist, with Buddhist, Daoist, Muslim and Christian minorities.

Time zone: Beijing time, which applies across China, is eight hours ahead of Greenwich Mean Time.

Currency: Renminbi; one *yuan* (known as *kuai*) equals ten *jiao* (also known as *mao*).

Weights and measures: China uses a mixture of metric and more traditional weights and measures. Distances are usually in kilometres, while weights are in *jin* (one *jin* is about half a kilo).

Electricity: 220 volts.

International dialling code: 86 (China) followed by 10 (Beijing).

Climate

The ideal time for travelling to Beijing is late spring (May to mid-June) and autumn (late August to mid-October).

The city has a continental climate, with four clearly defined seasons. Winter is cold and dry with little snow, and it is usually sunny. Sharp winds blow frequently from the northern steppes and desert regions to the west. Spring, which begins in April, is the shortest season: warm, dry and often windy. In early spring, sand storms blow in from Central Asia. These cease by mid-May at the latest. The average temperature then climbs quickly.

Summer begins around mid-June and reaches its peak in July and August. Both temperature and rainfall are highest in these two months. It is often muggy; temperatures climb to over 30°C and occasionally 35°C or more. About 75 percent of the annual rainfall occurs in June, July and August, when afternoon thunderstorms are common.

In autumn the sky is blue most of the time, and the air is cleaner (a noticeable cloud of smog hangs over the city much of the year). It is usually warm during the day and pleasantly cool in the evening. Early September to early November is considered the best season for touring. However, Beijing is crowded with tourists during these months, and hotels are sometimes fully booked.

Economy

Many people say Beijing lacks the economic vibrancy of its great rival, Shanghai. Yet the city's countless small shops, stalls and restaurants bear testimony to the growth of private enterprise since economic reform began in 1978. The city has a Chinese version of Silicon Valley at Zhongguancun, and is home to many of the big names of the Chinese computer, fashion, music and service industries. Hundreds of large Chinese, foreign and joint-venture companies, including most of the leading multinationals, have their China head offices here.

Government

Beijing has been a key city in northern China for more than 1,000 years. When it became the capital of the Mongol empire in the 13th century, the Mongols introduced a system of orthodox Confucian governance that remained in place, in various forms, until the early 19th century. Today, Beijing has a municipal government as well as local government congresses for each district. Members are elected by local Communist Party organisations. As with all levels of government in China, the party controls urban planning and management of all public affairs in the capital.

Etiquette

A short handshake is usual when being introduced to someone in China. Chinese people quite happily talk about such things as age, weight and other personal matters. This is not considered rude, and direct questions about the family or income are part of a normal conversation after quite a short acquaintance. Politics is best avoided between strangers. You will probably only make close friends after a longer stay.

In private company, and on tourist trips, it is not necessary to dress formally, though people on business trips should wear formal clothes for receptions and meetings. You don't need to wear an evening dress to go to the theatre or the Beijing opera. For Chinese men, smoking and drinking alcohol normally form an integral part of a business dinner. Women do not usually smoke or drink, though some younger urban women adopt both habits.

Keeping Your Cool

You need a lot of patience in China. If something doesn't happen as you imagined, stay calm and remain polite. Complaining, shouting and loud criticism often results in loss of face, and a deterioration of the situation. This doesn't mean you shouldn't openly and honestly state your view or criticise. As everywhere, it's the way it's done that counts.

Chinese people are usually polite to foreigners, but it is one of the numerous myths about the Chinese that politeness is deeply rooted in society. Once you've witnessed the rush hour on public buses, you will know how ruthless Chinese people can be. Well aware of this fact, the municipal government regularly exhorts Beijingers to become *wenming shimin* (civilised citizens). This means no spitting or swearing, being courteous towards visitors, and most of all obeying the law, especially traffic rules.

Loss of face is generally more serious in Chinese than Western culture. Taxi drivers shout and curse each other, but that's usually as far as it goes. Apparently shaking with rage one minute, the next minute they will calmly get back into their cars and drive off.

If you really encounter trouble, it may be best to try to explain this privately to the person concerned. In restaurants and hotels, service is sometimes poor or the food indifferent: feel free to give your opinion and, if necessary, ask to see the manager. If you are travelling in a group, you can always talk to the group leader.

Planning the Trip

Visas and Passports

A tourist visa is necessary for entering China. This can be applied for at the various embassies of the People's Republic of China. If you need to extend your visa in China, contact the Public Security Bureau, Visa Section, Andingmen Dongdajie (near the Lama Temple), Tel: 8401-5292.

On entry, a health declaration, entry card and customs declaration have to be completed. These forms are given out on the plane or at the airport.

Health

No vaccinations are required for China. It may be advisable to strengthen the body's resistance to hepatitis A infection by having a gammaglobulin injection before travelling. Malaria prevention, recommended by the World Health Organisation for some areas of southern China, is not necessary for Beijing.

Anyone planning to spend more than one year in China needs a health examination, which includes an Aids test. Travellers suffering from Aids, tuberculosis and other serious illnesses are not normally allowed to enter China.

Toilets: All hotels have good or acceptable Western-style toilets. Public toilets are normally the low, squatting kind, with little privacy. Older ones sometimes sit above infrequently flushed, open pits.

Money

The Chinese currency is called renminbi (RMB; literally, "people's

Customs

Be aware of customs regulations when entering or leaving China as some unexpected items may be on the restricted list.

A duplicate of the customs declaration which you received on arrival should be shown on departure. Expensive jewellery, equipment and the amount of foreign exchange should all be declared, and all imported items must be taken out again. Items that are imported and not taken out of the country again are subject to customs payments.

Many books, newspaper reports, magazines and videos that are legal in the West may be deemed illegal in China, especially political or pornographic works.

Export restrictions apply to antiques. Antiques that can be exported carry a special customs sticker, which normally has a Temple of Heaven symbol. It is advisable to keep receipts for items bought, in case of spot checks.

money"). The basic unit is the *yuan*, often called *kuai*. One *yuan* is worth 10 *jiao*, also called *mao*. Bank notes come in 100, 50, 10, 5, 2 and 1 *yuan* denominations; plus 5, 2 and 1 *jiao*. There are also 1 *yuan*, 5 *jiao*, 1 *jiao*, and 5, 2 and 1 *fen* (one-tenth of a *jiao*) coins.

Foreign currency and travellers' cheques can be changed in most hotels, and at branches of the Bank of China. Money exchange booths are also found in areas frequented by foreign shoppers. For credit card cash advances, there are automatic cash machines scattered throughout the city. The handiest for most people is inside the Friendship Store on Jianguomenwai. Banks will also issue cash advances, but charge a four percent commission. Major credit cards can be used in most large hotels, shops and restaurants.

When you change money, you get a receipt that allows you to change renminbi back to foreign currency within six months, but you can only change back up to 50 percent of the original sum.

Illegal money changers roam the streets offering a better rate than the banks, but beware: as with dealing on street corners anywhere, the chance of getting ripped off is high. If you must change money on the street, use people in stalls, as they have to be there the next day.

If you have problems changing money or getting a cash advance, the main branch of the Bank of China is at 410 Fuchengmen Dajie (at the Second Ring Road), Tel: 6601-6688. Or try the branches inside the China World Trade Centre, or at 8 Yabao Lu (Asia-Pacific Building).

What to Bring

There is a limit of 20kg for baggage on most international and domestic flights. It is advisable to take strong suitcases or other lockable bags.

The following items could be useful to take, depending on the type of accommodation you have planned: an adaptor, light raincoat, disinfectants, mosquito repellent (summer), medicine for digestive problems and colds, films and batteries; plus any prescription medicines you need. All of these items can be found in Beijing's upmarket hotels and shops, but it is usually more convenient to take them with you.

Photography

You can take photos of basically everything in Beijing, other than military installations. Inside some museums and temples, a fee has to be paid for taking photographs. Sometimes photography is prohibited to protect exhibits from flash damage, or to encourage sales of postcards and books. It is always polite to ask before taking pictures of individual people. Good slide and print film can be bought in larger hotels. Professional film is more expensive than in the West,

and can only be bought from specialist shops. AA and AAA size batteries are widely available.

Getting There

BY AIR

All visitors need a Chinese visa before embarking on a flight. Airports: the Capital Airport, Tel: 6456-3604, is about 30 km (18 miles) from the city centre. The journey takes about 30 to 40 minutes by taxi, but allow one hour

Public Holidays

The following are official non-working days in China:
1 January
Jan/February: Chinese New Year (4 days; exact date varies according to lunar calendar)
8 March: International Women's Day
1 May: International Workers' Day
1 October: National Day (2 days)

Information on China

You can obtain information about China from tour operators; of course, it is best to approach the ones specialising in China. While you can get tour brochures in travel agencies, you won't get much information about China. In the UK, you can approach the China National Tourist Office, 4 Glentworth Street, London NW1, Tel: (020) 7935-9787, Fax: (020) 7487-5842. In Australia: 19th Floor, 44 Market Street, Sydney, N.S.W. 2000, Tel: (02) 299-4057, Fax: (02) 290-1958. In the US, try China National Tourist Offices at 350 Fifth Avenue, Suite 6413 Empire State Building, New York, NY 10118, Tel: (212) 760-9700, Fax: (212) 760-8809; or 333 West Broadway, Suite 201, Glendale, CA92104, Tel: (818) 6545-7504, Fax: (818) 6545-7506, though you may not always get satisfactory and detailed answers. More information can be obtained from the Society for Anglo-Chinese

Understanding, 152 Camden High Street, London NW1, or from the National Committee for US-China Relations, 777 UN Plaza, New York NY 10017. In Hong Kong, try China International Travel Service, Rm 1213–15, Tower A, New Mandarin Plaza, 14 Science Museum Road, Tsimshatsui East, Tel: (852) 2732-5888, Fax: (852) 2721-7154.

China International Travel Service (CITS) has a website at *www.cits.com.cn*. Sites sponsored by Beijing Tourism Administration and other government bodies include: *www.bta.gov.cn*, *www.chinatour.com*, *www.beijingtour.net.cn* and *www.cbw.com*. Among several general China sites focusing on business, entertainment or news, but including some information for tourists, are: *ChinaSite.com*, *www.sinopolis.com.cn*, *china.muzi.net* and *www.chinaonline.com*.

or more at peak hours. Depending on the destination and category of taxi, the fare will be between 60 and 120 yuan. Beware of drivers who approach you before you reach the taxi rank; ensure the driver uses a meter, or make sure you agree a price before setting off.

Air China offers coach services from the airport to several stops in the city centre for 16 yuan. Destinations include the main Air China booking office on Chang'an Dajie, close to Xidan; the Lufthansa Centre; and the Beijing International Hotel, close to Beijing Railway Station. Taxis are available at all stops.

Most of the major hotels offer limousine pick-ups and free bus transfers.

Flight connections: Capital Airport has connections to more than 50 other cities in China. Most international flights use the newer Terminal 2, while domestic flights normally use Terminal 1. Hotels usually have flight booking services, and most major airlines have offices in Beijing. You must check in at least 30 minutes before departure for domestic flights – although delays are common on many domestic routes, and at least one hour before departure for an international flight. For shorter journeys within China, the train is generally more enjoyable.

Passengers leaving China by air must pay a 90 yuan airport tax; those taking domestic flights must pay 50 yuan. All international return flights departing from Beijing must be reconfirmed with your airline at least 72 hours before departure.

BY TRAIN

Beijing has two main railway stations: Beijing Station (Beijing Huochezhan) and Beijing West (Xi Huochezhan). Some trains to other parts of China run from the city's three smaller stations. Trans-Siberian trains leave from Beijing Station, the start of a fascinating five-day (via Mongolia) or six-day (via Northeast China) journey to Moscow. Tickets and visas are easier to obtain for Beijing-Moscow

than for Moscow-Beijing. The Beijing International Hotel has an international train ticket booking office. Allow at least a week to obtain Russian and, if necessary, Mongolian and Polish visas in Beijing. Don't forget to bring plenty of passport photos; otherwise there is a photo booth inside the main entrance to the Friendship Store, on Jianguomenwai, and another in the CITIC building next to the Friendship Store.

Independent Travel

Most individual travellers to Beijing are either people on business, who are generally looked after by Chinese partners, or the "backpackers" who arrive in China with just an air ticket and visa.

Independent travel in Beijing can prove difficult if you have no bookings and don't speak Chinese. Problems booking transport and accommodation can spoil your visit, particularly during the summer peak and if you are on a tight schedule. If you do want to organise your own trip, here are some tips:
Avoid the peak tourist season

(May–September). Get detailed information: when you arrive in Beijing, head for a travel agency such as CITS, which, for a small fee, will help you book rooms and tickets. Using agencies or hotel travel services can save a lot of hassle.

Besides the main travel agencies, Beijing has many small-scale, sometimes unlicensed tour operators. On some of the organised tours, as in many countries, the operators take tourists to shops and restaurants that pay the guides a commission. Others charge double for entrance tickets that you can buy yourself. But most tour companies are reasonably trustworthy, and usually cheap.

Booking by mail, fax or email is no problem for major hotels, but is unlikely to succeed in cheaper hotels because of the lack of English speakers. Ideally, you should ensure you have received confirmation of your booking before you arrive in Beijing.

A convenient way to purchase international train tickets departing from Beijing is directly through CITS

Airlines

Aeroflot, Jinglun Hotel (Beijing-Toronto). Tel: 6500-2412.
Air China, 15 Chang'an Xidajie, Xicheng dist. Tel: 6601-7755 (general information), 6601-3336 (domestic), 6601-6667 (international).
Air France, Rm 2716, China World Trade Centre. Tel: 6588-1388.
Alitalia, Rm 139–140 Jianguo Hotel. Tel: 6561-0375.
All Nippon Airways, 1st Floor, China World Trade Centre. Tel: 6505-3311.
Asiana Airlines, Rm 134, Jianguo Hotel. Tel: 6468-1118.
British Airways, Rm 210, Scitech Tower. Tel: 6512-4070.
Canadian Airlines, Lufthansa Centre. Tel: 6468-2001.
China Eastern Airlines. Tel: 6522-8627.
China Southern Airlines, 227 Chaoyangmenwai Dajie.

Tel: 6595-3622.
Dragonair, Rm L107, China World Trade Centre. Tel: 6518-2533.
Fesco Air Services (for domestic flights), 1st Floor, China World Trade Centre. Tel: 6505-3330.
Finnair, Rm 102, Scitech Tower. Tel: 6512-7180.
Garuda Indonesia, Rm 116A, West Wing, China World Trade Centre. Tel: 6505-2901.
Japan Airlines, Hotel New Otani Changfugong. Tel: 6513-0888.
KLM, 5th Floor, West Wing, China World Trade Centre. Tel: 6505-3505.
Korean Air, Rm L115C, West Wing, China World Trade Centre. Tel: 6505-0088.
Lufthansa, Beijing Lufthansa Centre. Tel: 6465-4488.
Malaysian Airlines, Rm 115A, West Wing, China World Trade Centre. Tel: 6505-2681.

MIAT (Mongolian), 1st Floor, Golden Bridge Plaza. Tel: 6507-9297.
Northwest Airlines, 5th Floor, West Wing, China World Trade Centre. Tel: 6505-3505.
PIA, 1st Floor, China World Trade Centre. Tel: 6505-1681.
Qantas, Rm 102, Lufthansa Centre. Tel: 6467-4794.
SAS, 1st Floor, Scitech Tower. Tel: 65183738.
Singapore Airlines, Rm L109, China World Trade Centre. Tel: 6505-2233.
Swissair, 2nd Floor, Scitech Tower. Tel: 6512-3355.
Thai International, Rm 207–209, Scitech Tower. Tel: 6460-8899.
Turkish Airlines, Rm 103, Lufthansa Centre. Tel: 6465-1867.
United Airlines, 1st Floor, Office Building, Lufthansa Centre. Tel: 6463-1111.

Embassies in Beijing

Australia, 21 Dongzhimenwai Dajie, Chaoyang District. Tel: 6532-2331/7, Fax: 6532-3101, Tlx: 22263 AUSTM CN.

Austria, 5 Xiushui Nanjie, Jianguomenwai. Tel: 6532-2061, Tlx: 22258 OEBPK CN.

Canada, 19 Dongzhimenwai Dajie, Chaoyang District. 19 Dongzhimenwai Dajie. Tel: 6532-3536, Fax: 6532-4972, Tlx: 222445 CANAD CN.

France, 3 Dongsan Jie, Sanlitun. Tel: 6531-1331.

Germany, 5 Dongzhimenwai Dajie, Sanlitun. Tel: 6532-2161, Tlx: 22259 AAPEK CN. Visa and Trade Section, Donsijie, Sanlitun. Tel: 6532-5556, Tlx: DDPEK CN.

India, 1 Ritan Donglu. Tel: 6532-1856.

Ireland, 3 Ritan Donglu, Chaoyang District. Tel: 6532-2691, Fax: 6532-6857.

Israel, 405 China World Trade Centre. Tel: 6505-2970.

Italy, Dong'er Jie, Sanlitun. Tel: 6532-2131.

Japan, 7 Ritan Lu, Jianguomenwai. Tel: 6532-2361.

Malaysia, 13 Dongzhimenwai Dajie. Tel: 6532-2531.

Mongolia, 2 Xiushui Beijie, Jianguomenwai. Tel: 6532-1203.

Nepal, Xilu Jie, Sanlitun. Tel: 6532-1795.

Netherlands, 4 Liangmahe Nanlu. Tel: 6532-1131.

New Zealand, Dong'er Jie, Ritanlu.

Tel: 6532-2731, Fax: 6532-4317.

Norway, 1 Dongyi Jie, Sanlitun. Tel: 6532-2261.

Pakistan, 1 Dongzhimenwai Dajie. Tel: 6532-2660/2021, Tlx: 22673 CMREP CN.

Philippines, 23 Xiushui Jie, Jianguomenwai. Tel: 6532-1872.

Poland, 1 Ritan Lu, Jianguomenwai. Tel: 6532-1235.

Russia, Dongzhimen Beizhongjie. Tel: 6532-2051, visas: 6532-1267, Tlx: 22247 SOVEN CN.

Singapore, 1 Xiushui Beijie, Jianguomenwai. Tel: 6532-3926.

South Africa, Suite C801, Lufthansa Centre, 50 Liangmaqiao Lu. Tel: 6465-1941, Fax: 6465-1965.

South Korea, 4/F China World Trade Centre. Tel: 6505-3171.

Spain, 9 Sanlitun Lu. Tel: 6532-1986.

Sweden, 3 Dongzhimenwai Dajie. Tel: 6532-3331.

Switzerland, 3 Dongwu Jie, Sanlitun. Tel: 6532-2736.

Thailand, 40 Guanghua Lu. Tel: 6532-1903.

United Kingdom, 11 Guanghua Lu. Tel: 6532-1961, Fax: 6532-1937, Tlx: 22191 PRDRM CN.

United States, 2 Xiushui Dongjie, Jianguomenwai. Tel: 6532-3431 ext.229 or 6532-3831 ext. 264, Fax: 6532-2483, Tlx: 22701 AMEMB CN.

Vietnam, 32 Guanghua Lu. Tel: 6532-1155.

via the internet, paid for by bank transfer. See the CITS website at *www.cits.com.cn* or email *xiemz@cits.com.cn*. On arrival in Beijing, tickets can be collected from the CITS office at 103 Fuxingmenwai Dajie, near Nanlishilu underground station.

Another possibility for independent travel to Beijing is to book a mini package or full "tailor made" package through a company that organises trips to China. They will book rooms, transfers and sightseeing, including an interpreter if you want one. One of the longer-established companies

organising individual packages to China is Regent Holidays in Bristol. See *www.regent-holidays.co.uk*.

Chinese Embassies Abroad

Chinese Embassies

UK, Consular Section, 31 Portland Place, London, W1N 3AG. Tel: (020) 7631-1430, (020) 7636-5637, recorded information (premium rate) 0891-880 808.

USA, 2300 Connecticut Avenue, Washington, DC 20008. Tel: (202) 6328-2515.

Practical Tips

Media

Print: Beijing has several Chinese daily papers, including the official party newspaper *Renmin Ribao* (*People's Daily*), *Guangming Daily*, which is mainly for intellectuals, the local *Beijing Daily* and *Beijing Evening Post*. For foreign visitors, *China Daily*, which is published daily except on Sundays, is a nationally distributed English daily. As well as propaganda, it includes daily listings of cultural events in Beijing, international news and good sports coverage. Several foreign daily papers can be bought in Beijing (a day late) from the big hotels and the Friendship Store. These include the *South China Morning Post* and *Hong Kong Standard*, which have the best coverage of China, the *International Herald Tribune* and *Financial Times*. Magazines available include *Newsweek*, *Time*, *The Economist*, and *Asiaweek*.

Television and radio: Chinese TV shows many foreign films, usually dubbed into Chinese but sometimes left in the original language and subtitled. CCTV broadcasts a daily English news programme at 10.30pm. Many large hotels carry CNN and satellite broadcasts from Hong Kong-based Star TV. *China Daily* prints a daily television programme schedule. Bilingual Beijing radio stations Easy FM and Joy FM broadcast Western and Chinese music on 91.5 FM. More bilingual programmes can be found on Your FM at 101.8 FM.

Postal Services

You will find postal facilities in most hotels. Letters and postcards to and from China take around six days. Postage rates are still cheap but sending parcels by air is more expensive. Parcels must be packed and sealed at the post office, to allow customs inspection. The main **International Post Office** for poste restante mail and for posting abroad is on the Second Ring Road, just north of Jianguomen intersection.

International express courier services, normally with free pick-up, are offered by: **DHL-Sinotrans**, 2nd Floor, East Wing, China World Trade Centre, tel: 6505-2173; **Federal Express**, Golden Land Building, Liangmaqiao Lu, tel: 6468-5566; **UPS**, Kelun Building, Tower 2, 12A Guanghua Lu, tel: 6593-2932.

Phone and Fax

Calls within Beijing from your hotel room are generally free. In most hotels you can telephone direct abroad, though in some you still need to ask the operator to call for you. In the leading hotels, you can use credit cards and international telephone cards. China's IDD rates have fallen but are still higher than most Western countries.

Many hotels, shopping centres and other public places now have card phones. Cards (30, 50 or 100 yuan) can usually be bought from nearby reception desks. Pre-paid internet phone cards offer rates as little as 25 percent of the standard cost of an international call. Several companies are selling internet phone cards on a trial basis, but the government has yet to decide whether to allow wider use of them.

Other options are the International Post Office on the Second Ring Road (open 8am–7pm). Besides long-distance calls, it handles remittances, money orders and telegraphic money transfers. The Long-Distance Telephone Building at Fuxingmen Dajie (7am–midnight) handles long-distance, conference and pre-booked calls. The Telephone Building on Chang'an Xidajie (24 hours) has a complete range of telephone and fax services.

Local calls can be made from the many roadside booths with attendants. They generally cost one jiao. These booths can also be used for long-distance calls but charges can be high.

Telex and fax: Almost all hotels have telex and fax services.

Telegrams: Telegrams are relatively expensive. Express dispatches, which take four hours, cost double

Travel Agencies

National Travel Agencies
China Comfort Travel, Head Office, 57 Di'anmenxi Dajie, Beijing 100009. Tel: 6603-5423, 6601-6288, Fax: 6601-6336, Tlx: 222862 KHT.

China Everbright Travel, 9/F East Bldg, Beijing Hotel, 33 Chang'an Dongdajie, Beijing 10004. Tel: 6513-7766/9022, Fax: 6512-0545, Tlx: 222285 CETI.

China Golden Bridge Travel, Head Office, 171A Tiananmen Xilu, Beijing 100035. Tel: 6601-5933, Fax: 6603-2628, Tlx: 222367 CGBT.

China International Sports Travel, 4 Tiyuguan Lu, Beijing 100061. Tel: 6701-7364, Fax: 6701-7370, Tlx: 222283 CIST.

China International Travel Service, Head Office, 103 Fuxingmen'nei Lu, Beijing 100800. Tel: 6601-2055, Fax: 6512-2068, 6601-2013, Tlx: 22350 CITSH. www.cits.com.cn

China M&R Special Tours, A7 Beisanhuan Xilu, Beijing 100088. Tel: 6202-6611/4166, Fax: 6201-0865, 6201-0802, Tlx: 222880.

China Merchants International

Travel, Tiandi Building, 14 Dongximennan Lu, Beijing 100027. Tel: 6501-9198, 6506-2288, Fax: 6501-1308, Tlx: 210390 CMITC.

China Rail Express Travel, Block 3, Multiple Service Bldg, Beifengwo Lu, Beijing 100038. Tel: 6324-6645, Fax: 6326-1824, Tlx: 222224 YTSRB.

China Rainbow Travel, Tel: 6501-7901, Fax: 6501-7901, Tlx: 211177 YAAH.

China Supreme Harmony Travel, Rm 944, Media Hotel, B11 Fuxing Lu, Beijing 100859. Tel: 6801-4422/3944, Fax: 6801-6218.

China Swan International Tours, Rm 2018–2020 East Building, Beijing Hotel, Beijing 100004. Tel: 6513-7766/2020, Fax: 6513-8487, Tlx: 222517 CSIT.

China Travel Service, Head Office, 8 Dongjiaominxiang Lu, Beijing 100005. Tel: 6512-9933, Fax: 6512-9021, Tlx: 22487 CTSHO.

China Women's Travel Service, Head Office, 103 Dongsinan Lu, Beijing 100010. Tel: 6655-3307, 6513-6311, Fax: 6512-9021, Tlx: 21160 CWTS.

China Youth Travel Service, Head Office, 23B Dongjiaominxiang Lu, Beijing 100006. Tel: 6512-7770, Fax: 6512-0571, 6513-8691, Tlx: 20024 CYTS.

CITIC Travel, 19 Jianguomenwai Dajie, Beijing 100004. Tel: 65005920, Fax: 6512-7514, Tlx: 22967 CTI.

Mongolia Juulchin Travel (for tours to Mongolia), Rm 4015, Beijing International Hotel, 9

Accessing the Internet

For e-mail and internet users, many hotels have facilities in their business centres. Some, such as the **Twenty-First Century Hotel**, 40 Liangmaqiao Lu, tel: 6466-3311, have separate internet centres. Beijing also has several internet cafes, including the **Unicom Sparkice Internet Cafe** at the China World Trade Centre, tel: 6505-2288 x8209 (*www.sparkice.com.cn*). Other

Sparkice internet cafes are at the **Capital Stadium**, West Wing, Baoshiqiao Lu, Haidian District, tel: 6833-5335; B1810 **Wantong New World Plaza**, 2 Fuchengmenwai Dajie, Xicheng District, tel: 6857-8794; and the **Parkson department store**, 101 Fuxingmennei Dajie (west of Changan Dajie, close to Fuxingmen underground stop), tel: 6205-2650.

Jianguomennei Dajie, Beijing 100005. Tel: 6525-4339, 6512 6688, Fax: 6525-4339, Tlx: 79318 JULN MH.

Beijing Travel Agencies

Beijing CITIC Guo'an International Travel Service, Rm 304, Guo'an Hotel, 1 Guangdongdian Beijie. Tel: 6501-0885, Fax: 6500-3263.
Beijing Youth Travel Service, Building 3, 96 Andingmennei Dajie. Tel: 6403-3521, Fax: 6403-3560, Tlx: 210098 BYTS.
China Air International Travel Service, 8 Dongsanhuan Beilu. Tel: 6508-2163, Fax: 6508-2163.
China International Travel Service (CITS), Beijing Tourism Building, 28 Jianguomenwai Dajie. Tel: 6515-8562, 6515-0515, Fax: 6515-8602, Tlx: 22047 CITSB. www.cits.com.cn
China Peace International Tourism, 14 Chaoyangmen'nan Dajie. Tel: 6512-2504, Fax: 6512-5860, Tlx: 222354 CLTI.
China Travel Service, Beijing Tourism Bldg, 28 Jianguomenwai Dajie. Tel: 6515-8844, 6515-2802, Fax: 6515-8557, Tlx: 22032 BCTS.
Beijing Divine Land Travel, 19 Xinyuan'nan Road, Dongzhimenwai Lu. Tel: 6467-7619, 6466-6887, Fax: 6467-7307, Tlx: 210347 DLTS.
Huayuan International Travel Service, Holiday Inn Crown Plaza, 48 Wangfujing Dajie. Tel: 6513-3388 x1212/13, Fax: 6513-2513, Tlx: 222872 HYITS.
New Ark Travel, 3 Zhaoying Lu. Tel: 6500-4385, Fax: 6500-4118, Tlx: 211229 BNATS.
North Star International, No. 10, Block 3, Anhuili Lu. Tel: 6491-0682, 6491-0683, Fax: 6491-0684, 6491-0691, Tlx: 210303 NSITC.
Sunshine Express, A101 Jingding Commercial Bldg, Langjiayuan Beilu. Tel: 6586-8069, 6586-8075, Fax: 6586-8077, E-mail: sunpress@public.bta.net.cn.

Business Travellers

Many foreign banks and companies have representatives in Beijing. Since the main ministries and important foreign trade organisations are based in Beijing,

China's capital is often the first point of contact for foreign business people. Trade fairs are held here regularly, and information on these and other aspects of doing business in China can be found on a growing number of websites, including:
www.chinabusinessworld.com,
www.sinopolis.com.cn,
www.chinonline.com,
www.clearthinking.com,
www.chinabis.com, *china.muzi.net*,
and *www.chinadaily.net*.

The following organisations can give more detailed information about business trips and arranging business connections:
UK: Department of Trade and Industry, China Desk, Northeast Asia Trade Unit, Bay 522, Kingsgate House, 66–74 Victoria Street, London SW1E 6SW. Tel: (020) 7215-4230, fax: (020) 7215-8797.
China-Britain Business Council (CBBC), 4th Floor, Abford House, 15 Wilton Road, London SW1V 1LT. Tel: (020) 7828-5176, fax: (020) 7680-5780, email: review@cbbc.org.
USA: National Council for US-China Trade, 1050 17th Street, NW, Washington DC 20036. Tel: (202) 6429-0340.
Chambers of Commerce:

Tourist Information

The state-run **China International Travel Service** (CITS) 28 Jianguomenwai Dajie, tel: 6515-8570, 6515-8562, fax: 6515-8602, *www.cits.com.cn*, has offices in several hotels and at some tourist venues. Most hotels offer guided tours to sites inside and outside Beijing. Larger hotels organise their own tours, others arrange trips through CITS or smaller travel companies.
Beijing Hutong Tourist Agency, Dianmenxi Dajie near the north gate of Beihai Park, tel: 6524-8482 or ask your hotel, runs guided pedicab tours through the old *hutong* (alleys) of what used to be one of Beijing's wealthiest areas, with stops at the Drum and Bell Towers. From the same area,

American Chamber of Commerce (Amcham), Rm 352, Great Wall Sheraton Hotel, 8 Dongsanhuan Beilu. Tel: 6500-5566 x2378/2379, Fax: 6501-8273.
British Chamber of Commerce, 2nd Floor, 31 Technical Club, 15 Guanghuali, Jianguomenwai Dajie. Tel: 6593-6610, Fax: 6501-8281. email: bccc@iuol.cn.net

Women Travellers

Women travelling alone generally experience fewer problems of harassment in China than in most countries. Travelling by public transport or bicycle is usually safe, but there have been occasional reports of Beijing taxi drivers harassing foreign women. When taking taxis, especially at night, or visiting smaller bars and clubs, it may be better to join other tourists.

Travelling with Kids

The main advantage for parents travelling with kids is that Western children usually draw more attention than adults. **Beijing Zoo** (especially the pandas), and the **China Puppet Theatre** are among the best bets for children. One new

starting at the southwest corner of Qianhai Lake, you can take boat tours as far as the Summer Palace.

For more information on tourism in Beijing, see these official websites:
www.beijingtour.net.cn,
www.bjta.gov.cn, *www.cbw.com*,
and *www.cits.com.cn*. Complaints or specific enquiries are handled by the Beijing Tourism Administration hotline on 6513-0828. If you want to book direct with a travel agency, several are listed below, divided into national travel agencies, which deal with mainly with tours booked outside China or travel to other provinces, and agencies that deal specifically with the Beijing area.

Tipping and Gifts

Tips are not usually expected and are often refused, but waiters in large hotels and restaurants, as well as a few taxi drivers, do court tips. Before you tip, remember that the average wage is relatively low – less than 1,000 yuan a month.

It is useful to bring a small stock of items such as lighters, badges, pens, calculators, penknives etc, to give to Chinese friends you may make. Other good gifts are cassettes, photo albums or typical souvenirs from your hometown. Foreign cigarettes, which are expensive in China, are also in demand.

attraction, for those who haven't seen similar things in the West, is the **Blue Zoo**, Workers' Stadium South Gate, tel: 6591-3397, where you admire the marine life by walking through tunnels inside giant aquariums. For Beijing's little emperors and empresses, Western fast-food outlets are a prime attraction. Many other attractions are linguistically or culturally inaccessible to Western kids.

Gay Travellers

Same-sex couples can share hotel rooms and there are generally no problems for gay travellers in China. Many Chinese people, however, are either completely ignorant of homosexuality or believe that gay men and lesbians exist only in the West. Beijing has a small gay scene, which the government appears to tolerate so long as it remains low-key. Some magazines carry contact advertisements and the city has at least one gay hotline. To avoid risk of publicity-induced closure, no gay bars or clubs are identified in this guide.

Travellers with Disabilities

Most major hotels have some form of ramp access, and good lifts, but it is difficult to avoid steps when visiting tourist sites. Ordinary shops and restaurants seldom provide ramp access. Some main streets have raised tracking to aid people with impaired vision.

Religious Services

Greater Beijing has more than 30 Christian churches with regular services on weekdays and Sundays. Catholic mass (including Sunday mass in English) is said in **Nantang Cathedral**, 141 Qianmen Dajie (right outside Xuanwumen underground station), Tel: 6602-5221, and **Beitang Cathedral**, 33 Xishiku Dajie, near Beihai Park, Tel: 6617-5098. Protestant services are held at **Gangwashi Church**, 57 Xisinan Dajie, Xicheng District, Tel: 6617-6181, and **Chongwen District Church**, Hougou Hutong, Chongwenmen, Tel: 6524-2193. Muslims can attend several mosques, including **Niujie Mosque** on Niu Jie in the south of the city. Buddhists have plenty of choice among Beijing's restored temples.

Medical Treatment

Getting used to a different climate and foreign food can affect one's health. It is worth taking medicines for colds, diarrhoea and constipation in your medical kit, as well as a stock of any regular medication you need. While traditional Chinese remedies are often excellent, language difficulties may make it hard to buy the right ones.

Most tourist hotels offer medical assistance. The Swissotel has its own pharmacy. In case of serious illness, foreigners can get treatment in special sections for foreigners at major local hospitals, but partly because of language problems, the service is not Western style.

The best hospitals with foreigner sections are the **Sino-Japanese Friendship Hospital**, Heping Donglu, Chaoyang District. Tel: 6422-1122; and **Capital Hospital**, 53

Dongdanbei Dajie. Tel: 6529-5269, emergency: 6529-5284.

More expensive, but the best place for treatment of serious illness, is the private **Beijing United Family Health Centre**, 2 Jiangtai Lu (close to Lido Hotel). Tel: 6433-3960, Fax: 6433-3963. All staff speak excellent English.

You will generally be given Western medicine in the foreigner sections of hospitals, and antibiotics are readily available. If you would like traditional Chinese medical treatment, whether herbs or acupuncture, you must request it specifically. Chinese hospitals are divided into those using Western medicine and those using traditional medicine, though some use both.

For non-emergency treatment, there are a few other foreign clinics, including the **International Medical Clinic**, Rm 106, Regus Office Bldg, Lufthansa Centre. Tel: 6465-1561, Fax: 6465-1984; and the **Hong Kong International Medical Clinic**, 3rd Floor, Swissotel, Dongsishitiao. Tel: 6501-2288 x2346, Fax: 6500-4660. Many hotels have in-house doctors who are trained in both traditional Chinese and Western methods, and the larger embassies have doctors who are willing to see patients in serious cases. They can also help arrange medical evacuation.

Security and Crime

Visitors don't need to take any special precautions in Beijing, though you should never leave money and valuables unguarded. Crime in China is low but rising. Beware of pickpockets on public buses, and always keep luggage locked.

Emergency Numbers

In case of emergency you can get help on the following numbers:
Police: 110
Ambulance: 120
Fire: 119

Getting Around

Orientation

Beijing has two main ring roads (the Second and Third), plus a partially completed fourth ring road. Most of the other main roads run north-south or east-west, making it relatively easy to find your way around. Main streets are commonly divided in terms of *bei* (north), *nan* (south), *xi* (west) and *dong* (east); and in terms of *nei* (inside) and *wai* (outside the Second Ring Road). On the other hand, many housing estates are full of indistinguishable (unless you can read Chinese) high-rise buildings, making it easy to get lost, especially at night. The words *jie*, *dajie*, *lu* and *men*, which you'll find on all maps, mean street, avenue, road and gate respectively.

City Maps: Reasonably accurate maps in English are available from most hotels. Bookshops and kiosks mainly sell Chinese maps, which usually include bus and underground routes. The most useful maps are those which have street and building names in both Chinese characters and English. Chinese name cards for hotels, restaurants, shops or other destinations are useful for showing taxi drivers or bus conductors.

Public Transport

UNDERGROUND

The city's underground system is limited to just two lines, but provides a useful link between Beijing Railway Station and some major tourist areas, such as Tiananmen Square, the Silk Market, Lama and Confucius temples, and the Drum and Bell towers. All journeys cost 2 yuan, irrespective of distance. One route runs parallel to the Second ring Road, more or less following the demolished city wall around the north of the city. The other runs under the western extension of Chang'an Jie from Fuxingmen out into the western suburbs. This line is gradually being extended eastwards.

A northern suburban light railway is also planned, to run from Xizhimen in the northwest to Dongzhimen in the northeast. Other routes are on the drawing board, such as a link from the Fragrant Hills to the airport and a north-south route, but it is likely to take the city many years to find the funds it needs to complete all these projects.

The first stretch of the Beijing underground was opened in 1971. It shares the advantages and disadvantages of most city underground routes the world over. It may be missing the baroque splendours of the Moscow metro and the gleaming chrome of many Western systems, but it is efficient

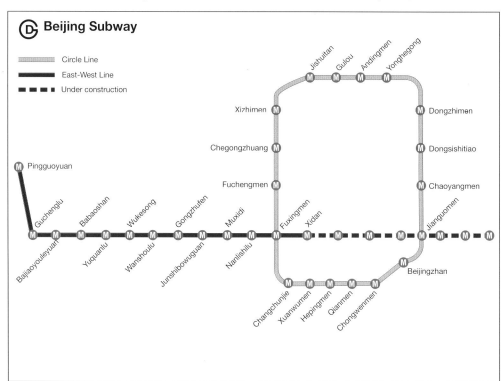

Beijing Subway

- Circle Line
- East-West Line
- Under construction

Fare Dodgers

According to the bus companies, only about 20 percent of passengers use single tickets, while the rest use monthly season tickets. But these figures ignore the fact that some passengers don't buy tickets at all, taking advantage of the chaotic tide to get a free ride. When the conductor confronts a fare-dodger, you get an idea of the explosive powers of the Beijing dialect. Buses are worth taking on at least one short journey, for that alone.

and quick, and outside the rush-hours, not quite as crowded as the buses. It is easy to find your way around as signs and announcements are bilingual.

BUSES

The network of red, yellow and blue buses is comprehensive, and operates from 5am to 11pm. Rides only cost a few jiao, depending on the distance. A few routes have been improved, with air-conditioned double-decker buses, but Beijing's buses are generally slow and crowded and the gaps between stops are sometimes long. They are extremely crowded during the rush-hours, and you will need to use your elbows, pushing and shoving like the locals do, just to get on the bus. Once on board, you will rarely get a seat and will probably be wedged securely against other passengers. Remember to secure money and other valuables before you board.

The conductors, mainly women, usually sit at tall metal desks close to the doors. They issue regular cries requesting passengers to pay their fares. Give the conductor a few jiao bills and rely on her help or on that of your fellow passengers, to whom you can perhaps show your destination on a map or name card. You will find people who just struggled violently to get on the bus in front of you will now be extremely helpful if you speak to them.

MINIBUSES

Minibuses ply the same routes as the buses but offer a faster, more comfortable service at several times the bus fare, though they are still cheap by Western standards (1 yuan to 10 yuan, depending on distance). They generally seat 16 people. For example, they run between the Summer Palace and the zoo, between the zoo and Qianmen gate (behind it is a main stop for minibuses), from the zoo to the Beijing railway station, from Qianmen to the station, from the Summer Palace to Xiangshan Park (and of course return the same way). They have official stops but, if they have space, will usually stop wherever they are flagged down

Private Transport

TAXIS

Taxis are cheap by Western standards (usually 1.2, 1.6 or 2.0 yuan per km), plentiful and convenient. Several types of taxi ply the roads of Beijing, from the cramped *xiali*, which costs 1.2 yuan per km, to Audis and other large saloons costing 3 yuan per km. Any waiting time is charged extra. At night, the basic fare and the cost per km are higher. All taxis have a meter. If you don't know your way around, ask your hotel receptionist how much your journey should cost.

Taxi drivers sometimes use the ignorance of foreign visitors as an extra source of income. Many drivers will try to quote a flat rate to your destination. Do not accept this, as it will never be cheaper than the meter charge. Always make sure the meter is switched on before setting off. The price per kilometre is indicated on a red sticker displayed in the taxi window, and they all have a minimum charge of 10 to 12 yuan. Once you've used up the minimum fare, the price jumps by 50 percent per km, unless you're using the taxi for a return trip before 11pm.

Drivers often refuse to take passengers – foreigners and locals –

to destinations they consider inconvenient. The growing number of complaints from passengers prompted the city to list an address where you can lodge a complaint if a taxi driver refuses to take you where you want to go or uses a different route from the one you instructed.

Most taxi drivers speak little or no English. If you are travelling with other people, make sure the driver doesn't try to charge the meter price for each passenger. Always carry enough change, since taxi drivers are often unable, or unwilling, to change a 100 yuan bill.

Taxis can also be hired for longer trips, such as whole-day tours or visits to the Great Wall or Ming Tombs. If you plan to do this, make sure you agree the total fare and the precise itinerary in advance. Plan to spend 300–500 yuan for a full day, depending on distance. Do not pay the full amount in advance. Here are some of the city's major taxi firms:
Beijing Car and Limousine Service, Bldg 14, Shuyunuanli. Tel: 6848-3312.
Beijing Taxi Corp, 26 Fuchengmenwai Dajie. Tel: 6831-2288 (24 hours).
Capital Taxi Co, 10 Yuetan Beijie. Tel: 6852-7084.

TOURIST BUSES

Most tour groups travel in comfortable, air-conditioned buses. There are bus companies in several places, for instance outside Beijing Railway Station and opposite the Chongwenmen Hotel, which organise regular excursions to the most important sights. There is another such company at 2 Qianmen Lu (northeast of Qianmen gate).

From mid-March to mid-October, Beijing also operates 18 special tourist bus routes suitable for independent travellers. These are more comfortable and faster than public buses, and much cheaper than hiring a taxi. On most routes, several buses leave each morning, starting from about 7am, and return the same afternoon, giving you some flexibility. Routes include

Qianmen to Badaling, the Ming Tombs, and the Eastern Qing Tombs, and Xuanwumen to Simatai.

BICYCLES

The vehicle most used by Beijingers is the bicycle; some 8.5 million bicycles use the city's streets. Cycling is also the most enjoyable way for tourists to see Beijing, but it requires steady nerves and basic fitness. If you have the time and energy, cycling will give you a completely different view of life in the city. You have to park your bicycle on one of the numerous parking places reserved for bicycles, which are guarded and normally cost 2 jiao. Bicycles here do not usually have lights but they do have rear reflectors. You can pump up the tyres or have repairs done almost anywhere in the city, as there are repair people on every street corner and in every alleyway.

If you do hire a bicycle, check the brakes first. Many hotels have bicycles for hire. Bikes can also be hired from the Ritan Bicycle Shop, at the eastern end of Ritan Donglu.

If you are not used to urban cycling, it is a good idea to practise before going to China. If you want to experience travelling through Beijing at a cyclist's pace but don't feel up

Renting a Car

Foreign tourists are not allowed to drive in China. You can hire a car with driver via most travel agencies and hotels, or from taxi companies; minibuses are also available. Try **Beijing Minibus Co**, Tel: 6721-1558; or **Beijing Transport Co Service for Foreigners**, Tel: 6502-2616. Alternatively, try negotiating a whole-day or half-day price direct with a driver. If you ask at the front desk of your hotel, most will arrange a car for the day for you, giving the driver clear instructions where you want to go and what time you want to return. Do not pay in advance.

to cycling yourself, pedicabs (or trishaws) can be hired near many tourist sites.

Domestic Travel

As China's capital, Beijing is the main traffic centre for the country. All traffic routes converge on the city: Beijing has flights and trains to all other parts of China.

BY AIR

China's national tourist offices and travel agencies, including many hotel travel desks, can give you the current flight schedules of the state airlines. The number of domestic airlines has been growing rapidly in the last few years. All are, effectively, under the umbrella of the Civil Aviation Authority of China (CAAC). Accompanying this growth in the aviation business have been improvements in service. But tight budgets, especially for the smaller airlines, and the rapid growth of the industry, have led to overused airports and frequent flight delays. This was one of the reasons behind the extension of Beijing's Capital Airport. Some people have also voiced safety concerns over domestic flights, although there is no clear evidence to suggest that it is a particular problem in China.

You can buy tickets from travel agencies or airline booking offices. Travel agencies may be more convenient as, although they charge more, they are more likely to have English-speaking staff. Try **Fesco Air Services**, 1st Floor, China World Trade Centre. Tel: 6505-3330. Or try CITS, near the Gloria Plaza Hotel, or China Youth Travel Service (CYTS), round the corner from the CITIC building, east of the Friendship Store. It is best to buy your tickets as far as possible in advance.

BY RAIL

Beijing has two main railway stations: Beijing Station (Beijing Huochezhan) and Beijing West (Xi Huochezhan). Some trains to

Seat/Berth Categories

There are four different classes on Chinese trains: soft sleeper (*ruanwo*; four beds in one compartment), hard sleeper (*yingwo*; six beds in an open compartment), soft seat (*ruanzuo*) and hard seat (*yingzuo*). All are comfortable for both long and short journeys, except for the hard seats, which are not recommended for anything other than short trips.

other parts of China run from the city's three smaller stations.

The easiest way to buy tickets is through your hotel travel desk, or through China International Travel Service (CITS). Alternatively, you can go to the foreigners' booking office inside Beijing Station, where you can also buy tickets for trains leaving from Beijing West. Beijing West also has a foreigners' booking office on the first floor. If you want a sleeper berth, especially in summer, it is best to buy your ticket two or three days in advance. Return tickets can be purchased for Hong Kong–Beijing but not for other routes. However, because of the complicated system for selling advance tickets, you will need to queue, and you may need to visit the station more than once. **Beijing Huochezhan** (Central Station) Information Tel: 6563-4432/52, 6512-9525. Booking Office (some English): 6563-3662. **Xi Huochezhan** (Beijing West) Information Tel: 6321-6263 /4215/ 4269.

Where to Stay

In recent years, Beijing has experienced a boom in hotel construction, especially at the higher end of the market. Many of the most palatial hotels, some with glass fronts, rotating rooftop restaurants or classical Chinese adornments, are now prominent landmarks on the city's skyline. Many of the international-standard hotels are either joint ventures or wholly owned by a foreign hotel chain. Top managers are often foreigners, many of them from Hong Kong or Singapore. These hotels, of course, charge international prices. Beijing has more than 4,000 hotels but only one hundred or so are open to foreigners. With the recent concentration on luxury hotels, there is a shortage of good hotels at medium and low prices.

The largest international hotels are like enclaves in the Chinese capital, and give the impression of small, independent towns that have little connection to their surroundings. This is partly because they are used by long-stay business people, and have Western-style restaurants, shops and other facilities that cater for homesick expats. Some foreign firms also have offices in these hotels.

All the leading hotels have telex, fax, email, post and banking facilities, restaurants, swimming pools and other sports facilities, doctors, masseurs, nightclubs and discos. Some include supermarkets, delicatessens or bakeries. In most hotels you can make direct international phone calls, and in many you can use credit cards and international telephone cards.

All hotels have air-conditioning and nearly all rooms have television. Some hotels stock their own videos. In general, all hotels have bathrooms and shower facilities, though in some of the cheapest you may have to use a communal shower. Rooms always have hot and cold running water. This is probably safe to drink, but most locals drink boiled water. Hotel rooms are always supplied with flasks of boiled water.

The top hotels usually have their own bars, sometimes with a 24-hour service. Taxis wait in front of most large hotels, otherwise, they are normally easy to find on the street. In the peak tourist season (especially June to October) some hotels are fully booked. At less popular times, hotels may offer discounts or special packages. Many hotels will accept reservations from abroad via fax or e-mail.

Price Guide

Prices are per night for two people sharing a standard double room, including taxes:

$$$$	more than $240
$$$	$130–$240
$$	$60–$130
$	less than $60

$$$$
China World Hotel
1 Jianguomenwai Dajie
Tel: 6505-2266
Fax: 6505-167
www.shangri-la.com
Top class service and accommodation, with health club, swimming pool, shopping and business centres, plus several Western and Asian restaurants. Well located for business.

Diaoyutai State Guest House
Sanlihe Lu (east of Yuyuantan Park)
Tel: 6859-1188
Fax: 6851-3362
www.chinadyt.com
Once reserved for senior Chinese officials and state guests, this hotel is still used to accommodate VIPs. As a result, expect high security and high prices (reportedly US$20,000 a night for suites used by world leaders).

Grand Hotel Beijing
35 Chang'an Dongdajie
Tel: 6513-7788
Fax: 6513-0049
www.grandhotelbeijing.com, e-mail: sales@grandhotelbeijing.com
This Hong Kong joint venture, attached to the Beijing Hotel, offers the height of luxury a stone's throw from Tiananmen Square. Its facilities include a rooftop terrace with views over the square.

Hilton Hotel
1 Dongfang Lu
Dongsanhuan Beilu
Tel: 6466-2288
Fax: 6465-3052
e-mail: reserve@hiltonbeijing.com.cn
Next to the airport expressway, this has, like all Hiltons, every comfort. Among the highlights are Japanese and Cajun restaurants.

Great Wall Sheraton Hotel
Dongsanhuan Beilu
Tel: 6590-5566
Fax: 6590-5938
www.sheraton.com
This luxury US joint venture is handy for the airport and downtown areas. Its many tours and activities include hikes on the Great Wall.

Kunlun Hotel
2 Xinyuan Nanlu (opposite Lufthansa Centre)
Tel: 6590-3388
Fax: 6590-3228
www.hotelkunlun.com
Well established hotel which holds regular art auctions and houses a popular disco. Across the road from the Lufthansa shopping and business complex.

Palace Hotel
8 Jinyu Hutong
Wangfujing Dajie
Tel: 6512-8899
Fax: 6512-9050
Modern, functional construction with Chinese imperial flourishes. A waterfall cascades down into a lobby full of Chinese antiques, while designer labels compete in the shopping arcade. Located in a lively street ideal for shopping and Tiananmen.

Shangri-La Hotel
29 Zizhuyuan Lu
Haidian District
Tel: 6841-2211
Fax: 6841-8006

www.shangri-la.com
This tasteful high-rise hotel has meeting rooms, a ballroom, French and Asian cuisine, and a full range of other facilities. On the western edge of the city, the Shangri-La provides a shuttle-bus service to downtown areas.

$$$

Beijing Hotel
33 Chang'an Dongdajie
Tel: 6513-7766
Fax: 6513-7703, 6513-7307
e-mail: business@chinabeijinghotel.com.cn.
Opened in 1917, with a long list of famous guests, this is still considered one of the best hotels in Beijing. Period features give it an air of tradition, in contrast to many newer competitors. Centrally located, on the corner of Wangfujing shopping street, near Tiananmen Square.

Beijing International Club Hotel
21 Jianguomenwai Dajie
Tel: 6460-6688
Fax: 6460-3299
Matching Chinese tradition with modern furniture, this chic hotel opened in late 1997 in a prime location behind the International Club. The hotel's elegant Press Club Bar quickly became a favourite of the foreign business community.

Gloria Plaza Hotel
2 Jianguomen Nandajie
Tel: 6515-8855
Fax: 6515-8533
www.hotel-web.com/gloria/beijing
With a great location on a major intersection, opposite the Ancient Observatory, and next to one of the main CITS offices, the Gloria has several restaurants and a lively sports bar.

Holiday Inn Crowne Plaza
48 Wangfujing Dajie
Dengshikou
Tel: 6513-3388
Fax: 6513-2513
Located on one of central Beijing's busiest shopping streets, close to the Imperial Palace, the Crowne Plaza has its own gallery of modern Chinese art, and a salon for performances of traditional Chinese music.

Holiday Inn Lido
Jiangtai Lu
Tel: 6437-6688
Fax: 6437-6237
www.lidoplace.com
e-mail: info@lidoplace.com
A haven for foreigners, the Lido has shops, including a deli and a bakery, supermarket, offices and apartments. Just 20 minutes from the airport.

Jianguo Hotel
5 Jianguomenwai Dajie
Tel: 6500-2233
Fax: 6500-2871
e-mail: jhpsales@chinaonline.com.cn.net
Convenient for the Friendship Store, Silk Market and most embassies, this is a favourite with long-term business visitors.

Kempinski Hotel
Beijing Lufthansa Centre
50 Liangmaqiao Lu
Tel: 6465-3388
Fax: 6465-3366
www.kempinski_beijing.com
Attached to Youyi (Friendship) Shopping City, this hotel has all facilities, including health club, restaurants and the authentic Paulaner Brauhaus.

Movenpick Hotel
Xiaotianzhu Village
Shunyi County
PO Box 6913
Tel: 6456-5588
Fax: 6456-5678
Very close to the airport, this hotel is a little isolated from the city, but makes up for this with excellent facilities, including horseriding nearby, summer barbecues, and a chance to eat hotpot in a real Mongolian yurt.

New Otani Changfugong Hotel
26 Jianguomenwai Dajie
Tel: 6512-5555
Fax: 6512-5346
www.newotani.co.jp/ihotels/chang
A Japanese joint venture to the east of the city centre and close to the embassy district, the New Otani caters mainly for Japanese tourists and business people. Its rooms, lobbies, and restaurants are immaculate, but its main advantage · is its central location.

Peace Hotel
3 Jinyu Hutong
Wangfujing Dajie
Tel: 6512-8833
Fax: 6512-6863
In the same lively street as the Palace Hotel, close to Tiananmen and the Imperial Palace, this joint venture provides spacious rooms.

Radisson SAS Royal Hotel
6A Dongsanhuan Beilu
Tel: 6466-3388
Fax: 6465-3186
Excellent facilities, including CITS office and tennis courts. You can choose from Scandinavian, other Western and Chinese food.

Price Guide

Prices are per night for two people sharing a standard double room, including taxes:

$$$$	more than $240
$$$	$130–$240
$$	$60–$130
$	less than $60

Swissotel Beijing
Hong Kong-Macau Centre,
Dongsishiqiao Lu
Tel: 6501-2288
Fax: 6501-2501
www.swissotel.com
A semicircular, mirrored facade dominates one of Beijing's busy intersections. Popular with business travellers.

Traders' Hotel
1 Jianguomenwai Dajie
Tel: 6505-2277
Fax: 6505-3144
www.shangri-la.com
Well located at the northern end of the China World Trade Centre business complex, with solid service, food and accommodation, this is a cheaper option than the neighbouring China World Hotel.

Zhaolong Hotel
2 Gongren Tiyuchangbei Lu
Tel: 6500-2299
Fax: 6500-3319
Convenient for the nightlife of Sanlitun, Beijing's main bar area, the Zhaolong has its own theatre and restaurants.

$$
Beijing Bamboo Garden Hotel
24 Xiaoshiqiao Hutong
Jiugulou Dajie
Tel: 6403-2229
Fax: 6401-2633
Simple, clean rooms open onto a classical Chinese garden, close to the Drum Tower. What it lacks in facilities compared with large, modern hotels, it more than makes up for in atmosphere.

Beijing International Hotel
19 Jianguomenwai Dajie
Tel: 6512-6688
Fax: 6512-9961
With a good location near Beijing Railway Station and the Henderson and Cofco Plaza shopping centres, this 1,000-room hotel offers full facilities including booking offices for international flights and trains.

Dragon Spring Hotel
Shuizha Beilu
Mentougou
Tel: 6984-3366, 6984-3362
Fax: 6984-4377
For atmosphere and facilities, this international hotel built in classical Chinese style beats most similarly priced hotels in Beijing. But it is out towards the Western Hills, an hour from the city centre.

Fragrant Hills Hotel
inside Fragrant Hills Park
Tel: 6259-1166
Fax: 6259-1762
A modern sanctuary from urban noise, in the lush hills northwest of Beijing, beyond the Summer Palace. Swimming pool, Chinese and Western restaurants.

Friendship Hotel
3 Baishiqiao Lu
Haidian district
Tel: 6849-8888
Fax: 6849-8866
www.cbw.com/hotel/friendship
Part of a huge state-run hotel spread out in pleasant grounds close to the Summer Palace and university district, the hotel has several sections offering a range of prices and facilities. It is also home to many foreigners working for Chinese state employers.

Grand View Garden Hotel
Nancaiyuan (on southwest corner of Second Ring Road)

Tel: 6326-8899
Fax: 6326-3139
Ideal if you like classical gardens and buildings, but a little isolated.

Hademen Hotel
A2 Chongwenmenwai Dajie
Tel: 6701-2244
Great location diagonally opposite the Xinqiao Hotel, and convenient for Beijing Railway Station and the Temple of Heaven.

Jing Guang New World Hotel
Hujia Lou
Dongsanhuan Lu
Tel: 6597-8888
Fax: 6597-3333
A 53-storey building dominating the eastern Third Ring Road, the New World is almost a self-contained town, with bakery, restaurants, nightclubs, play areas, medical centre and supermarket – and, of course, some of the best views of Beijing.

Jinglun Hotel (Beijing-Toronto)
3 Jianguomenwai Dajie
Tel: 6500-2266
Fax: 6500-2022
Next to the Jianguo and known for its cuisine, the Jinglun is another business person's favourite.

Minzu Hotel
51 Fuxingmennei Dajie
Tel: 6601-4466
Fax: 6601-4849
www.minzuhotel.com
About 3 km (2 miles) west of Tiananmen, the Minzu is favoured by long-stay business people. It has a Turkish restaurant, with regular belly dancing, and it stands next to the Nationalities Cultural Palace, which stages performances and exhibitions showcasing the cultures of China's 56 minorities.

Qianmen Hotel
175 Yongan Lu
Tel: 6301-6688
Fax: 6301-3883
Offering standard accommodation in the old outer city, near the Temple of Heaven, the Qianmen stages nightly Beijing opera performances.

Ritan Hotel
1 Ritan Lu
Tel: 6512-5588
Fax: 6512-8671
Intimate little hotel inside Ritan Park, near the main embassy area.

Peaceful and reasonably priced.

Twenty-First Century Hotel
40 Liangmaqiao Lu
Tel: 6466-3311
Fax: 6466-3311
www.21st.cn.net
e-mail: sale@21st.cn.net
Just 1 km east of the Lufthansa Centre, this hotel is part of a modern complex including shops, a small internet centre, Korean, Chinese and Western restaurants, business facilities, theatres and a cinema. Several lively bars are across the road.

Xinqiao Hotel
2 Dongjiaomin Xiang
Chongwenmen
Tel: 6513-3366
Fax: 6512-5126
This elegant old-style hotel has been fully refurbished and modernised. At the southeast corner of the former Legation Quarter, it is close to Tiananmen Square and Beijing Railway Station.

Ziyu (Purple Jade) Hotel
55 Xisanhuan Beilu
Xicheng District
Tel: 6841-1188
Fax: 6841-1355
Through a traditional gateway, you enter a compound containing both ancient and modern architectural styles. Traditional rooms enclose small courtyard gardens, while the main block has Western style rooms with full facilities. Situated in Beijing's western suburbs, the Ziyu is convenient for Beijing West Railway Station, the Summer Palaces and the Fragrant Hills.

$
Beifang Hotel
45 Dongdan Beidajie
Dongcheng District
Tel: 6525-2831
Fax: 6525-2928
Retaining touches of traditional Chinese architecture, this small hotel was completed in 1953. It is conveniently located in the city centre near Wangfujing, with a restaurant serving Beifang (northern) Chinese dishes.

Haoyuan Hotel
Shijia Hutong
Dongsinan Dajie

Dongcheng District
Tel: 6512-5557
Fax: 6525-3179
Hidden away in a narrow alley near the busy Dongdan shopping street, and close to the Palace Hotel, the Haoyuan's rooms surround two quiet courtyards. The buildings are a traditional combination of brick and red lacquered wood, with curved tiles on the roofs. A small restaurant serves hearty traditional fare.

Jianguomen Hotel
Building 12
Jianhua Road (south of Jianguomenwai Dajie)
Tel: 6500-5577
Fax: 6502-2707
Cheap hotel close to Beijing Railway Station and the Friendship Store.

Price Guide

Prices are per night for two people sharing a standard double room, including taxes:

$$$$	more than $240
$$$	$130–$240
$$	$60–$130
$	less than $60

Jinghua Hotel
Xiluoyuan Nanlu (past Yongdingmen)
Fengtai District
Tel: 6722-2211
Fax: 6721-1455
The cheap and cheerful Jinghua is in the far south of Beijing, on the Third Ring Road. Though this is a backpacker favourite, the rooms have showers, telephones, and air-conditioners. Dormitory beds are also available.

Jingtai Hotel
65 Yongwai Jingtaixi
Tel: 6721-2476
This popular backpacker hotel in south Beijing is close to a food market and a row of small restaurants. Cheaper rooms are without bath.

Longtan Hotel
15 Panjiayuan Nanlu
Second Ring Road South
Tel: 6771-1602
Fax: 6771-4028

Long a favourite with budget travellers who want to get away from the more crowded backpacker hotels, this hotel is opposite Longtan Park in the south of the city. Facilities are basic, and it is away from the tourist areas, but the modern hotel offers relatively cheap, modern comfort. Single travellers are usually allowed to share three and four-bed rooms.

Lusongyuan Hotel
22 Banchang Hutong
Kuanjie
Dongcheng District
Tel: 6401-1116
Fax: 6403-0418
This courtyard hotel was established in 1980 in a former Qing dynasty official's residence. Rooms are refined and airy. Stone lions still guard the traditional wooden gate, which leads to the pavilions, trees, rockeries and potted plants that fill the courtyards. The Chinese restaurant gets good reviews.

Yinghua Hotel
17 Huixin Dongjie
Tel: 6422-4455
Clean, basic hotel in one of north Beijing's liveliest restaurant streets. Rooms are modern and functional, and the karaoke can sometimes be noisy, but the hotel offers good value.

Youhao Guesthouse
7 Houyuanensi
Jiaodaokou
Dongcheng District
Tel: 6403-1114
Fax: 6401-4603
Not to be confused with the giant Friendship Hotel, the Youhao (Friendly) Guesthouse lies behind brick walls in a traditional alley close to the Drum Tower. The rooms, part of a large compound where Nationalist leader Chiang Kai-shek once stayed, surround Chinese courtyard gardens. The hotel makes a great base for exploring one of Beijing's best-preserved *hutong* (alley) areas.

Hotels outside Beijing

Chengde
Qianwanglou Hotel
Bifengmen Lu
Tel: (0314) 202-4385
For atmosphere alone this is the best option in Chengde. The small, exquisitely refurbished hotel occupies a Qing dynasty mansion set just inside the grounds of the imperial resort. **$$**

Yunshan Hotel
6 Nanyuan Jie
Tel: (0314) 202-4657
Is the main tourist hotel in Chengde, close to the station and with the best facilities. **$$**

Mongolian Yurt Holiday Village
Tel: (0314) 216-2710
In summer, the cheapest option is a yurt (circular felt tent) inside the imperial resort. You don't have to rough it too much, as the yurts have washrooms and televisions. **$**

Shanhaiguan/Beidaihe
Beidaihe Guesthouse for Diplomatic Missions
1 Baosan Lu
Beidaihe
Tel: (0335) 404-1807 (or 6532-4336 in Beijing)
Just five minutes from the main beach, this hotel has friendly staff and a good seafood restaurant. All rooms have balconies with sea views. **$$**

Jinshan Guesthouse
4 Dongsan Lu
Beidaihe
Tel: (0335) 404-1338
Fax: (0335) 404-2478
On a quieter beach, 4 km (2½miles) north of the town centre, the Jinshan has full facilities including a business centre and a bowling alley. **$$**

Jingshan Hotel
Dong Dajie
Shanhaiguan
Tel: (0335) 505-1130
Next to the famous East Gate of the Shanhaiguan garrison on the Great Wall, the Jingshan has comfortable rooms in the heart of the small town. **$**

North Street Hotel
Bei Dajie
Shanhaiguan
Tel: (0335) 505-1683
This popular backpacker hotel is set around a quiet courtyard, close to the Jingshan Hotel in the old walled town. **$**

Tianjin
Geneva Hotel
32 Youyi Lu
Hexi
Tel: (022) 2835-2222
Fax: (022) 2835-9855
A little way out of the city centre, this relatively cheap hotel has four restaurants, a nightclub, a bowling centre, a health club, and smart, Western-style guestrooms. **$**
New World Astor Hotel
33 Tai'er Zhuang Jie
Tel: (022) 2331-1112
Fax: (022) 2331-6282
Refurbished in 1997, the Astor opened in 1863. It retains much of its late 19th century elegance and atmosphere, facing the Hai River, while providing full 21st century services. **$$$**
Tianjin Hyatt Hotel
219 Jiefang Beilu
Tel: (022) 2331-4222
Fax: (022) 2331-1234
The Hyatt backs onto the river. Rooms are light, and the facilities, including Chinese, Japanese and Western restaurants, are top-class. **$$$**

Where to Eat

After shopping, eating is Beijing's most popular pastime. The city teems with restaurants, from streetside noodle vendors and full meals served at sidewalk tables, to the famous Peking Duck served in five-star hotels. Sichuan restaurants stand between Korean and Xinjiang Muslim barbecues, surrounded by numerous four-table outlets where the toilet is "out the door, down the alleyway and turn left."

Eating out is definitely better value in local spots. At most Chinese restaurants you can eat a simple meal, with beer or soft drinks, for less than 50 yuan per person. At the more expensive restaurants, where you might have Peking Duck or better quality Western food, you could pay 100–200 yuan per person.

The major hotels contain some excellent restaurants, especially for Guangdong and Imperial-style dishes. But they are expensive, charging Western prices for all food. The alternative is to hit the smaller, independent restaurants that are giving the hotel restaurants a run for their money.

If you tire of Chinese food, there are plenty of alternatives. Most large hotels have reasonable Western restaurants. In recent years, Korean, Japanese and Western restaurants have mushroomed, though the quality and authenticity of some is disappointing. Middle Eastern, Brazilian and African food can all be found in Beijing.

As Western culture continues to infiltrate Beijing, so does its food. McDonald's and Kentucky Fried Chicken have outlets all over the city. In the Sanlitun embassy area, and to a lesser extent the

Jianguomenwai and Chaoyang Park areas, Western-style bars and restaurants open almost weekly. These places, some of which are hard to distinguish, cater for expats and affluent young locals.

The main meal times are 11am–2pm for lunch and 5–9pm for dinner, but Beijing also has several 24-hour restaurants. Listed below are some of the better-known local establishments. They are not classified, but experience indicates you should get good food and service in them. Some restaurants, including most of those listed and those in the large hotels, take telephone reservations. For Peking Duck, you normally have to make a reservation because of the preparation time involved. Outside the hotels, even some of the larger restaurants have no English menus, so be prepared to point.

Peking Duck Restaurants
Bianyifang Roast Duck Restaurant
2A Chongwenmenwai Dajie
Tel: 6712-0505
113 Qianmenwai Xianyukounei
Tel: 6511-2092
A long-established favourite with two central locations, Bianyifang offers a choice of canteen-style dining with the locals, or restaurant service. The courses of roast duck, duck soup and side dishes are the same in both sections. **$$$**
Tuanjiehu Peking Roast Duck Restaurant
Building 3
Tuanjiehu Beikou
Dongsanhuan
Tel: 6507-2892
At one of the classiest duck restaurants, every part of the duck is served in a range of exquisite side dishes including deep-fried heart with coriander, and stir-fired intestines. The roast duck is a little crisper than that of many competitors. **$$$$**
Quanjude Roast Duck Restaurant
14 Qianmen Xidajie. Tel: 6301-8833; 32 Qianmen Dajie. Tel: 6511-2418; 13 Shuaifuyuan, off Wangfujing. Tel: 6525-3310.
The first Quanjude opened its doors in 1852. It continued as a state-

owned restaurant during the communist era, and now has several palatial branches. The atmosphere can sometimes be a bit conveyor-belt. **$$$**

Old Beijing Cuisine

Jinghua Shiyuan
8A Longtan Xilu
Tel: 6711-5331
Set around a large courtyard perfect for summer dining, Jinghua offers traditional specialites including dainty meat-filled pastries, barbecued meat and cold snacks. Look for a giant copper teapot, 200 yards south of the northwest gate to Longtan Park. **$$**

Old Beijing Noodle King
Chongwenmen
Tel: 6705-6705
Close to the Temple of Heaven, this restaurant has revived the lively tradition of Beijing fast food. Waiters bellow at the diners to announce the arrival or departure of each customer. Look for the rickshaws outside. **$**

Tangenyuan
East Gate
Ditan (Temple of the Earth) Park
Tel: 6428-3358
Take a rickshaw ride to the door of a courtyard-style building. Inside is a recreation of old Beijing streets (the TV sets look a bit out of place). Acrobats, opera singers and magicians entertain you, though sometimes the Peking opera is a little too loud. Easily combined with

The Good Old Days

One of the latest trends to sweep the capital is a return to the "Old Beijing" food and lively dining style common before 1949. Dressed in traditional clothes, waiters shout across the restaurant to announce those coming and going. Diners usually order a range of snacks and fried dishes, which are whisked through the restaurant and clattered down. Instead of rice, noodles are the standard staple, usually eaten with a thick sesame and soy based sauce.

trips to the park, Lama Temple or Confucius Temple, this is the ideal place for a lively group dinner. Reservation essential. **$$$**

Yiwanju Old Beijing Noodles
Fangzhuang branch
6 Pufang Lu
Tel: 6766-6667
Yayuncun (Asian Games Village) branch, Building 6, Anhuili District 4.
Tel: 6765-4321
Popular with locals, Yiwanju is a cheaper, more understated version of the old-time Beijing noodle house. Plates still clatter, and waiters still holler, in the mock-Qing setting. Both branches of Yiwanju have talking mynah birds. **$**

Mongolian Hotpot

Hongbinlou
82 Chang'an Dajie (near the main post office)
Tel: 6601-4832
This famous Muslim restaurant offers not only some of the capital's best hotpot, but also a whole range of other specialities, including Beijing duck and shish kebabs. **$$$**

Nengrenju
5 Taipingqiao
Baitasi
Tel: 6601-2560
Many claim Nengrenju is the best hoptpot restaurant in Beijing, with good service and fine food. Take the plunge with several curls of finely sliced lean lamb. After that, select from the restaurant's array of seafood, mushrooms, vegetables, noodles, beancurd and many other ingredients. **$$$**

Minzu Wenhua Gong (Minorities' Cultural Palace) Fuxingmen Dajie
Tel: 6666-0544
This Mongolian hotpot restaurant is one of several restaurants showcasing some of China's 56 minorities inside an exhibition centre and concert venue, next to the Minzu Hotel. **$$**

Imperial

Fangshan
inside Beihai Park
Tel: 6401-1889
Opened in 1925 by three imperial chefs in a traditional courtyard on

the shore of Beihai Lake, Fangshan produces dishes once served to Qing emperors. Calligraphy and antique furniture adorn the stylish dining rooms. An extensive menu features haute cuisine from across China. Set banquets start at 150 yuan per person for a relatively simple meal to more than 1,000 yuan for a truly imperial feast. **$$$$**

Tingliguan (Pavilion for Listening to the Orioles Singing)
inside the Summer Palace
Tel: 6258-1608
Enjoy fine imperial cuisine in an idyllic, imperial setting opened in 1949 close to Kunming Lake. Reservations essential. **$$$$**

Price Guide

Average price of dinner per person, without wine:

$$$$	more than 150 yuan
$$$	100–150 yuan
$$	50–100 yuan
$	less than 50 yuan

Regional Chinese cuisine

Afanti
2 Houguaibang Hutong
Chaoyangmennei Dajie
Tel: 6525-1071
Renamed "A-fun-ti" to reflect the fun-pub atmosphere, this lively Xinjiang Muslim restaurant has belly dancers and other shows. Afanti encourages you to join him on the tables. The roast mutton, kebabs and nans are good, too. Reservations advised. **$$$**

Daijiacun (Dai Village)
13 Tiyuguan Lu
Chongwen District
tel: 6714-0145; and Guandongdian Nanjie, Chaoyang District, tel: 6594-2454.
The Dai people of China's southwestern Yunnan province are related to Thais. Their slightly spicy food often uses pineapple and coconut. Among the specialities are rice and other dishes steamed in bamboo tubes, wild mushrooms, snake, and rice wine. Dancers entertain you during your meal, and invite you to join them. **$$$**

Fengzeyuan
11 Liujiayao Beilu, Yongdingmenwai.
Tel: 6761-1331; 83 Zhushikou
Xidajie. Tel: 6318-6688.
Shandong cuisine is the hallmark of
one of the city's most praised
restaurants. Many dishes feature
delicately flavoured seafood. **$$$**

Kangle
259 Andingmennei Dajie
Tel: 6404-2223
A block east of the Bell and Drum
Towers, Kangle serves a wide range
of southern cuisine, especially
Fujian and spicy Yunnan dishes. **$$**

Ritan Park Restaurant
Southwest corner of Ritan
Gongyuan. Tel: 6500-5837.
This courtyard restaurant also has
outdoor tables by a small lake. The
menu is dominated by spicy
Sichuan dishes, like Mapo Doufu
and Gongbao Chicken, and *jia
chang cai* – standard "homestyle"
dishes. Steamed *jiaozi* (pasta
parcels) are also popular. **$$**

Sichuan Restaurant
51 Xirongxian Hutong
Tel: 6603-3291; 37A Donganmen
Jie, Wangfujing, Tel: 6513-7591.
Long a favourite of Party cadres and
even leaders, the original Sichuan
occupies a beautiful courtyard
house hidden away in a hutong. The
Wangfujing branch serves the same
combination of Sichuan standards
laced with hot chillies and peppers,
with specialities like *guoba* (sizzling
rice-crust), hot pepper soup and
cold noodles. **$$**

Sunflower Village
51 Wanquanhe Lu
Haidian District
Tel: 6256-2967
Bringing back the bad old days of
the Cultural Revolution might not be
everyone's idea of fun, but the
Sunflower recreates some of the
dishes from a time of great
austerity. You can sit on a *kang* (a
heated brick platform common in
northern China), while you admire
period newspaper clippings, and
pictures of the Great Helmsman
and his heroic workers and
peasants. Some of the dishes
feature leaves, grass or insects.
More immediately appealing are
stewed beancurd, *songren yumi*

(stir-fried corn and pine-nuts), and
wotou (steamed cornbread). **$$**

Tibet Shambala
301 Xinjiang Xiao Lu
Baishiqao
Haidian District
Tel: 6842-2631
The Tibetan owner has attempted to
bring a touch of high-plains cuisine
to far-off Beijing. Diners sit in small
white-washed rooms draped with
Tibetan Buddhist paintings. Try
tsampa (barley flour blended with
yak butter), *momos* (dumplings
filled with minced yak meat), and
thukpa noodles with lamb. **$$**

Vegetarian

Beijing Sucai Fanguan
74 Xuanwumen Dajie
south of Xidan crossing
Tel: 6605-6130
This simple eatery serves mainly
stir-fried vegetable and beancurd
dishes, and several kinds of
vegetarian *jiaozi*. **$**

Gongdelin
158 Qianmen Nandajie
Tel: 6702-0867
The Beijing branch of a Shanghai
restaurant opened in the early
1920s, Gongdelin specialises in
amazing mock meat dishes,
carefully crafted from beancurd,
mushrooms and vegetables. A few
dishes are so realistic that some
vegetarians are put off by the
appearance. **$$**

Tianshi
57 Dengshikou Dajie
Dongcheng District
Tel: 6524-2349
Don't be fooled by the menu, which,
like that at Gongdelin, lists a large
selection of meat and fish dishes.
They are all fake, from the Tea-
Marinated Duck to the Sweet-and-
Sour Mandarin Fish. The restaurant,
which has a shop downstairs,
claims its Buddhism–inspired
dishes are all selected for their
health benefits. **$$**

Western

Adria
Lanmaqiao Lu, opposite Kempinski
Hotel. Tel: 6460-0896;
14 Dongdaqiao Lu. Tel: 6500-6186.
Great pizza, pasta, salad and wine

are the staples of this Italian
restaurant with two locations. **$$$**

Bleu Marine
5 Guanghua Xilu
Tel: 6500-6704
The chefs buy fresh ingredients
daily and the exquisite French menu
changes regularly. The authentic
atmosphere is irresistible to
homesick Europeans. Reservations
essential. **$$$$**

Mexican Wave
Dongdaqiao Lu
Tel: 6506-3961
A long-time expat favourite serving
not only Mexican standards like
enchiladas and tortillas, but also
decent pizzas and burgers. **$$$**

Kebab Kafe
Sanlitun Beilu
Tel: 6415-5812
Fairly authentic German food in the
heart of one of Sanlitun's two main
bar streets. **$$$**

Culture

Sources of Information

Weekly Beijing listings magazines *City Edition*, *Metro Weekly* and *Beijing Scene*, plus the China Daily publication *Beijing Weekend* and the Beijing Tourism Administration publication *Beijing This Month*, all have useful guides to entertainment, the arts and expat events. For those who read Chinese, *Beijing Youth Daily* and *Beijing Evening Post* are recommended. Or check these web listings: *www.xianzai.com* *www.beijing-cityedition.com* *www.beijingscene.com* *www.chinabuzz.com* For information on the latest exhibitions at Beijing musuems, see *www.bjmuseumnet.org*
   A Chinese language site with details of classical music concerts is *www.artstoday.com*

Acrobatics

Acrobatics are a traditional form of street theatre in China, with special performances at Chinese New Year fairs. It is also an important element in Beijing opera and in many Chinese martial arts. Most regular acrobatics shows in Beijing are performed by young students, usually including children. Venues include:
Chaoyang Theatre, 36 Dongsanhuan Beilu, Hujialou. Tel: 6507-2421.
Poly Plaza, 14 Dongzhimen Nandajie. Tel: 6500-1188 x5127.
Universal Theatre, Dongsishi Qiao. Tel: 6502-3984.

Teahouses

In addition to the ordinary teahouses, which simply serve as a refuge from family, work, shopping, or whatever over a pot or two of a fine brew, a few teahouses entertain their guests. They stage short performances of Beijing opera, acrobatics, magic shows, crosstalk and other entertainment.
Lao She Teahouse, 3rd Floor, 3 Qianmenxi Dajie. Tel: 6303-6830.
Tianqiao Happy Teahouse, 113 Tianqiao Market, Chongwen District. Tel: 6303-0617.

Theatre

Theatres attract larger audiences than Beijing opera venues. Both local plays, including many avant garde pieces, and foreign plays are performed. The main theatres are:
Capital Theatre, 22 Wangfujing Dajie. Tel: 6524-9847.
Beijing Drama Theatre, 11 Hufang Lu. Tel: 6303-8149.
21st Century Theatre, Sino-Japanese Youth Centre, 40 Liangmaqiao Lu. Tel: 6466-3311.

Classical Music

If you are lucky, you may be able to see one of the foreign artists or conductors on tour in Beijing — they come in increasing numbers. Beijing's main venues for Chinese and Western classical music concerts, as well as ballet, dance and song ensembles and other performances, are:
Beijing Concert Hall, 1 Beixinhua Jie. Tel: 6605-5812.
Beijing Exhibition Centre Theatre, Xizhimenwai Dajie. Tel: 6835-1383.

Cinema

Despite the number of pirated video CDs on the streets, Beijing still has many cinemas. Most have morning, matinee and two evening showings. The latter usually start around 6.30pm and 8.30pm. Cinemas showing foreign films are especially popular, but more expensive. *Titanic* is as well known in China as anywhere, and Hong Kong comedies and action films remain popular. Foreign films are usually dubbed into Chinese. You can buy tickets at each venue, but it is often not possible to book in advance by telephone. If you are travelling with a group or on a package tour, you can ask your tour guide. Every second Friday, at the Sino-Japanese Youth Exchange Centre, **Cherry Lane Movies** (Tel: 6522-4046; *www.cherrylane.com*) shows a Chinese film with English subtitles. Cinemas showing both Chinese and foreign films, without subtitles, include:
Dahua Cinema, 82 Dongdan Beidajie. Tel: 6527-4420.
Victory Cinema, 55 Xisi Dongdajie. Tel: 6617-5091.

Peking Opera

Young people in Beijing seldom appreciate the often complex plays and style of Beijing opera, and they prefer disco, karaoke or television. Some of the traditional Beijing opera theatres have adapted to modern trends and stage pop concerts, performances of *Xiangsheng* (crosstalk, or comic dialogues) or similar pieces. But most visitors will surely want to see a typical Chinese production, and some of the best-known opera venues are:
Chang'an Theatre, Jianguomen Nei Dajie (next to the International Hotel). Tel: 6510-1309.
Grand View Garden Theatre, 12 Nancaiyuan Jie, Xuanwu. Tel: 6351-9025.
Guanghe Theatre, 46 Qianmenroushi Jie, Qianmen Dajie. Tel: 6701-8216.
Huguang Guildhall, 3 Hufang Qiao, Xuanwu. Tel: 6351-8284.
Liyuan Theatre, Qianmen Hotel, 175 Yongan Lu. Tel: 6301-6688 x8860.
Zhengyici Theatre, 220 Xiheyuan Dajie, Xuanwu District. Tel: 6722-6787. This authentic wooden theatre holds nightly performances in a traditional setting.

Ziguang Cinema, 168 Chaowai Dajie. Tel: 6500-3868.

Art Galleries

For an overview of the best of Chinese art, visit the China National Art Gallery. Small commercial galleries have also flourished in Beijing since the early 1990s. These sell the work of many innovative artists, as well as masters of traditional watercolour, ceramics and sculpture techniques. Exhibitions change frequently. Several websites showcase fine art in Beijing and other Chinese cities: *www.chinese-art.com*, *artscenechina.com*, and *china-avantgarde.com*.

China National Art Gallery, 1 Wusi Dajie, Chaoyangmennei. Tel: 6401-7076.

Hualai Gallery, 74 Donghuamen Dajie, northeast of Tiananmen Square. Tel: 6523-8182. *www.hlgallery.com*.

Red Gate Gallery, 3rd Floor, China World Hotel, Jianguomenwai Dajie. Tel: 6505-2266 x6821.

Wan Fung Gallery, 136 Nanchizi Dajie. Tel: 6512-7338.

Xu Beihong Memorial Hall, 53 Xinjiekou Beidajie. Tel: 6225-2265. Xu Beihong is one of China's most celebrated watercolour artists.

Children's Shows

Most performances of acrobatics and Beijing opera, and variety shows at teahouses, are suitable for children. Programmes usually begin and end early. Other possibilities include:

Blue Zoo, Workers' Stadium, South Gate. Tel: 6591-3397. Tunnels below the extensive tanks allow some great views of marine life.

China Puppet Theatre, 1 Anhuaxili. Tel: 6425-4798.

Nightlife

Many people will tell you that Beijing is not China. The quality and quantity of entertainment available supports that claim. Karaoke no longer dominates the capital's nightlife, especially for more affluent people. Youngsters dance the night away under the laser lights of huge discos. Businessmen frequent garish clubs where hostesses offer *san pei* — three accompaniments: drinking, dancing and sex.

Once you could only find bands, dancing, foreign beer and mixed drinks in the large hotels, but now several areas popular with affluent locals or expats have whole streets full of bars. Some bars close around 2am, though many stay open until 4am or 5am, especially at weekends. In some, you can find live rock music or jazz; in others, DJs spin dance tunes. Discos break up the dancing and laser shows with performances by singers and cage dancers.

Because new places appear so quickly, it is sometimes best to aim for one of the three main bar areas: Sanlitun, Jianguomenwai, and the Haidian university district. The local government has already begun to move some Sanlitun bars to a specially built bar area at the south gate of Chaoyang Park. Though many Sanlitun and Chaoyang Park bars are depressingly similar attempts to recreate European or North American style, some Beijing entrepreneurs have opened bars specializing in punk rock, jazz, sportscasts, film and other entertainment. All of the music venues listed stage live performances on Friday and Saturday; phone or check publications for other days.

Live Music

Arcadia, Building 3, Jindu Apartments, Fangchengyuan. Tel: 6764-8271. Decorated by the owner-artist, this bar has a distinctive, modern atmosphere in which house singers cover Chinese and Western pop classics.

CD Cafe, Dongsanhuan Lu. Tel: 6501-6655 x5127. Jazz and blues bands attract a regular crowd of aficionados to this otherwise unremarkable bar.

Get Lucky Bar, Taiyanggong Market, Huixin Dongjie. Tel: 6429-9109. Raucous punk and rock bands explore the Chinese pop fringe in suitable surroundings.

Henry J Bean's, China World Trade Centre. Tel: 6505-2266. House bands cover Western standards in an American-style burger bar.

Hotline 1950, 4–5 Liangmaqiao Lu. Tel: 6461-1950. Amidst imported Americana, the Hotline house band belts out cover versions of Western and Chinese standards, aided by dancers, drag acts and (sometimes) comedians.

Jam House, Sanlitun Nan Jiuba Jie. Tel: 6506-3845. Chinese and expat bands play all kinds of Western and Chinese pop in a bar frequented by young foreigners.

Minder Cafe, Dongdaqiao Xiejie. Tel: 6599-6066. A mainly Filipino house band enlivens one of the best-known, or most notorious, expat bars, bringing a touch of Benidorm to Beijing.

Mother Earth Cafe, 1 Baijiazhuang Lu, Dongsanhuan Lu. Tel: 6503-1099. Bizarre and, like many Beijing bars, eclectic. A haunted house exterior masks a spacious "rainforest" interior, complete with

Where's Hot

Weekly listing magazines *City Edition*, *Metro Weekly* and *Beijing Scene* have the best nightlife guides. Or check: *www.xianzai.com*, *www.beijing-cityedition.com*, *www.beijingscene.com*, or *www.chinabuzz.com*.

kitsch animals, where many Beijing pop and rock bands perform.
Sanwei Bookstore, 60 Fuxingmenwai Dajie. Tel: 6601-3204. At this former teahouse, above a bookstore, Friday is jazz night, while Saturday is reserved for Chinese classical music played on pipa and guzheng.

Bars

Bus Bar, Xuesi Lukou, Beisanhuan Lu, Haidian. This sixties-style bar, housed in two old buses, is a popular hang-out for arty students.
Goose and Duck, Ritandongyi Jie. Tel: 6509-3777. One of several partly successful attempts to create an English pub.
Half Dream, 5 Xingbu Yicun Xili (near the Leyou Hotel). Tel: 6415-8083. Ancient Egyptian motifs grace one of Beijing's trendiest bars, popular with local dancers, artists and actors, plus a few expat groupies.
Hidden Tree, 12 Sanlitun Nan Jiuba Jie. Tel: 6509-3642. Pop classics complement the pleasant European style, with drinks including pricey bottled Belgian beer.
Jazz Ya, 18 Sanlitun Bei Jiuba Jie. Tel: 6415-1227. Japanese owned, this bar offers an extensive cocktail menu and a mellow mood aided, of course, by plenty of good jazz.
Pretty Bird, Anhuali Xiqu, behind the Jiangsu Hotel. Tel: 6427-7025. A former bomb shelter now houses a cavernous club full of experimental sculpture and experimental people.
Schiller's, Liangmaqiao Lu, opposite the Kempinski Hotel. Tel: 6461-9276. An unpretentious Western bar, which serves decent bar meals.

Discos

Banana Club, Top Floor, Sea Sky Shopping Centre, 12 Chaoyangmenwai Dajie. Tel: 6599-3351. More affluent locals favour this upmarket club, which features a dancefloor, karaoke rooms, and a lounge area where the house band plays.

The Den, Gongti Lu, next to City Hotel. Tel: 6592-6290. A fluid clientele, and an international cattle market around the crowded, sweaty dancefloor, recreate Ibiza in Beijing.
Hotspot, Sanhuan Donglu. Tel: 6531-2277. One of the pioneers of industrial décor, drag acts and cage dancers wearing little but long boots, Hotspot maintains its popularity despite competition from newer and bigger imitators.
JJ's Rock 'n' Roll, 1 Nongzhan Nanlu, south gate of Chaoyang Park. Tel: 6618-9305. A monster of dance, JJ's has multiple levels in a building that resembles the inside of a power station cooling tower.
Nightman, 2 Xibahe Nanlu. Tel: 6466-2562. Young Beijingers dance away the night to a mixed bag of sounds served up by local and imported DJs, among slightly seedy, multi-level dancing and posing areas.

Festivals

Apart from Spring Festival – new year according to the Chinese lunar calendar – the other public holidays in modern China are observed according to the Gregorian calendar. National Day and International Workers' Day, the two most important public holidays, reflect the political changes since 1949 in China. Other important political celebrations that are not public holidays are July 1, the day of the foundation of the Chinese Communist Party, and August 1, the founding day of the People's Liberation Army. Several other traditional festivals have revived since the Cultural Revolution, though these are more evident in Beijing's rural areas.

The origins of these traditional festivals go back a long way, some to the Shang dynasty (16th to 11th centuries BC). Some lost their original meaning over time, changed in content, or gained a religious meaning; others marked historical events or were reserved for the worship of ancestors or gods. The Spring Festival, the Qingming Festival (Day for Remembering the Dead) and the Moon Festival survive more or less intact. These form one half of the ancient six festivals: three "festivals of the living" (Spring Festival, Dragon Boat Festival, and Moon Festival) and the three "festivals of the dead" (Qingming Festival, All Souls' Day, and the Songhanyi Festival – for sending winter clothes to ancestors).

Traditional Western holidays, including Christmas, are not usually celebrated in China, except by expats and small local Christian communities. Shops and restaurants, however, have latched on to the chance of another seasonal boost to trade. Young, educated people often exchange Christmas cards or presents.

Spring Festival

The most important traditional festival is Chinese New Year or **Spring Festival** (Chunjie). It usually falls in late January or early February. If you travel in China at that time, expect restricted and crowded public transport services, because many people return to their home towns for this festival. Trains are often fully booked. The Chinese new year celebrations are traditionally a family gathering, similar to Christmas in the West. On New Year's Eve, the entire family gathers for a special meal. In Beijing and the north, families make and eat *jiaozi* (pasta parcels filled with minced meat and vegetables). At midnight, they welcome the new year with a volley of firecrackers – though officially, fireworks have been banned in Beijing since the mid-1990s.

The first day is taken up with meals and visits to relatives. The second and third days are for friends and acquaintances. People visit each other, always taking food, drink or other gifts, and offering good wishes for the new year. During Spring Festival, many Beijing parks and temples hold fairs where you can still see stilt walkers, dragon dancers, wrestlers, jugglers,

Spring Cleaning

In the past, it was customary that all debts had to be paid before Spring Festival. This is because the earth god leaves the earth a few days before the festival to report to the Jade Emperor about the behaviour of each family. During the one-week festival, all work had to stop in the house, which had been cleaned and renovated. Today, people still clean and tidy thoroughly before festivals.

snake charmers, Yang Ge dancers, and opera singers. Some of the best fairs are held in Ditan Park, the Summer Palace, and the Temple of the White Cloud. Longtan Park hosts a spectacular national folk arts competition.

Lantern Festival

The **Lantern Festival** used to signify the official end of the new year celebrations. Today, people work normally on that day. Only the meal of *yuanxiao* (sticky rice balls, usually filled with sweet red bean or sesame paste) follows the old customs. In recent years, Beijing has again promoted Qing-style processions, inlcuding musicians, lion dancers, Yang Ge groups, and banners with pictures of deities.

Festival of Light

The **Qingming Festival** (Festival of Light) was originally a day to celebrate the renewal of life in springtime. Later it became a day to remember the dead. In the past, those who could afford it would make a pilgrimage to the graves of their ancestors, taking cooked chicken, pork, vegetables, fruit, incense and candles. They would burn paper money, often printed with "Bank of Hell," and sometimes paper clothes, furniture and houses to ensure their ancestors fared well in the spirit world. After the sacrifice, the cleaning of the graves would begin. Many people, especially in rural areas, have resumed the customs of sweeping graves and burning paper money. In Beijing, schoolchildren lay wreaths and flowers in Tiananmen Square in memory of those who gave their lives for the revolution.

Moon Festival

The **Moon Festival** or Mid-Autumn Festival (Zhong qiu jie), celebrated according to the lunar calendar on the 15th day of the eighth month (usually mid-September) also remains popular in Beijing. On this day, people eat moon cakes filled

with various combinations of meat, fruit, sugar, spices, seeds and nuts. The cakes are to remind people of the revolt against Mongol rule in the 14th century, when similar cakes were used to transport secret messages between Chinese leaders. According to ancient Chinese myth, the hare and toad live on the moon. Stories about the moon hare and Chang'e, the "woman in the moon," are still told. If the weather is good, people sit together outside on the day of the Moon Festival (which is a normal working day), chat, look at the moon, and eat moon cakes.

Cricket Matching

The Moon Festival is also the time for the cricket championships. Hundreds of cricket fanciers, many of them members of informal clubs, prepare for the annual contest. If you own a white jade-tailed or a double-toothed cricket, you have a good chance of winning. The crickets are put into elaborate containers, or into simpler ones made of bamboo strips, and taken for walks under the coats of their owners. During competition, the owners put opposing crickets into one container and wait for one to send the other packing. Professional cricket fanciers divide their fighting insects by weight, just like boxers. Gambling is strictly controlled in China, and mostly illegal, but a small flutter is part of the fun on these occasions.

Outdoor Activities

Sports

Chinese people are generally very keen on sport. Many sports halls and stadiums, some of them built to bolster Beijing's Olympic Games bids, host regular competitions and tournaments. Early each morning, the parks fill with people practising taiji, qi gong, martial arts, badminton and table tennis. Chinese television broadcasts local and international sporting events, and stars like Ronaldo and Michael Jordan are as well known in China as Marx and Engels.

Walking the Wall

An unusual place to hike – and hopefully get away from the crowds – is on one of the less visited stretches of Great Wall, such as Jinshanling or Huanghuacheng.

The Great Wall Sheraton Hotel offers weekend hikes led by expert William Lindesay along a spectacular stretch of wall not far from Mutianyu, combined with a stay in a modernised farmhouse. Lindesay also arranges clean-ups of the wall. See *www.wildwall.com* or e-mail *wildwall@netchina.com.cn*

You can arrange your own hike along the wall but be warned that accommodation is rudimentary. A guard tower on the eastern stretch of Mutianyu has been converted into Gubao Villa (tel: 6962-6867), with bunks and simple meals but no washing or toilet facilities. Simatai has a modern, off-wall guesthouse (tel: 6993-1095) and a tourist village.

Facilities for Visitors

Many large hotels, including the **Lido, Shangri-la, New Otani, SAS Radisson** and **Great Wall Sheraton**, have sports facilities including gymnasia, tennis courts and swimming pools. **Dongdan Sports Centre** (Dongdan Dajie, near Chang'an Dajie. Tel: 6523-1241) has a swimming pool, indoor tennis and squash courts and other facilities right in the city centre. **China World Hotel** (Tel: 6505-2266 ext.33) has good indoor tennis courts open from 6am to 10pm. China World shopping centre also has an ice-skating rink. In winter, the frozen Kunming Lake at the Summer Palace is Beijing's premier ice-skating venue.

Wealthy locals and expats dabble in horse riding or golf at a growing number of centres in suburban Beijing. The **Movenpick Hotel** (Tel: 6456-5588) organises horse riding, or try **Beijing Green Equestrian Club** (by the Wenyu River, east of Lijing Garden Villa, close to the airport) or **Beijing Horsemanship Club** (Shili Nanlu, Jiuxianqiao. Tel: 6435-4756). Among the golf course options are **Beijing International Golf Club** (50 km/30 miles north of Beijing near Changping. Tel: 6974-5678), and **Beijing Country Golf Club** (35 km/22 miles northeast of Beijing in Shunyi County. Tel: 6944-1005).

Spectator Sports

Soccer has overtaken basketball as the most popular spectator sport in China. Naturally, the capital has one of the top professional soccer teams, Beijing Guo'an. Like many Chinese teams, Guo'an regularly attract crowds of more than 50,000. They have also bought several foreign players, though the overall level of skill remains far behind that of leading European and South American teams. But it is worth watching a game to sample the unique atmosphere. Unfortunately – or perhaps fortunately – most visitors will not understand the crude chants. Professional basketball has also taken off, aided by many ex-NBA players.

Tickets for Guo'an soccer games, and for basketball games featuring the Beijing Ducks in the CBA league, can be bought from the ticket office on the north side of the Workers' Stadium or from the Li Sheng Sports Store (74A Wangfujing Dajie. Tel: 6525-0581)

Hiking and Cycling

The Beijing area offers plenty of opportunities for **hiking** and **cycling**. The Ming Tombs, Eastern Qing Tombs, and the former imperial summer resort of Chengde are all set in picturesque hiking country.

There are no Western style campsites in China, but wild camping is possible so long as you stay far enough away from villages and fields. Cycling remains the best way to see the city (see Getting Around). It is also possible to cycle to sights around Beijing, though some of the distances make a day-trip too demanding. For cycling tours and other information about cycling in China, see *www.BikeChina.com*

Shopping

What to Buy

Beijing offers a wide variety of shopping, from table-top stalls on the street to vast new plazas full of famous brands. For visitors, silk, jade, cloisonné, lacquerware, jewellery, carpets, watercolour paintings and clothing all make popular gifts or souvenirs. Prices vary considerably, and good items can be expensive.

All hotels have shops, and the top hotels have elegant shopping arcades, usually with some exquisite antiques for sale. But the most interesting and inexpensive way is to wander around one of the main shopping areas in the capital, such as Wangfujing or Qianmen. Here you will find a typical Chinese shopping atmosphere and you will get a vivid impression of the huge number of shoppers in China. Many of the people you see shopping are

Shopping Tips

Examine everything you buy carefully, especially at streetside stalls; bargain hard at all markets and private shops. If you like something buy it, otherwise you may later regret a lost opportunity because what you see today will probably be gone tomorrow. And don't miss a shopping spree in one of the big shopping centres; at the same time, you will get a chance to see Chinese shoppers in action. Especially in the free markets, it is advisable to compare prices and watch how much the locals pay. All too often, free market traders will happily fleece unwary customers.

not Beijing residents but visitors from other regions on holiday or business. Shops generally open from 9am–8pm every day. In department stores, chain stores and larger shops, prices are usually fixed, but bargaining is definitely expected elsewhere.

Shopping Areas

Below are the main shopping centres and some important shops and markets.

Wangfujing

Beijing's premier shopping street received a huge facelift in 1999, in preparation for the 50th anniversary of Communist China. It is now a paved street that has two of China's biggest and glitziest shopping centres, the Sun Dongan Plaza and the Oriental Plaza, at either end. Among the stores that survived the redevelopment are China Star Silk Store (No. 133), Beijing Medical Department Store (No. 153) and the refurbished Beijing Department Store (No. 255). At the northwest corner, close to a crossroads, is the Foreign Languages Bookstore, a good place to buy English books about China. Diagonally across the crossroads from the bookstore is the Luwu Jewellery and Craft Store (No. 268). Small stalls inside the Luwu store sell many craft items and souvenirs, including silk, jade, musical instruments and carved stone and wood items. Other interesting shops are a musical instrument shop (on the corner with Dong'anmen), and an art shop with scroll paintings and stone rubbings (No. 265). At No. 289, the Beijing Huadian, a gallery, sells paintings by modern artists in both contemporary and traditional styles.

Xidan

Xidan is an old commercial quarter to the east of the Minzu Hotel, about a mile west of Tiananmen Square. Like Wangfujing, its main street Xidan Beidajie runs north from Chang'an Avenue and has also undergone major rebuilding, so that

it is almost unrecognisable as the collection of bustling clothes markets it was in the early 1990s. Plush department stores now line Xidan Beidajie, the oldest of which is the Xidan Baihuo Shangchang. Xidan offers far less of interest to visitors than Wangfujing. A new multilevel bookshop on the west side might be worth a look. And a basement restaurant at the southeastern corner gives a glimpse of both traditional food and 1970s-style eating, where you queue up to buy tokens before going to collect your food. Look for the traditional doorway painted red and green.

Qianmen

Qianmen Dajie runs south from Qianmen gate at the southern end of Tiananmen Square. This was part of Beijing's busiest commercial quarter during the Qing dynasty. A walk around the area is also an exploration of old Beijing. Along Qianmen Dajie you will find the Beijing Silk Shop (Beijing Sichou Shandian, No. 5), a music shop (Xinsheng Yueqidian, No. 18) that specialises in traditional instruments, the Hall of Eternal Youth (Changchun Tang, No. 28), a traditional pharmacist, the Hunan Pottery Shop (Hunan Taoci Shangdian, No.99) and the Jingdezhen Porcelain Shop (Jingdezhen Yishu Cipi Fuwubu, No.119). On the east side of the street is Quanjude (No. 32), one of the capital's best-known Peking duck restaurants.

Dazhalan

Just 300 metres long, Dazhalan (Large Wicker Gate) dates from the Ming dynasty and remains one of the liveliest shopping streets in Beijing. It runs southwest from the northern end of Qianmen Street. Among the highlights of the narrow lane is Ruifengxian, an old silk shop with a marble gate and a traditional wooden interior. On the same street is the capital's best-known traditional pharmacist, Tongrentan pharmacy, which dates from the mid-17th century.

Dazhalan and the streets around

it have a long history as an entertainment centre. Five of the biggest Peking opera houses used to be here, and you can still buy opera clothes, masks and props at the Peking Opera Costume Shop. Two old shoe shops, Neiliansheng and Buyingzhai, make traditional handmade cotton shoes. President Jiang Zemin, like Mao before him, orders his cotton shoes from Dazhalan.

If you take a right turn off Dazhalan, you can continue west until you reach Liulichang (*see below*). The walk takes under 20 minutes, not including browsing time, and takes you through some quiet, unspoilt *hutong* (alleys). Because taxis are not allowed to stop at the Dazhalan end of Qianmen Street, it may be better to start from Liulichang. Alternatively, to start from Qianmen you can take the underground to the Qianmen stop, or walk south from Tiananmen Square.

Liulichang

This is often known as Antique Street because of the large number of antiques and art and craft items on sale. You can buy original paintings and woodblock print reproductions, materials for traditional Chinese painting, and old (and new) books.

Liulichang means glazed tile factory. The Ming dynasty tile factory that gave the street its

Buying Antiques

Although many low-quality household items are much cheaper than they are in the West, antiques and works of art often fetch surprisingly high prices. Objects dating from before 1840 can not be exported. Most antiques date from the early 20th century, which covered the final period of the late Qing dynasty and the early republic. In recent years, factories have produced many replicas of antiques, and it is harder to find really beautiful pieces, such as woodblock prints of traditional pictures.

name has long gone, but it once made the imperial yellow tiles that crown the Forbidden City. The street has been completely renovated in Qing style in recent years and has regained its splendour with even more shops. Even if you don't want to buy anything, Liulichang is fun to wander round and window shop. The street runs east-west either side of Nanxinhua Jie, which you can cross via a footbridge. The most famous shop, Rongbaozhai, is on the western stretch. Rongbaozhai is known for its paintings, calligraphy, and brilliant woodblock prints. You can find expensive, as well as many cheap, souvenirs and gifts in the shops along Liulichang, including nice stone rubbings. This is also a good place to buy artist's materials. But genuine antiques have become scarcer and are generally limited to the more expensive shops. Some of the pictures on sale here are of rather poor quality.

If you are really interested in the chance of finding the genuine antiques at a bargain price, plus plenty of cheap reproductions, there are three other markets you won't want to miss. The **Chaowai Market**, at the northern end of Ritan Lu, has two warehouses that are well worth perusing: one is devoted to furniture, the other to small antiquities. Prices are generally reasonable and, as with all markets, bargaining is the norm. Two others are Hongqiao market (*see below*) and the Panjiayuan "Ghost Market" (*see below*).

Shopping Centres

Diagonally opposite the Friendship Store, across Jianguomenwai Dajie, is the **Scite** shopping centre. Like several of Beijing's new upmarket shopping centres, Scite is full of luxury imports. Just half a mile west along Chang'an Dajie are the neighbouring **Cofco Plaza** and **Henderson Centre**. Other alternatives are the **Parkson** department store, conveniently reached from the Fuxingmen underground station, and the **Sun Dongan** and **Oriental** plazas on Wangfujing.

The Friendship Store

A visit to the Friendship Store (Youyi Shangdian) is definitely one of the most comfortable ways to shop in Beijing. It is located on Jianguomenwai Dajie, the eastern extension of Chang'an Dajie. You can buy most things produced in China at the store, from dried mushrooms to exquisite cloisonné. There is a large carpet section and a stock of good silk. The Friendship Store can arrange to send any goods abroad and deal with the customs formalities for you. It also has a dressmaking department, a watch repair counter, a bookshop, a coffee shop, a supermarket and a dry cleaner's.

The **Friendship Shopping City** (usually known as Yansha), at the Lufthansa Centre, takes in a broader price range. Its five floors cover everything from ginseng to roller blades. The basement has a small supermarket and there are plenty of restaurants and snack bars in the Kempinski Hotel, which also forms part of the Lufthansa complex.

Markets

Once the shops and offices have closed, Beijing families hurry to the food markets to find eggs or a cabbage for supper. Even with prices as low as a few jiao, you can still bargain. Be aware though, that foreigners buying fruit or vegetables are often quoted much higher prices than locals. If you are concerned about this, watch what someone else pays first.

Every neighbourhood has some kind of food market. Until the mid-1990s, many main roads had long rows of market stalls, often supplemented by farmers selling direct from their trucks. Many such markets sold services as well as goods. Barbers, masseurs, tailors and cobblers all offered their skills. You can still find these people plying their trades on the street, but most outdoor markets have disappeared. The municipal government now has a policy of moving all markets indoors and discouraging roadside stalls. If you see a group of vendors suddenly bundle up their wares and rush off, this probably means they have spotted a tax officer.

Hongqiao
One of the new-style markets is **Hongqiao.** Located across the road from the Temple of Heaven, it occupies a modern shopping centre. It sells a bewildering variety of food and the whole effect of the market is a confusing and intense assault on the senses.

But Hongqiao market is no longer just for food. On the first floor are stalls with bird cages, plant pots, bamboo bicycle seats for children, plastic bowls and other household items. Watches, radios, cassette players and pagers can all be found here. At the eastern end is a section devoted to toys, gifts and stationery. Up on the second floor you'll find jeans, leather jackets, fur coats, furniture and luggage being sold by competing stalls.

Food for all Tastes

Hongqiao Market sells almost every kind type of food imaginable, from live scorpions to tropical fruit, The basement is devoted to food stalls. Here, grain and dried fruit are sold next to fresh fruit and vegetables. The aroma of fresh coriander, ginger and leeks, aniseed and fennel seeds, dried shrimps and pepper, the basic ingredients of Chinese cuisine, mingle with the fascinating sight of black "tree ear" fungus, melon seeds and steaming sweet potatoes, and the noise of rapid, loud bargaining. In the seafood section, barrels of live fish, turtles and shrimps stand beside cages of crabs, frogs and snakes. Next to this is the meat section, where you sometimes find dog on a table besides goats' heads and sides of beef and pork.

But the third floor is the one not to miss. Here you'll find strings of pearls by the hundreds, at a fraction of their cost in the West. About 50 stalls stock antiques or reproductions, selling mostly smaller items. You can find everything from brass containers turned an "ancient" green that belies their youth, to ceramic Buddhas, wooden masks, and Red Guard alarm clocks and other Cultural Revolution kitsch. If you shop carefully, you can find some great deals. Take your time and look around before you buy. Sometimes the price in one stall can be many times that at another. Bargaining is expected.

Hongtan
Across the road from Hongqiao, at the northeast corner of the Temple of Heaven Park, is the newer **Hongtan** market. Originally specialising in potted plants, flowers, and gardening and pet supplies, Hongtan has expanded to include antiques, reproductions, souvenirs and gifts. It is a good place to buy teapots and cheap ceramic items, and carved wood salvaged from demolished courtyard houses.

Panjiayuan
Not far from Hongqiao, near the southeast corner of the Third Ring Road, **Panjiayuan** is the liveliest place to buy genuine and reproduction antiques. Known as the Ghost Market (because it begins by 6am) and the Farmers' Market (because farmers come from outside Beijing to sell goods here), it is largely a weekend market, though some stalls open on weekdays. Early Sunday morning, before 9am, is the best time to visit. Everything is sold here, often in large quantities. Rows of vases, pots and other ceramic items are laid out in one section, while another section is devoted to art and antiques. A separate compound specialises in all kinds of secondhand goods.

Guanyuan
Another market that still offers something unique is **Guanyuan.**

The Silk Market

Perhaps the best-known market for foreign visitors, the **Silk Market** has grown with the city. Beginning 500 yards east of the Friendship Store, on the north side of Jianguomenwai Dajie, it is likely to be moved to an indoor site within the next two years. It now covers more than one alley, and sells much more than silk. The best bargains are seconds or surplus fashion clothes from designer names, as well as traditional-style silk and cotton garments, outdoor shoes, and down jackets. In recent years, the number of stalls selling reproduction antiques and souvenirs has increased. The market has also become a magnet for illegal vendors of all kinds of counterfeit goods, from Video CDs to rucksacks.

Specialising in wildlife, curious visitors are attracted by the colourful birds in long rows of cages, either piled on top of each other or hanging from poles and branches. On the western side of the market, which is near Fuchengmen, are brilliantly-coloured ornamental fish swimming in huge glass containers or small enamel bowls.

The Bird Market
To the west of Longtan Park, in southeast Beijing, is the city's biggest **bird market.** Hundreds of people crowd into the narrow street to buy or look, especially on weekend mornings.

Traders set up stalls in the open, selling birds, dogs, cats, rabbits, and sometimes more exotic animals like snakes or monkeys, from the back of their tricycle carts. In late summer, cricket fanciers also sell their insects here. Orioles, thrushes and budgies twitter and hop about in their cages. The "bird with a hundred souls," as the Chinese call Mongolian larks, is among the most popular and expensive of birds.

Bamboo cages start from 10

yuan. However, if you want a skillfully-crafted antique cage with fancy brass fastenings, you will have to pay at least 200 yuan.

Bookstores

The state-owned Xinhua bookshop has over 100 branches in Beijing, though these usually stock few books in English, other than language textbooks. The **Xidan** bookstore is one of the largest, while Haidian, which is home to many universities, has a **Book City** full of small bookstores.

Many hotels stock good selections of books about China in English, as do several department stores, including Yansha, the Friendship Store, Parkson and the China World Shopping Centre. Probably the best place to find books on Chinese history, medicine, language and culture is the **Foreign Languages Bookstore** on Wangfujing.

Language

People in Beijing speak *putonghua*, or common language, known in the West as Mandarin Chinese. Putonghua is promoted as the standard language across the country, though most Chinese people also, or only, speak a local dialect. In most Beijing hotels you will find someone who can speak at least some English; in the top hotels good English is spoken. You can generally manage in English in tourist areas. However, taxi drivers usually speak little or no English.

Language and Writing

Putonghua or other Chinese dialects such as Cantonese is the first language of 93 percent of the population of China. Based on the northern dialect, one of the eight dialects of China, putonghua is taught throughout the country. There is considerable difference in the pronunciation of different dialects, though written forms are the same everywhere. Many ethnic minorities, such as Tibetans and Mongolians, have their own written and spoken

language. In Beijing, a slightly different dialect is spoken. Although the pronunciation in Beijing is very close to standard Chinese, it also has some distinctive characteristics, particularly the "er" sound added to the end of many syllables.

Since 1958, the *pinyin* system has been used to represent Chinese characters phonetically in the Latin alphabet. Pinyin has become internationally accepted, so that Peking is today written Beijing (pronounced Bay-jing), Canton is Guang-zhou, and Mao Tsetung is Mao Zedong. At first this may seem confusing to Westerners, but it is a useful, practical, if imperfect system that is increasingly popular in China. You will find many shop names written in pinyin above the entrance, and the names at railway stations are written in pinyin, so it is helpful to learn the basic rules of the pinyin system.

Most modern dictionaries use the pinyin system. (Taiwan, however, usually uses the older Wade-Giles transliteration system.) This transcription may at first appear confusing if one doesn't see the words as they are pronounced. The city of Qingdao, for example, is pronounced *chingdow*. It would definitely be useful, particularly for individual travelers, to familiarise yourself a little with the pronunciation of pinyin. Even when asking for a place or street name, you need to know how it is pronounced, otherwise you won't be understood. This guide uses the pinyin system

A Language of Character

Written Chinese uses thousands of characters, many of which are based on ancient pictograms, or picture-like symbols. Some characters used today go back more than 3,000 years. There are strict rules in the method of writing, as the stroke order affects the overall appearance of the characters. Because of the slowness of formal calligraphy, ordinary people develop their own simplified handwriting for everyday

use. In the past the script was written from right to left and top to bottom, but today it is usually written from left to right.

Some 6,000 characters are in regular use; 3,000 characters are sufficient for reading a newspaper. Mainland China has reformed written Chinese several times since 1949, and simplified characters are now used. In Hong Kong and Taiwan the old characters remain standard.

Names and Forms of Address

Chinese names usually consist of three, or sometimes two, syllables, each with its own meaning. Traditionally, the first syllable is the family name, the second or two others are personal names. For instance, in Deng Xiaoping, Deng is the family name, Xiaoping the personal name. The same is true for Fu Hao, where Fu is the family name, Hao the personal name. Until the 1980s, the address *tongzhi* (comrade) was common, but today *xiansheng* and *furen*, the Chinese equivalent of Mr and Mrs, are more usual. A young woman, as well as female staff in hotels and restaurants, can be addressed as *xiaojie* (Miss), Address older men, especially those in important positions, as *xiansheng* or *shifu* (Master).

throughout for Chinese names and expressions on occasion.

Pronunciation

The pronunciation of the consonants is similar to those in English: b, p, d, t, g, k are all voiceless; p, t, k are aspirated, b, d, g are not aspirated. The i after the consonants ch, c, r, sh, s, z, zh is not pronounced, it indicates that the preceding sound is lengthened.

Pinyin/Phonetic/Sound
a/a/f**ar**
an /un/r**un**
ang/ung /l**ung**
ao/ou/l**ou**d
b/b/**b**ath
c/ts/ra**ts**
ch/ch/**ch**ange
d/d/**d**ay
e/er/d**ir**t
e (after i,u,y)/a/tr**am**
ei/ay/m**ay**
en/en/wh**en**
eng/eong/**ng** has a nasal sound
er/or/honour
f/f/**f**ast
g/g/**g**o

h/ch/lo**ch**
i/ee/k**ee**n
j/j/**j**eep
k/k/ca**k**e
l/l/**l**ittle
m/m/**m**onth
n/n/**n**ame
o/o/b**o**nd
p/p/tra**pp**ed
q/ch/**ch**eer
r/r/**r**ight
s/s/me**ss**
sh/sh/**sh**ade
t/t/**t**on
u/oo/sh**oot**
u (after j,q,x,y)/as German
   u+/m**u+d**e
w/w/**w**ater
x/sh/as in **sh**eep
y/y/**y**ogi
z/ds/re**ds**
zh/dj/**j**ungle

Tones

It is sometimes said that Chinese is a monosyllabic language. At first sight, this seems to be true, since each character represents a single syllable that generally indicates a specific concept. However, in modern Chinese, most words are made up of two or three syllables, sometimes more. In the Western sense, spoken Chinese has only 420 single-syllable root words, but tones are used to differentiate these basic sounds. Tones make it difficult for foreigners to learn Chinese, since different tones give the same syllable a completely different meaning. For instance, *mai* with a falling fourth tone (*mài*) means to sell; if it is pronounced with a falling-rising third tone (*mâi*), it means to buy. If you pay attention to these tones, you can soon tell the difference, though correct pronunciation requires much practice. Taking another example, the four tones of the syllable ma: first tone, *mä* means mother; second tone, *má* means hemp; third tone, *mâ* means horse; and fourth tone *mà* means to complain.

   The first tone is pitched high and even, the second rising, the third falling and then rising, and the fourth falling. There Is also a fifth,

"neutral" tone. The individual tones are marked above the main vowel in the syllable.

Grammar

Chinese sentence structure is simple: subject, predicate, object. Many Chinese words serve as nouns, adjectives and verbs without altering their written or spoken forms. Verbs have single forms and do not change with the subject. There are no plural forms for verbs or nouns. All of these have to be inferred from the context. The easiest way to form a question is to add the interrogative particle *ma* (neutral tone) to the end of a statement.

Language Guide

The list on the following pages uses diacritical marks to indicate which of the four tones is used:

umlaut: m**ä** = high and even tone
acute: m**á** = rising tone
circumflex: m**â** = falling then rising tone
grave: m**à** = falling tone

GREETINGS

Hello	Nî hâo	你好
How are you?	Nî hâo ma?	你好吗?
Thank you	Xièxie	谢谢
Goodbye	Zài jiàn	再见
My name is...	Wô jiào...	我叫...
My last name is...	Wô xìng...	我姓...
What is your name?	Nín jiào shénme míngzi?	您叫什么名字?
What is your last name?	Nín guìxìng?	您贵姓?
I am very happy...	Wô hên gāoxìng...	我很高兴...
All right	Hâo	好
Not all right	Bù hâo	不好
Can you speak English?	Nín huì shuö Yīngyû ma?	您会说英语吗?
Can you speak Chinese?	Nín huì shuö Hànyû ma?	您会说汉语吗?
I cannot speak Chinese	Wô bù huì Hànyû	我不会汉语
I do not understand	Wô bù dông	我不懂
Do you understand?	Nín dông ma?	您懂吗?
Please speak a little slower	Qîng nín shuö màn yìdiânr	请您说慢一点儿
What is this called?	Zhège jiào shénme?	这个叫什么?
How do you say...	... zênme shuö?	...怎么说?
Please	Qîng	请/谢谢
Never mind	Méi guänxì	没关系
Sorry	Duìbùqî	对不起

PRONOUNS

Who/who is it?	Shéi?	谁?
My/mine	Wô/wôde	我/我的
You/yours (singular)	Nî/nîde	你/你的
He/his	Tä/täde	他/他的
She/hers	Tä/täde	她/她的
We/ours	Wômen/wômende	我们/我们的
You/yours (plural)	Nîmen/nîmende	你们/你们的
They/theirs	Tämen/tämende	他们/他们的
You/yours (respectful)	Nín/nínde	您/您的

TRAVEL

Where is it?	... zài nâr?	...在哪儿?
Do you have it here?	Zhèr... yôu ma?	这儿有...吗?
No/it's not here/there aren't any	Méi yôu	没有
Hotel	Fàndiàn/bìnguân	饭店/宾馆
Restaurant	Fànguânr	饭馆
Bank	Yìnháng	银行
Post Office	Yóujú	邮局
Toilet	Cèsuô	厕所
Railway station	Huôchë zhàn	火车站
Bus station	Qìchë zhàn	汽车站
Embassy	Dàshíguân	大使馆
Consulate	Lîngshìguân	领事馆
Passport	Hùzhào	护照
Visa	Qiänzhèng	签证
Pharmacy	Yàodiàn	药店
Hospital	Yiyuàn	医院
Doctor	Dàifu/yïshëng	大夫/医生
Translate	Fänyì	翻译
Bar	Jîubä	酒吧
Do you have...?	Nín yôu... ma?	您有...吗?
I want/I would like	Wô yào/wô xiäng yào	我要/我想要
I want to buy...	Wô xiäng mâi...	我想买...
Where can I buy it?	Nâr néng mâi... ma?	哪儿能买吗?

This/that	Zhège/nèige	这个/那个
Green tea/black tea	Lûchá/hóngchá	绿茶/红茶
Coffee	Kāfēi	咖啡
Cigarette	Xiāngyān	香烟
Film (for camera)	Jiāojuânr	胶卷儿
Ticket	Piào	票
Postcard	Míngxìnpiàn	明信片
Letter	Yī fēng xìn	一封信
Air mail	Hángkong xìn	航空信
Postage stamp	Yóupiào	邮票

SHOPPING

How much?	Duöshâo?	多少
How much does it cost?	Zhège duöshâo qián?	这个多少钱?
Too expensive, thank you	Tài guì le, xièxie	太贵了, 谢谢
Very expensive	Hên guì	很贵
A little (bit)	Yìdiânr	一点儿
Too much/too many	Tài duö le	太多了
A lot	Duö	多
Few	Shâo	少

MONEY MATTERS, HOTELS, TRANSPORT, COMMUNICATIONS

Money	Qián	钱
Chinese currency	Rénmínbì	人民币
One yuan/one kuai (10 jiao)	Yī yuán/yì kuài	一元/一块
One jiao/one mao (10 fen)	Yī jiāo/yì mâo	一角/一毛
One fen	Yì fēn	一分
Traveller's cheque	Lûxíng zhīpiào	旅行支票
Credit card	Xìnyòngkâ	信用卡
Foreign currency	Wàihuìquàn	外汇券
Where can I change money?	Zài nâr kêyî huàn qián?	在哪儿可以换钱?
I want to change money	Wô xiâng huàn qián	我想换钱
What is the exchange rate?	Bîjià shì duöshâo?	比价是多少?
We want to stay for one (two/three) nights	Wômen xiâng zhù yì (liâng/sān) tiān	我们想住一(两, 三)天
How much is the room per day?	Fángjiān duöshâo qián yì tiān?	房间多少钱一天?
Room number	Fángjiān hàomâ	房间号码
Single room	Dänrén fángjiān	单人房间
Double room	Shuángrén fángjiān	双人房间
Reception	Qiántai/fúwútai	前台/服务台
Key	Yàoshì	钥匙
Clothes	Yīfù	衣服
Luggage	Xínglî	行李
Airport	Fēijichâng	飞机场
Bus	Gönggòng qìchë	公共汽车
Taxi	Chüzü qìchë	出租汽车
Bicycle	Zìxíngchë	自行车
Telephone	Diànhuà	电话
Long-distance call	Chángtú diànhuà	长途电话
International call	Guójì diànhuà	国际电话
Telephone number	Diànhuà hàomâ	电话号码
Telegram	Diànbào	电报
Computer	Diàn nâo/jìsuànjī	电脑/计算机
Check e-mail	Chá diànxìn	查电信
Use the internet	Shàng wâng	上网

TIME

When?	Shénme shíhòu?	什么时候?
What time is it now?	Xiànzài jídiân zhöng?	现在几点种?
How long?	Duöcháng shíjiān?	多长时间?

One/two/three o'clock	Yì diân/liâng diân/sän diân zhöng	一点/两点/三点种
Early morning/morning	Zâoshang/shàngwû	早上/上午
Midday/afternoon/evening	Zhöngwû/xiàwû/wânshang	中午/下午/晚上
Monday	Xïngqïyï	星期一
Tuesday	Xïngqïèr	星期二
Wednesday	Xïngqïsän	星期三
Thursday	Xïngqïsì	星期四
Friday	Xïngqïwû	星期五
Saturday	Xïngqïliù	星期六
Sunday	Xïngqïtiän/xïngqïrì	星期天/星期日
Weekend	Zhöumò	周末
Yesterday/today/tomorrow	Zuótiän/jïntiän/míngtiän	昨天/今天/明天
This week/last week/	Zhègexïngqï/shàngxïngqï/	这个星期/上星期/
next week	xiàxïngqï	下星期
Hour/day/week/month	Xiâoshí/tiän/xïngqï/yuè	小时/天/星期/月
January/February/March	Yïyuè/èryuè/sänyuè	一月/二月/三月
April/May/June	Sìyuè/wûyuè/liùyuè	四月/五月/六月
July/August/September	Qïyuè/bäyuè/jiûyuè	七月/八月/九月
October/November/December	Shíyuè/shíyïyuè/shíèryuè	十月/十一月/十二月

EATING OUT

Restaurant	Cänting/fànguän'r	餐厅/饭馆儿
Attendant/waiter	Fúwúyuán	服务员
Waitress	Xiâojiê	小姐
Eat	Chï fàn	吃饭
Breakfast	Zâofàn	早饭
Lunch	Wûfàn	午饭
Dinner	Wânfàn	晚饭
Menu	Càidän	菜单
Chopsticks	Kuàizi	筷子
Knife	Däozi	刀子
Fork	Chäzi	叉子
Spoon	Sháozi	勺子
Cup/glass	Bëizi/bölìbëi	杯子/玻璃杯
Bowl	Wân	碗
Plate	Pán	盘
Paper napkin	Cänjïn zhï	餐巾纸
I want...	Wô yào...	我要
I do not want...	Wô bú yào...	我不要
I did not order this	Zhège wô méi diân	这个我没点
I am a vegetarian	Wô shì chï sù de rén	我是吃素的人
I do not eat any meat	Wô suôyôude ròu döu bù chï	我所有的肉都不
I do not eat any meat or fish	Wô suôyôude ròu hé yú, döu bù chï	我所有的肉和鱼都不吃
Please fry it in vegetable oil	Qïng yóng zhíwù yóu châo châo	请用植物油炒炒吃
Beer	Píjiu	啤酒
Red/white wine	Hóng/bái pútaojiu	红/白葡萄酒
Liquor	Bái jiu	白酒
Mineral water	Kuángquánshuï	矿泉水
Soft drinks	Yînliào	饮料
Cola	Kêlè	可乐
Tea	Cháshuï	茶水
Fruit	Shuïguô	水果
Bread	Miànbäo	面包
Toast	Kâomiànbäo	烤面包
Yoghurt	Suän nâi	酸奶
Fried/boiled egg	Châo/zhû jïdàn	炒/煮鸡蛋
Rice	Mîfàn	米饭
Soup	Täng	汤
Stir-fried dishes	Châo cài	炒菜

Beef/pork/lamb/chicken	Niú/zhū/yáng/jī ròu	牛肉/猪肉/羊肉/鸡肉
Fish	Yú	鱼
Vegetables	Shūcài	蔬菜
Spicy/sweet/sour/salty	Là/tián/suān/xián	辣/甜/酸/咸
Hot/cold	Rè/liáng	热/凉
Can we have the bill, please	Qǐng jié zhàng/mǎidàn	请结帐/买单

Specialities

Peking Duck	Běijīng kǎoyā	北京烤鸭
Hotpot	Huǒ guō	火锅
Phoenix in the Nest	Fèng zài wōlǐ	凤在窝里
Mandarin fish	Tángcù guìyú	糖醋鳜鱼
Thousand layer cake	Qiān céng bǐng	千层饼
Lotus prawns	Ǒu piànn'r xiārén	藕片儿虾仁
Homestyle cooking	Jiā cháng cài	家常菜

Appetizers

Deep-fried peanuts	Zhá huāshēngmǐ	炸花生米
Boiled peanuts	Zhǔ huāshēngmǐ	煮花生米
Soft beancurd	Bàn dòufu	拌豆腐
"Hairy" green beans	Máo dòu	毛豆
Mashed cucumber	Pái huángguā	排黄瓜
Pressed beancurd strips	Dòufu sī	豆腐丝
Thousand Year-Old Eggs	Sōnghuā dàn	松花蛋
Smoked beancurd with celery	Qíncài dòufu gān'r	芹菜豆腐干儿

Meat dishes

Aubergine/eggplant fritters stuffed with minced pork	Qié hé	茄盒
Spicy chicken with chillies	Làzi jīdīng	辣子鸡丁
Spicy chicken with peanuts	gōngbào jīdīng	宫爆鸡丁
Pork with egg and "tree ear" fungus	Mùxū ròu	木须肉
Shredded pork with bamboo shoots	Dōngsǔn ròusī	冬笋肉丝
Beef in brown sauce	Hóngshāo niúròu	红烧牛肉
Sizzling "iron plate" beef	Tiěbǎn niúròu	铁板牛肉
Beef with potatoes	Tǔdòu niúròu	土豆牛肉

Seafood

Prawns with cashew nuts	Yāoguǒ xiārén	腰果虾仁
Carp in brown sauce	Hóngshāo lǐyú	红烧鲤鱼
Boiled prawns	Shuǐzhǔ xiārén	水煮虾仁
Stir-fried prawns	Qīngchǎo xiārén	清炒虾仁
Sweet and sour mandarin fish	Tángcù guìyú	糖醋鳜鱼
Hot and sour squid	Suānlà yóuyú juàn	酸辣鱿鱼卷

Vegetable dishes

Sweetcorn with pine kernels	Sōngrén yùmǐ	松仁玉米
Mange tout/snowpeas	Hélán dòu	荷兰豆
Spicy "dry" green beans	Gānbiān biǎndòu	干煸扁豆
Spicy "fish flavour" aubergine	Yúxiāng qiézi	鱼香茄子
Greens with dried mushrooms	Xiānggū yóucài	香菇油菜
Spicy beancurd with chilli	Málà dòufu	麻辣豆腐
Stir-fried egg and tomato	Xīhóngshì chǎo jīdàn	西红柿炒鸡蛋
Fried shredded potato	Tǔdòu sī	土豆丝
Clay pot with beancurd soup	Shāguō dòufu	沙锅豆腐
Sour cabbage with "glass" noodles	Suāncài fěnsī	酸菜粉丝
Potato, aubergine and green pepper	Dì sān xiān	地三鲜

Staple food

Steamed bread	Mántou	馒头
Cornbread	Wōtou	窝头
Fried rice	Dàn chāo fàn	蛋炒饭
Plain rice	Bái fàn	白饭
Sizzling rice crust	Guōbā	锅巴
Noodles	Miàntiáo	面条
Pancakes	Bīng	饼

Soups

Hot and sour soup	Suānlà tāng	酸辣汤
Egg and tomato soup	Xīhóngshì jīdàn tāng	西红柿鸡蛋汤
Beancurd soup	Dòufu tāng	豆腐汤
Lamb and marrow soup	Yángròu dōngguā tāng	羊肉冬瓜汤
Fish-head soup	Yútóu tāng	鱼头汤

Fast food

Noodles	Miàntiáo	面条
Stuffed pasta parcels (meat/vegetable filling)	Jiāozi	饺子
meat/vegetable filling	ròu xiàn/sù xiàn	肉馅/素馅
Steamed meat buns	Bāozi	包子
"Pot stickers" (fried jiaozi)	Guōtiē	锅贴
Egg pancake	Jiàn bīng	煎饼
Wonton soup	Húndùn	混沌
Soy milk	Dòu jiāng	豆浆
Deep-fried dough sticks	Yóutiáo	油条

Numbers

One	Yī	一
Two	Èr	二
Three	Sān	三
Four	Sì	四
Five	Wū	五
Six	Liù	六
Seven	Qī	七
Eight	Bā	八
Nine	Jiū	九
Ten	Shí	十
Eleven	Shíyī	十一
Twelve	Shíèr	十二
Twenty	Èrshí	二十
Thirty	Sānshí	三十
Forty	Sìshí	四十
Fifty	Wūshí	五十
Sixty	Liùshí	六十
Seventy	Qīshí	七十
Eighty	Bāshí	八十
Ninety	Jiūshí	九十
One hundred	Yìbāi	一百
One hundred and one	Yìbāi língyī	一百零一
Two hundred	Liāng bāi	两百
Three hundred	Sān bāi	三百
Four hundred	Sì bāi	四百
Five hundred	Wū bāi	五百
One thousand	Yìqiān	一千

Further Reading

Beijing

On a Chinese Screen by Somerset Maugham, Oxford University Press, 1997. Maugham, who first published this travelogue in 1922, wrote brief but engaging sketches of some of the local and foreign characters he met in Beijing.

The Forbidden City: Centre of Imperial China (Discoveries) by Gilles Beguin and Dominique Morel. Abrams, 1997. A brief account details the daily lives of Ming and Qing emperors in the former imperial palace.

Hiking on History by William Lindesay. Oxford University Press, 2000. Indispensable for hikers, this is a guide to walking on several unrestored, less-visited sections of the Great Wall near Beijing.

Old Peking: City of the Ruler of the World by Chris Elder (Editor). Oxford University Press, 1997. This is a collection of passages written by foreigners who visited Beijing at various times during its long history as China's imperial capital.

Peking Opera by Colin MacKerras. Oxford University Press, 1997. A simple explanation of the history and standard forms of Peking opera, in the Oxford Images of Asia series.

The Private Life of Chairman Mao: The Memoirs of Mao's Personal Physician by Li Zhisui. Random House, 1996. As the Great Helmsman loses control, Dr Li chronicles the degeneration of the revolutionary leader into a callous, drug-dependent tyrant and gives an insight into life in Zhongnanhai, Beijing's new "Forbidden City."

General

Behind the Forbidden Door by Tiziano Terzani, Unwin Counterpoint, 1985. This correspondent's book gives a personal and very readable insight into the early, not always smooth processes of reform and opening up to the outside world.

China Wakes: The Struggle for the Soul of a Rising Power by Nicholas Kristof and Sheryl Wudunn. Random House, 1995. Another Beijing correspondent and his wife detail personal experiences in China.

Real China: From Cannibalism to Karaoke by John Gittings. Pocket Books, 1997. In an attempt to portray life beyond Beijing, one of China's longest-serving foreign correspondents travels through several provinces to examine the problems faced by 800 million rural Chinese.

History

China Remembers by Zhang Lijia and Calum MacLeod. Oxford University Press, 1999. A fascinating and accessible look at New China through the eyes of 33 people who have vivid memories of five decades.

Dragon Lady: The Life and Legend of the Last Empress of China by Sterling Seagrave and Peggy Seagrave. Vintage Books, 1993. Blaming the fabrications of the "Hermit of Peking," Edmund Backhouse, for the myth of "evil" empress dowager Cixi, this book shows how Cixi was herself manipulated by princes and eunuchs.

From Emperor to Citizen by Aisin-Gioro Puyi. Foreign Languages Press, 1989. The quite readable autobiography of the last emperor, Puyi, covers his progress from a childhood in the confines of the imperial throne, to an adult life as a puppet of the Japanese, prisoner of the communists, and comrade of new Beijing.

Hungry Ghosts, Jasper Becker. John Murray, 1996. Using meticulous research, Becker tells the grim truth about the darkest period of post-1949 China: the death of some 30 million in the famines of the Great Leap Forward.

Red Star over China by Edgar R. Snow. Grove Press, 1973. A classic first-hand account of the years of guerilla war leading up to the 1949 revolution, when Snow followed

Mao and other communist leaders.

The Search for Modern China by Jonathan Spence. Norton, 1990. Bringing to life Chinese society and politics over the past 400 years, this has become a standard text for students of Chinese history.

Wild Swans: Three Daughters of China by Jung Chang. Anchor Books, 1991. Adding plenty of historical detail, Wild Swans records 20th century China through the lives of three generations of women, starting with the author's concubine grandmother.

Politics

The Era of Jiang Zemin by Willy Wo-lap Lam. Prentice Hall, 1999. **China after Deng Xiaoping** by Willy Wo-lap Lam. Wiley, 1995. Often considered the leading political commentator on China, Lam explains the inner workings of Beijing politics as well as any outsider can.

Mandate of Heaven: The Legacy of Tiananmen Square and the Next Generation of China's Leaders by Orville Schell. Touchstone Books, 1995. Schell explores the issues facing China's political leaders from the perspective of writers, artists, musicians, dissidents, underground publishers and venture capitalists.

Culture

China Pop: How Soap Operas, Tabloids, and Bestsellers Are Transforming a Culture. Zha Jianying. New Press, 1995. Zha takes an offbeat look at the explosion of Chinese popular culture in the 1980s and 1990s.

In the Red, Geremie Barme, Columbia University Press, 1999. An academic examination of literary trends in China since 1989, especially the role of dissenting voices.

Travels Through Sacred China, Martin Palmer, Thorsons 1996. After brief but helpful introductions to the main religious beliefs and practices, the rest of this book is devoted to detailing the most important among hundreds of temples and sacred sites in China.

Other Insight Guides

Over 200 titles in the acclaimed *Insight Guides* series cover every continent. Those highlighting destinations in the East Asian region include guides to *China*, *Hong Kong*, *Taiwan*, *Korea*, *Japan* and *Tokyo*. The entire region is detailed in *Insight Guide East Asia*.

There are also over 100 *Insight Pocket Guides*, with an itinerary-based approach designed to assist the traveller with a limited amount of time to spend in a destination. Titles include *Beijing*, *Canton (Guangzhou)*, *Hong Kong*, *Macau* and *Tibet*.

Insight Compact Guides offer the traveller a highly portable encyclopedic travel guide packed with carefully cross-referenced text, photographs and maps. Titles include *Beijing*, *Shanghai* and *Hong Kong*.

Insight Fleximaps combine clear, detailed cartography with essential travel information. The laminated finish makes the maps durable, weatherproof and easy to fold.

ART & PHOTO CREDITS

Gonzalo M. Azumendi 6/7, 57, 114, 119, 188, 207T, 238L
Bodo Bondzio 65R, 70L, 77, 132/133, 134, 151, 175, 177T, 187L, 201, 206, 214, 220, 226, 257, 264
Lance Dawning 208
R. Dorel 246/247, 251, 252
Helmut Forster-Latsch 84
Robert Fried 50, 74, 90, 92, 117T, 130
Peter Hessel 24L, 29L
Hans Höfer 123, 222/223
Jack Hollingsworth 88
Andrew Holt back cover top right, 4B, 110T, 112, 142, 153, 159, 162T, 192/193, 230, 236T
Image Bank 27, 60, 102, 125, 138, 238R
Volkmar E. Janicke 8/9, 219T
Catherine Karnow 37, 51, 64, 69, 72, 73, 108, 137, 152, 152T, 166/167, 172, 172T, 177, 179, 190T
Gloria Maschmeyer 218
Ulrich Menzel 75
Manfred Morgenstern 18/19, 22, 23, 24R, 25, 26, 28, 29R, 30, 31, 32, 33, 34, 35, 36, 39, 42, 56, 63, 65L, 68, 71L, 71R, 93, 105, 109, 115, 128, 141, 178, 180/181, 183, 185, 190, 196, 199, 200, 200T, 202, 211, 213, 215, 216, 219, 221R, 224, 227, 228, 229, 249, 250, 253, 254T
Collection of the National Palace 66
Panos Pictures 38, 46/47, 138T, 150, 174, 189, 240, 242, 242T, 243
Erhard Pansegrau 1, 20, 43, 62,

67, 70R, 79, 81, 82, 85L, 91, 100/101, 149, 161, 236
Photobank 41R, 96/97, 120/121, 194/195, 204
Andrea Pistolesi back flap bottom, 14, 76, 78, 86, 111, 146/147, 148, 174T
Rex Features 2/3, 10/11, 12/13, 17, 21, 45
David Sanger 41L, 85R, 122, 124R, 131, 156, 157, 158T, 197, 205, 210, 239, 241
Peter Scheckmann 255, 256
Blair Seitz 232/233
Bill Smith 230T, 231
Hilary Smith 4/5, 40, 48/49, 52, 53, 59, 61, 98/99, 112T, 113, 118, 124L, 127, 140L, 140R, 165L, 165R, 169, 179T, 204T, 214T, 254, 258, 259, 260T, 261, 262L, 262R, 263, 263T
Tom Till 234
Trip/Bryce Atwell 220T
Trip/M Barlow 237
Trip/T Bognar 176
Trip/M Good 168
Trip/W Mathew 256T
Trip/Streano/Havens 171
Trip/P Treanor 240T
Elke Wandel 80, 83, 162, 209
Kosima Weber-Lui 58, 143R, 144, 182, 217, 248
Andrew Wheeler 89, 124T, 202T, 207, 208T, 250T
David Wilkins 235
Marcus Wilson-Smith all small cover pictures except back cover top and back flap bottom, 5B, 44, 87, 116, 127T, 129, 130T, 135, 136T, 139, 140T, 143L, 143T,

145, 145T, 150T, 160, 163, 164, 164T, 171T, 173, 184T, 187R, 187T, 188T, 191, 216T, 221L, 226T, 239T

Picture Spreads

Pages 54/55 *Top row, left to right*: Trip/K Cardwell, David Sanger, Gonzalo M. Azumendi, Hilary Smith. *Centre*: Robert Fried. *Bottom row*: La Belle Aurore, Hilary Smith, Gonzalo M. Azumendi, La Belle Aurore.
Pages 94/95 *Top row, left to right*: Frank Broekhuizen, Hilary Smith, Hilary Smith, Gertrud & Helmut Denzau. *Centre row*: Mary Evans Picture Library, Frank Broekhuizen, Andrew Wheeler. *Bottom row*: John Walmsley, Panos Pictures.
Pages 154/155 *Top row, left to right*: Hilary Smith, Jayawardene, Jayawardene, Panos Pictures. *Centre row*: Andrea Pistolesi, Alastair Scott. *Bottom row*: Trip/A Tovy, Andrew Wheeler, Hilary Smith, Jayawardene.
Pages 244/245 *Top row, left to right*: The Hulton Getty Collection, Bill Smith, Trip/M Barlow, Bill Smith, Bill Smith. *Centre row* Bill Smith, Manfred Morgenstern. *Bottom row*: Bill Smith, David Sanger, Bill Smith, Manfred Morgenstern.

Map Production Phoenix Mapping
© 2000 Apa Publications GmbH & Co. Verlag KG (Singapore branch)

INSIGHT GUIDE
BEIJING

Cartographic Editor **Zoë Goodwin**
Production **Stuart A Everitt**
Design Consultants
Carlotta Junger, Graham Mitchener
Picture Research **Hilary Genin, Monica Allende**

Index

Numbers in italics refer to photographs

The Insight Approach

The book you are holding is part of the world's largest range of guidebooks. Its purpose is to help you have the most valuable travel experience possible, and we try to achieve this by providing not only information about countries, regions and cities but also genuine insight into their history, culture, institutions and people.

Since the first Insight Guide – to Bali – was published in 1970, the series has been dedicated to the proposition that, with insight into a country's people and culture, visitors can both enhance their own experience and be accepted more easily by their hosts. Now, in a world where ethnic hostilities and nationalist conflicts are all too common, such attempts to increase understanding between peoples are more important than ever.

Insight Guides:
Essentials for understanding

Because a nation's past holds the key to its present, each Insight Guide kicks off with lively history chapters. These are followed by magazine-style essays on culture and daily life. This essential background information gives readers the necessary context for using the main Places section, with its comprehensive run-down on things worth seeing and doing.

Finally, a listings section contains all the information you'll need on travel, hotels, restaurants and opening times.

As far as possible, we rely on local writers and specialists to ensure that information is authoritative. The pictures, for which Insight Guides have become so celebrated, are just as important. Our photojournalistic approach aims not only to illustrate a destination but also to communicate visually and directly to readers life as it is lived by the locals. The series has grown to almost 200 titles.

Compact Guides:
The "great little guides"

As invaluable as such background information is, it isn't always fun to carry an Insight Guide through a crowded souk or up a church tower. Could we, readers asked, distil the key reference material into a slim volume for on-the-spot use?

Our response was to design Compact Guides as an entirely new series, with original text carefully cross-referenced to detailed maps and more than 200 photographs. In essence, they're miniature encyclopedias, concise and comprehensive, displaying reliable and up-to-date information in an accessible way. There are almost 100 titles.

Pocket Guides:
A local host in book form

However wide-ranging the information in a book, human beings still value the personal touch. Our editors are often asked the same questions. Where do *you* go to eat? What do *you* think is the best beach? What would *you* recommend if I have only three days? We invited our local correspondents to act as "substitute hosts" by revealing their preferred walks and trips, listing the restaurants they go to and structuring a visit into a series of timed itineraries.

The result: our Pocket Guides, complete with full-size fold-out maps. These 100-plus titles help readers plan a trip precisely, particularly if their time is short.

Exploring with Insight:
A valuable travel experience

In conjunction with co-publishers all over the world, we print in up to 10 languages, from German to Chinese, from Danish to Russian. But our aim remains simple: to enhance your travel experience by combining our expertise in guidebook publishing with the on-the-spot knowledge of our correspondents.

66 I was first drawn to the
Insight Guides by the
excellent "Nepal" volume.
I can think of no book
which so effectively
captures the essence of
a country. Out of these
pages leaped the Nepal
I know – the captivating
charm of a people and
their culture. I've since
discovered and enjoyed
the entire Insight Guide
series. Each volume deals
with a country in the
same sensitive depth,
which is nowhere more
evident than in the
superb photography. 99

Sir Edmund Hillary

The World of Insight Guides

400 books in three complementary series cover every major destination in every continent.